# The Cabin in the Mountains

# The Cabin in the Mountains

## A Norwegian Odyssey

# Robert Ferguson

*An Apollo Book*

Head of Zeus Ltd
First Floor East
5–8 Hardwick Street
London EC1R 4RG

WWW.HEADOFZEUS.COM

*For Nina*

# Contents

*Wessel Zapffe – Næss's mountain cabins – how smoking saved Bertrand Russell's life – Næss, Else Herzberg and Zapffe climb Stetind – failure of my efforts to clear the snow – on Zapffe's 'Anti-Natalist' philosophy – Zapffe's extreme environmentalism – we sit down to eat*

# 1

## Friday afternoon,
## 21 December 2018

Christmas 2018 – the drive to the cabin –

ice on the roads – problem of getting onto

the roof – clearing snow from the roof –

losing a snow shovel – lighting the fire – an

alternative method of clearing the snow not

used – I check the Blackpool result –

Geirr Tveitt's music on the radio

I t was about three o'clock on a Friday afternoon and snowing heavily as we pulled up outside the cabin after the two-hour drive from Oslo. The sky had hardly opened its eyes all day and already it was closing them. The last half hour of the journey was a heart-stopping series of bends along a country road considered too insignificant to be regularly cleared by the snowploughs that chugged up and down the main roads like giant insects. Long sections of it were covered in what Norwegians call *panseris*, a dense and rock-hard layer of ice made doubly hazardous by the emergence, over the winter weeks, of rutted tracks that seemed, at first glance, in their subtle, asphalt greyness, to be actual road. You had constantly to resist the temptation to let the VW Golf slide into the comfort of the fit, and instead concentrate on keeping the offside wheels just holding the far side of the camber. It gave a feeling of control over the car, however slight.

Arriving at the village of Veggli after the last, twisting section of road through the Numedal valley always brought a false sense of 'journey over'. There remained one final leg, as you leave the Fv 40 (County Road 40) just past the Circle K petrol station for the ten-kilometre climb up the mountainside to Mykstulia, and the eastern limits of the great Hardangervidda, the mountain plateau that extends from Eidsfjord in the west to Rjukan and Kongsberg in the east. For about half of its length this is a metalled road, becoming a cinder track as it passes across sheep grids and arrives at a toll barrier, operated by a plastic key card. After the barrier the track continues to twist and turn upwards, passing half-hidden tiny shacks belonging to the mountain's original cabin-owners, the people who built cabins there thirty or forty years ago, when the cabin life Norwegians dreamed of was simpler than the one they dream of now.

Glancing constantly in the rear-view mirror as the track twisted upwards through the steadily falling snow, I saw a familiar sight: a line of cars on our tail, other cabin-owners anxious to reach base, or locals on their way up to Veggli Fjellstue for a beer. The locals are easy to spot in their enormous pickups, usually with an array of hunting lights mounted on the roof or the front crash bar, sometimes on both. Cabin-owners as often as not are in more subdued 4x4s –VW Tiguans and Range Rovers, family-sized vehicles with plenty of room at the back for toboggans and a Thule ski-box on the roof. The four-wheel drives and studded winter tyres seem to make them fearless and impatient and you have to struggle to resist the temptation to speed up in response to their imagined exasperation. I could almost hear the young Oslo professional in the white Volvo station wagon driving right on my tail turning to his wife and saying 'It's probably some old farmer. He's wearing one of those hats with earflaps.'

Determined to get rid of my tail, I accelerated away once we passed the toll barrier and headed up the mountain between dense fields of snow, the track climbing and twisting all the way, past six or seven rather ominous-looking metal rubbish containers parked off the track on the left-hand side. They looked like tanks without caterpillar tracks. Even up here, the Norwegian concern for the environment was in evidence, each container colour-coded: green for Paper and Cardboard, black for Glass, blue for Other Rubbish. Two more bends and now we saw high above us, where the track took yet another

upward turn and twisted back on itself, a string of coloured
lights in the shape of a fir tree tethered outside Veggli Fjellstue,
the café that functions as a sort of social centre for the cabin
community in the winter.

I indicated and made a right turn off the track as it twisted
on up towards that festive fir tree and saw with relief that
Jørgen, the landowner who had sold us the land and whom we
paid three thousand kroner a year to clear the snow with his
giant yellow plough, had been within the last few hours, and
we were able to drive the last hundred metres up to the cabin
through a layer of snow no more than ten centimetres deep.

I almost wished he hadn't, and that we had been obliged
to turn round and drive back to Oslo again. Turning off the
engine, I sat for a moment, looking upwards through the
window in astonishment at the almost unbelievable quantity
of snow piled up on the cabin roof. It added something like
an extra twenty per cent to its height. A great white quiff
of it reared up dramatically, like Hokusai's wave about to
smash down, while below it dangled down over the gable
in what looked like a gravity-defying suspension. Left to its
own devices, exuberant nature had abandoned all self-control.
Since our last visit three weeks earlier, it had spent the days
and nights whipping and scouring the open area separating
the cabin from the dense stand of pines at the top of the
steep slope behind it, whirling the snow up onto the roof into
a monstrous cowlick of compacted flakes. My first thought
was that the roof couldn't possibly take even one more
snowflake – and the local forecast was for more. My second
thought was: I need to get up there on the ladder and clear it.
My third thought was: how? Even before getting out of the
car I could see that the cabin was surrounded by a wall of
snow about waist-high: where could I even plant the ladder

in order to climb up onto the roof and start shovelling the snow down?

No answer. But no option either. We climbed out of the car. Jørgen had managed to get the scoop of his giant plough almost up to the door of our shed, so after unlocking the door we took out two snow scoops and for the next twenty minutes worked together to clear a narrow track to the main door of the cabin, on the long side wall facing the shed and about a metre and a half away from it. The shed too wore a crown of snow that almost doubled its height. Then, as Nina ferried the plastic bags of shopping into the cabin from the car, I got down on my hands and knees and dragged and wiggled the two halves of the sliding ladder out from their storage space beneath the planks of the terrace at the front of the cabin. Having locked them together I staggered across the terrace to the long, eastern-facing wall of the cabin and, after several attempts at a manoeuvre that involved lifting the ladder up high enough to plunge its legs down through the snow until they hit something solid at the bottom, I finally managed to lean it up against the roof at an angle of about forty-five degrees and about two metres to the right of the weatherboards. With a snow scoop for the heavy clearing gripped in my right hand and an ordinary shovel for more detailed work dangling from my left I then began the slow ascent, one step at a time, keeping my body pressed as close to the rungs as possible, the tools banging and snagging against the rungs, until finally I was above the level of the guttering and able to reach out and anchor them both in the snow. In my almost insane haste to get on with the job I was still wearing the clothes I had driven up in – a zip-up fleece jacket over a merino wool vest with a high collar, denim jeans with merino wool long johns underneath, and a pair of ordinary Ecco sports shoes.

The next problem was how to get from the ladder onto the roof without immediately sliding over the edge. The snow was still quite fresh, but as I discovered from my first tentative step off and to the right of the top rung, it was wet enough to be stamped down into a flat platform large enough to stand on. Transferring my weight from the safety of the ladder onto this first step I made five further such platforms, each one of which brought me closer to the safety of the ridge, until finally I reached it.

I stood upright, slightly out of breath. The mere fact of being up on the roof at all seemed half the battle. Shovelling the snow down over the sides would, I thought, be a relatively easy matter. It was only snow, after all. Soft and white. Superficially impressive, but insubstantial stuff. Keen to make a huge and dramatic inroad on the problem as rapidly as possible, I waded along the ridge towards the front of the cabin, and that man-high quiff of snow I had identified as my principal opponent. From observations made below I knew that it extended out-wards and downwards from the point of the gable for at least a metre. Stopping short of where I calculated the roof ended and the snow began, I leaned forward and peered over the edge. Down below I saw the bent back of my wife in her red parka as she chipped away at widening a track through the snow between the car and the door. Then I took a deep breath, raised the blade of the shovel in a two-handed grip high above my head and, shutting my eyes tightly, brought it down into the snow, like a picador lancing the neck of a great white bull. With a swish a small slice of the quiff detached itself and slipped away over the side.

After several further repetitions I had made what seemed to me, from my vantage point on the roof, visible inroads on the quiff. Resting briefly, with one hand leaning on the chimney, close to the middle of the ridge, and studying the less dramatic aspects of the job, I now realised that what at first glance had looked like relatively modest build-ups of snow on the lower slopes of the roof were, on closer inspection, thigh-deep deposits that continued all the way down to the guttering. Carefully wading back towards the steps I had cut in the snow, I grabbed the wide-mouthed snow scoop and began energetically pushing it up and down the lower slopes with a sort of old-fashioned lawnmower movement, wondering even as I did so whether or not what I was doing – shaving away the deep snow that lay just beyond my feet – might not have the very result I feared the most, namely a sudden rushing and uncontrolled slide over the edge of the roof.

Instead, following one of my more ferocious lunges, it was the snow scoop itself that flew out of my hands. Propelled by

the full force of an outward thrust, it skimmed away and flew off into the blinding whiteness. Taking a few tentative sideways steps downwards, I bent my knees and peered over the edge. I couldn't see it anywhere. It had disappeared as swiftly and surely as if it had gone overboard on an ocean liner. I shouted to my wife, told her what had happened, and watched as she searched the region behind the cabin in which I believed it had landed. After wading around for some five minutes she called up that she had found it. It was broken. The scoop had snapped off at the junction with the handle. A clean break. By a wretched piece of luck it must have landed directly on a submerged rock.

Still improvising, and now with the shovel as my only weapon, I went back to work, this time targeting areas in which the minimum of judicious wedging of snow with the shovel would produce the most dramatic avalanches. These turned out to be along the front and rear gables of the cabin. I soon discovered that, with the blade of the shovel inserted at the right place, I was able to send chunks of snow the size of hay bales somersaulting over the edge. The higher up the roof I stood, the better the avalanche I was able to generate, but the more likely the avalanche was to stall on its way over. When that happened I had to make my way down and, approaching as close as I dared, attempt to poke it over the edge with an extended foot, or the handle of the shovel. More often than not I succeeded only in breaking it up into smaller lumps that still refused to complete the journey over the edge.

And yet, plan or no plan, as time passed and the afternoon began to grow dark, I felt the approach of a sense of satisfaction at the results: there *was* less snow now, and my visions of our picking our way about inside the cabin among the rubble of fractured roof-timbers, a snowed-under table and a sofa strewn with the sodden mass of the turf roof were less frequent. In this more relaxed frame of mind, with the job almost done, I began thinking about how I *should* have approached it. In particular I recalled a conversation with Jens, the pint-sized and dark-bearded caretaker at our block of flats in Oslo, a person much given to *mansplaining* and so finding the ideal audience in me, on the general subject of clearing snow from cabin roofs, in the course of which he had described a technique that, in its simplicity and manifest efficiency, struck me as genius. You need two people, he told me. And a length of three-ply rope about thirty metres long – they sell it at Maxbo. You need to tie knots in the rope, one about every half metre. Then you need to toss the rope over the roof, as close to the ridge as you can. One of you needs to stand at the front of the cabin with one end of the rope, and the other at the back holding the other end. Then you just walk the snow down. Five minutes and it's all gone, the whole lot of it.

Why didn't you do that? I said to myself. Why didn't you listen to Jens? Why don't you listen when people give you good advice? Why did you just climb up onto the roof and start, with no idea of what you were going to do, without even changing your clothes? As so often before, my own inefficiency appalled me. But then – as so often before – I realised that the application of a technique to the specific version of the problem the technique was supposed to solve ran up against a difficulty *unique to my version of the problem*; in this particular case, the sheer impossibility of anyone manning the other end of the rope at the back of the cabin on account of the wall of snow surrounding it.

My wife was saying something to me from the front of the house and I slowly plodded back up to the ridge and then along to the point of the gable to see what she wanted. She was standing between the parked car and the open shed door, looking up, shading her eyes against the glare of the snow with one hand. Below me I noticed for the first time what looked like a satisfyingly large quantity of snow piled in front of the terrace and the main door. It would have to be cleared away in due course, but at least it wasn't on the roof any more. I leaned on my shovel, waiting. With all due modesty I would not have been surprised to hear a few words of wifely admiration: *You've done a great job. It looks a lot better now.* Something along those lines. She spoke again, gesticulating in my direction as she did so. I still couldn't hear. With my head slightly to one side I pointed in the direction of my right ear: *Please say again.* Again she pointed, then cupped her hands to her mouth and said, with exaggerated slowness: 'You missed a bit there. Hanging down over the front.'

Somewhat deflated by this, I toyed briefly with the idea of pretending I still couldn't hear, but then thought better of it.

'I can't stand that close to the edge,' I called back irritably.

And then, urging upon her the level of fear I had been living with over the past ninety minutes, added: 'I can't see where I'm putting my feet.' Still, I took a cautious half-step closer to the point of the gable and, peering as far forward as I dared, saw the bulging overhang of snow she was pointing to, dangling from the junction of the gable boards like a swollen eyelid. Still mysteriously, after thirty years of marriage, concerned to impress her, I made a sudden lunge forward and stabbed sharply down with the blade of the shovel. The reward was instantaneous. A thunderous, powdery white whoosh, the most dramatic of all my avalanches thus far. Suddenly, a mere eighteen inches below and in front of me, I saw the scarred tops of the weatherboards lining the gable. Victory.

'I'm coming down now. Put the kettle on.'

★

Even before I changed out of my drenched clothes I laid a fire inside the glass-fronted wood-burning stove. A crunched-up sheet of newspaper on the small grate of the Jøtul, then two handfuls of thick twigs sprinkled across it. I stepped outside again and, brushing the snow off the birch logs stacked along the nearside wall of the shed, picked out four, which I carried back inside and arranged into a small structure on top of the twigs, two longitudinally, two latitudinally. I then added a second layer of twigs on the top, nesting a single white firelighter within it, before crossing to the kitchen section of the open-plan living room, opening the drawer next to the sink and taking out a box of matches. Standing in front of the stove I opened the two dampers located immediately below the glass front, one to its left extremity, the other to its right, struck a match and applied it to the firelighter at the top, so that the fire would burn downwards into the logs, and the flames ignite the gases released by the logs on their way up towards the chimney and so maximise the heat potential held within them. I closed and fastened the heavy glass door, stepped back, watched and waited. For a moment there was no sign of life at all. Suddenly, the chamber was filled with a rapidly rotating ball of dense, milky-white smoke. It was a fascinating sight and, as the ferocity of the rotation increased, increasingly alarming. Abruptly there was a muted, whooshing explosion and smoke burst in swift, synchronised puffs from the top and bottom and sides of the door. Then the glass was clear, with rich tongues of flame licking across its surface. I realised the logs must have been wet, and as I headed towards the bathroom for a shower made a mental note always to carry in enough wood to start the next fire before closing down the place.

After showering I changed into a pair of black fleece trousers and a warm, zip-up Bergans cardigan, pulled up a stool and sat drying my hair in front of the Jøtul. I was exhausted. My back was aching. I felt old, like those Russian rats I read about once on the BBC website that went through their entire lives without any illnesses and then suddenly, just before they died, all the illnesses they should have had fell upon them in an unremitting shower, as though they'd simply been waiting their turn. Thinking back over my adventures on the roof I found myself wondering whether to be proud of myself or dismayed at my own foolishness. I was nearly seventy years old: why on earth was I still trying to impress my wife? Hadn't she urged, even as we sat in the car and contemplated the awesome dimensions of that quiff of snow atop the gable, that there were local firms, some based in Veggli itself, that advertised their services for jobs exactly like this, knowing that most cabin-owners on the mountain didn't live locally and couldn't follow such developments themselves? But I hadn't built the place. I hadn't driven the digger that cleared the site, I hadn't chopped down the pines, I hadn't sawn the logs, hadn't raised a hammer in anger nor burned my skin on a screwdriver, I had done none of the jobs I had expected to do when, in my dreams, I imagined myself the owner of a cabin in the Norwegian mountains: surely the very least I could do was clear the snow off my own roof? It was a matter of self-respect.

I switched off the hairdryer, checked the time, picked up my phone to check the Blackpool result. Lost three–two to Fleetwood. I put the phone down and regretted, not for the first time, that we'd agreed to internet access up here. It only left you vulnerable to idiotic and random sources of disappointment. It was part of a curious sense of guilt that had haunted me throughout so much of the process of realising this dream, at just how luxurious and comfortable the cabin had turned out to be. At how little resemblance it bore to the dream of a mountain cabin I had been secretly nurturing almost from the time, over thirty years earlier, when my interest in Norway and Norwegian culture turned into a passion.

I enumerated the luxuries we had access to: as well as the internet there was a shower, an electric towel rail, hot and cold running water and a flushing toilet. There was underfloor heating in the bathroom and in the hallway, both of which could be controlled using an app called *Ring Hytta Varm* (Ring-the-Cabin-Warm). From a simple digital interface you navigate to a Control page that gives an option between two temperature settings for the bathroom and the hallway, one entitled Comfort, the other Economy. About twelve hours before you intend to set out for the cabin you move from Economy to Comfort by sliding a digital bubble, and by the time you arrive, once you've dug your way from the car to the door and entered the cabin, there's no need to rub your hands together and slap your shoulders, no shivering hurry to find the matches and light the log fire you hopefully had the good sense to lay before leaving on your last visit, no need to empty your luggage from the car at a brisk trot to raise your body temperature while you wait for the logs to warm the place up: from the moment you step inside you're breathing in warm air that is in stunning contrast to the nostril-stinging pinch of seventeen degrees below that you've just shut the door on. You could almost walk around in a T-shirt. At times I feel this capitulation to comfort as a shameful and disheartening decadence, a betrayal. But of what? The cabin life I once dreamed of, with an earth closet twenty-five icy metres away that you have to put on thick, outdoor clothing to visit, with no electricity but only candles and oil lamps, no running water but instead water collected at physical cost, water carried in wooden buckets from a hole broken into the frozen surface of a nearby lake that can only be reached on skis, with logs the only form of fuel available not just for heating but for cooking too, with washing limited to a cold-water splash of the face first thing in the morning, and sleeping at night in a bunk bed with wooden slats for a mattress wearing a scarf, two pullovers and a woollen hat against the cold?

This dream cabin life is still a reality, but for a dwindling minority of Norwegians. Despite the mountain views and the pine forests and scrawny birch trees, there is little sense of remoteness or isolation up here in Mykstulia. Planning restrictions, reflecting an enduring and almost elegiac concern for the integrity of what was once remote mountain pasture inhabited only by flocks of grazing sheep in the short summer months, insist that all new cabins follow the contours of the landscape. Along with the turf roofs and the forty shades of brown used to paint the exteriors, it means that the cabins disappear into the landscape during the day. It's only at night, and on winter evenings in particular, when the lights start to go on, that you realise there are cabins everywhere.

I stood up, opened the stove door and put another log on. My wife was still outside, clearing the track between the door and the shed that my avalanches had almost obliterated. I could hear the scrape of her snow shovel now and then as it struck the shingle beneath the snow. Then I heard the door opening and she came in, panting as she stamped the snow from her boots on the mat. Alex, our miniature schnauzer, ran past her to greet me in bustling enthusiasm, his little black tail wagging furiously.

'Finished?'

'Yes.'

She sat on the bench by the front door and began pulling off her heavy blue snow shoes.

'I need a shower. Is there any water left?'

'Plenty of water left.'

'I'll give his feet a shower first. It's wet snow. I should've put his bootees on but I forgot.'

She picked up the dog and disappeared into the bathroom, closing the door behind her. As she always did on entering the cabin in the evening she had instinctively turned on the lights, and as I always did as soon as she had left the room I got up and turned them off again. There is something deeply restful about the fading of natural light within a room on an overcast winter afternoon such as this and I try never to miss it. I switched on the radio, turned the chair sideways to the stove, facing the window on the long, eastern wall of the cabin, and looked out across the valley at the view that was the real reason we bought this plot of land and this cabin in the first place: the seven Blefjell peaks in a jagged line that formed the furthermost limit of sight in that direction. From the radio came the sounds of Leif Ove Andsnes playing *Vél Komne med æra*, the first of Geirr Tveitt's *Fifty Folk Tunes from Hardanger*. As I watched from the window I saw, as though conjured by the piano notes, the slow formation of three thin, pinkish bars of dusky light above the Blefjell peaks. The snow had stopped. Not a breath of wind stirred in the tops of the small stand of pines just visible low down the slope on my right. I heard a far-off bleat from one of the two goats the proprietor of the Veggli Fjellstue further up the hill keeps as pets. As though at a given signal, lights began going on in the valley below. First one, then another, then two, three more,

more and more of them. It was like seeing stars appear in the sky for the first time. Quite suddenly I was overcome with an intense sensation of happiness. It was as though rain were falling inside my head. Closing my eyes, I abandoned myself to it.

# 2

## Sunday, 31 December 2017

Selling a dream – baptism in the

mountain chapel – origins of the cabin

dream – the dog gets bored – chance

meeting with a landowner

ater I was to realise it was a boom time for cabin building in the Norwegian mountains, and that similar hoardings could be seen all over the mountainside at Vegglifjell. But that December morning two years ago, as we left the cabin belonging to my brother-in-law, Paul, and his wife, Trine, and set out for the walk to the little mountain chapel where the christening was to take place, was the first time I had seen one:

### HER KAN VI BYGGE DIN HYTTEDRØM
*(We can build your cabin dream here)*

it said. I stopped a moment to reflect on the bold nature of the claim. In the midst of that dense white wilderness it was hard

to imagine anything being built exactly where that sign stood. Then my wife was calling on me to hurry up, the ceremony was about to start in five minutes.

In the vestibule I picked up a booklet on the history of the chapel. We took our seats, and as we waited for the priest to begin I glanced idly through it. *The mountain chapel at Veggli,* I read, *is two thousand six hundred and twenty-five feet above sea level. It has seating for a hundred people. It was designed by Hans Halvorsen, of Sandefjord, built by Einar Eriksrud, and consecrated by Bishop Osberg in 1992.* A large, wine-dark curtain bisected the nave from corner to corner, focusing attention on the altar in the corner on which there was a painting of a man looking out over the mountains. Beneath it was an inscription: I WILL LIFT UP MINE EYES TO THE HILLS. PSALM 121. To the right of it, the panels on the small pulpit continued the mountain landscape theme. Further round the right-hand wall, half-hidden by the curtain, there was a green wooden door, which could be opened by a thumb latch to give access, via a small ladder, to the wooden bell-tower attached to the outside of the church. The church was built of stone brought down from the Hardangervidda. In the area behind the partitioning curtain through which we had entered the church was a kitchen, a toilet, a small bedroom and an open fireplace serving a space large enough to accommodate a family gathering such as ours, consisting of some thirty people. It was slightly surreal to read that the organ of that tiny and remote chapel had been imported from Queen Elizabeth's Chapel in Windsor Castle, although on looking round I couldn't see an organ anywhere. The Ten Commandments had been inscribed in gold leaf on the green beams that criss-crossed the roof space above our heads.

Almost all the guests that Sunday were from the father's

side of the family, our Norwegian side. Kelly, the baby's mother, was Chinese-Mauritian. She and Marius had got married in Stavanger a few months previously. There was to be a second leg of the wedding for the benefit of Kelly's family in six months' time in July, on Mauritius. Mathias' christening came in the middle of the two ceremonies, bridging as it were the two halves of the wedding.

Alex was sleeping on the floor at my feet in my black Fjällräven rucksack. We'd only had him for about six weeks and I was far from certain his toilet training was complete. Each time he made a move I was afraid he might have weed, or worse, inside the bag. Or that suddenly he would become aware that Halvorsen, a sparky little Jack Russell belonging to one of Marius's friends, was sitting on the other side of the aisle just two rows in front of us. Twice, during the arrival-mingling that had taken place before the baptism, Halvorsen had tried to mount Alex. Unsuccessfully, I was pleased and even proud to note. But I knew that if either one of them got wind of the other now a barking match would ensue, which not even the wrath of God would be able to subdue.

The priest looked to be no more than thirty and wore one of those *presteskjegg* you only get in Lutheran countries, a moustacheless beard that instantly imparted four centuries of Lutheran authority to the office that was a little compromised by the dark blue trainers visible below the rim of his white surplice. What with worrying about the dog and the unruly children I failed to follow the service for at least the first ten minutes, but from the printed order of service I know that things got under way with a rendition of a Christmas song, *Julekveldsvisa*, to a text by Alf Prøysen, one of the country's favourite songwriters, long dead but still fondly remembered. This was followed by the baptismal psalm *En krybbe var vuggen* ('A crib was the cradle'). Then came the baptism itself. Little Mathias, swathed in a white christening robe about three metres long, duly howled in protest at the sudden shock of cold water on his forehead. The priest then intoned the proclamation of faith: *Jeg forsaker djevelen og alle hans gjerninger og alt hans vesen. Jeg tror på Gud Fader, den allmektige himmelens og jordens skaper* ('I forsake the devil and all his works and his being. I believe in God, the Father almighty, creator of heaven and earth'). This was followed by a reading from the Prologue to the Gospel of St John: 'In the beginning was the Word, and the Word was with God, and the Word was God. The same was in the beginning with God. All things were made by him; and without him was not any thing made that was made. In him was life; and the life was the light of men. And the light shineth in darkness; and the darkness comprehended it not.'

The traditionally Christian nature of the proceedings surprised me. I had known Marius since he was born and neither he nor his parents had ever struck me as being religious. Perhaps it came from Kelly's side. The baptism was followed by the sermon, followed by two rousing hymns. The Norwegian hymnal is unique to Norwegian culture and the melodies were unfamiliar to me. But long ago, when I first began attending the confirmation ceremonies that are still such an important part of Norwegian social life, I had made the decision to groan along anyway, as a courtesy, and because I found it strangely enjoyable. I respond in the same way when the priest says *let us pray*, and did so on this occasion too, bowing my head, closing my eyes, savouring the vacuum that briefly arose before my thoughts hurried off and I was once again outside and once again contemplating that sign we had passed on our way over to the chapel. The naked directness of the claim impressed me. My cabin dream was a secret: how could the company who were making it know what it was?

It was a dream I'd been nurturing for decades, ever since the early 1970s, when I was living and working in London and met a woman who had recently returned to England after spending two years among the hippies of Haight-Ashbury in San Francisco. We moved in together, and among the books she unpacked from her cardboard boxes was a green Noonday American paperback edition of Knut Hamsun's novel *Pan*, originally published in Norwegian in 1894. I recognised the name. I had come across it in one of Henry Miller's books. Miller described him as 'that Dostoevsky of the north' and that was enough to arouse my curiosity. I picked it up, opened it and read the first paragraph:

These last few days I have thought and thought about the Nordland summer's endless day. I sit and think of it, and of a cabin I lived in, and of the forest behind the cabin, and I feel like writing something down, just to make the time pass, and because it amuses me. Time drags now, I can't make it pass as fast as I would like, although nothing troubles me and I lead the most enjoyable of lives. I'm well satisfied with everything, and thirty is no great age. A few days ago someone living far away from here sent me two feathers in the post. It was amusing to see two such fiendishly green feathers. And I have no health problems, apart from a touch of arthritis in my left foot from an old shotgun wound that healed a long time ago. I remember how quickly the time passed two years ago, incomparably quicker than it does now. A summer was gone almost before I had noticed it. It was two years ago, in 1855.

With a strange and almost diffident passion, the narrator, Lieutenant Thomas Glahn, goes on to describe the young woman he met and fell in love with that summer. Her name is Edvarda and she is the daughter of the local squire. She lives in a big white house in a coastal settlement called Sirilund. He can just about see it from the door of his cabin, perched at the edge of a forest high above the village. Edvarda falls in love with him too, but their complexity as individuals dooms the relationship. Both have too much pride to be able to give of themselves completely, and as the first signs of autumn begin to appear in the forest, Glahn leaves Sirilund. Two years later he writes the memoir we have just been reading. In a brief coda set in India Hamsun brings in a second narrator, another hunter, who describes how Glahn provoked him so greatly that in the end he shot him. It's a suicide by proxy.

I was a fast reader, used to devouring books, but that short book hypnotised me. As I read I *became* Thomas Glahn. I could smell the stale blood on the hides nailed to the walls of the cabin, see the glints of spectral colour in the wings pinned there, hear the faint whimpering of our dreaming dog Æsop, the explosive pop and crackle of the firewood as we sat and roasted the game we had shot in the forest. And afterwards we would lie back and rest on our primitive wooden bed, smoking our pipe and listening to the approach of night in the forest outside, completely alone, completely content.

I had never come across anything like *Pan* before. In marking the start of my lifelong fascination with Norway, a country that up until that time I could hardly have shown you on the map, in a quite literal sense it dictated the course of my future life. Much later I learned that *Pan* has similarly obsessed generations of young Norwegians – men as well as women – since its publication in 1894, and that attempts to mimic its stylistic originality have been the ruin of many a young Norwegian writer.

It was the dream of this cabin, and a life like this lived in the cabin, that took hold of me at that early age and contrived, through all the subsequent years in which my life did not resemble Glahn's in the slightest, to sustain itself in the belief and the hope that these dreams might one day come true. Gripped as I was by the hypnotic quality of the prose, even in James McFarlane's English translation, and curious to know whether this quality derived from something unique to the Norwegian language, or whether it was directly attributable to the genius with which Hamsun used the language, I started teaching myself Norwegian. At the time I was working behind the counter at a newsagent's at the lower end of Charing Cross Road, and on afternoons with few customers my head would be buried in the copy of Hugo's *Teach Yourself Norwegian in Three Months* that we carried on our shelves. After a few months this obsession with Norway developed to a point at which I enrolled as an undergraduate at University College London and took a degree course in Scandinavian Studies, specialising in Norwegian. Part of the attraction of the course was that in the first of its four years students got to spend three months in Norway.

I remember the mixture of pleasure and sadness that descended on me after the four years of study were over. I was thirty-two years old. I'd been to Norway. I'd learned that the effects Hamsun was able to achieve in *Pan* and the other novels and short stories I subsequently devoured owed more to his inspired use of Norwegian than to any special quality in the language itself. Now this brief engagement with the dreamland was over, and it was time to go back to – well, back to what? The four years had left me with nothing save an extensive and probably useless knowledge of what was still, at that time, an obscure and minor European culture.

By 1980, towards the end of my studies, I had managed to sell a couple of ideas to the drama department at BBC Radio that included a dramatisation of Knut Hamsun's first novel *Hunger*, his fraught account of the travails of a young writer living rough and starving on the streets of Kristiania* as he struggles to write something that will make his name. But my infatuation with *Pan* and life as a doomed hunter–lover living in a cabin in the far north of Norway remained as strong as ever, and on the back of the broadcast of the much more radiophonic *Hunger* I was able to persuade the drama department to follow it up with an adaptation of Hamsun's great novella.

It was during the recording of this play, at Bush House just off Oxford Circus, that I came as close as I would ever actually get to *becoming* Lieutenant Glahn and moving *not just into his cabin but into his life*. With the hindsight of years, of course, my obsession with this novel might easily seem ridiculous, but in defence of the old young man I was I might add that at a reception I attended in Oslo some twenty-five years ago to honour Ibsen's biographer, Michael Meyer, Meyer told me that his friend Graham Greene had been similarly fascinated by Hamsun's *Pan*, and that traces of this can be glimpsed in Greene's 1952 novel *The End of the Affair*, for example in the way Greene gives his narrator, Bendrix, the limp that he shares with Hamsun's Glahn.

An actor called Robin Ellis, well known at the time as the male lead in the original television dramatisation of *Poldark*, had been cast as Lieutenant Glahn. The film version of John

---

* Oslo was known as Christiania until 1877, when the spelling was changed to Kristiania. In 1925 the name was changed to Oslo.

Fowles' novel *The French Lieutenant's Woman* had just opened in the West End and Lynsey Baxter, who played the part of Ernestina, Charles Smithson's fiancée in the film, was Edvarda. Lynsey was small and blonde, with a beautiful forehead and mysterious eyes. I was infatuated with her from the moment she entered the studio and struggled desperately to hide the fact. But with the innate intensity of the story further intensified by the claustrophobic and windowless environment of the recording studio at Bush House, over the three days that the recording spanned I just couldn't do it. On the final afternoon of the recording session, as she stood buttoning her coat to leave, still clutching a bunch of flowers the producer had given her, in front of a grinning array of studio technicians I plucked up the courage to ask if I could see her again.

'Yes,' she said.

*Yes!*

How my heart sang!

I never wanted to leave that stuffy, airless little studio with its blinking consoles and coloured lights and microphones high up in Broadcasting House. Suddenly, in the middle of London, it had become my cabin at the edge of my forest in the remote north of Norway. My dream had come true. I had entered completely into the world of a book. In a bewildered ecstasy I shook everyone's hand twice and wished them all goodbye several times before heading for the studio door. There I almost tripped over a tin wastepaper bucket that had toppled over from the weight of the copies of the script tossed into it by the actors on their way out. The sight of those scripts spilling from the mouth of that upended bucket was like a dagger to my heart. To the actors it had been just another day's work, just another day at the office. On the lift down I recalled how the urbane Ellis had even laughed during rehearsal as he read a line of Glahn's about 'thirty being no great age'. At one point he also made some in-character crack about 'fishes and loaves of bread' and in general he had made no attempt to hide the fact that he disliked the character. As far as I could tell Ellis was a perfectly nice man and a good actor, but Glahn he wasn't. How could he be? *I* was Glahn.

And what did it matter? Edvarda, Edvarda – my Edvarda had said yes!

*

Two days later, out in the world of big red Routemasters and newspaper vendors, things weren't quite the same. Edvarda and I met in the coffee bar in the basement of Dillon's, as the university bookshop on Malet Street was then known. Her forehead was still beautiful, but away from the cabin, away from the studio, things weren't quite the same. When we had finished our coffee she took me straight to the department stocking New Age books, probably the only type of book in the world I would pay not to have to read. Already I could sense our budding romance was doomed to fail, and in the midst of a kind of joyous misery it made me all the more desperate to see her again. The whole point of the exercise was to fail, and it seemed to me there was a very good chance I might succeed.

At the entrance to Goodge Street tube station, as the street lights were coming on to lighten the November gloom, I said goodbye to her. We were standing next to a newspaper vendor who smelt of beer and hawked copies of the *Evening Standard* in such a loud voice he nearly drowned out my attempts to make her understand how much I needed to see her again. Looking back, I imagine she was alarmed and puzzled by the fervour of my demeanour, especially since it was obvious to both of us that we had little in common. She had already discreetly suggested that my interest in her might have something to do with the play. It was a stunningly accurate insight, which I dismissed as absurd. But she agreed to meet me the following Monday, at a BBC lunchtime concert at St John's Church in Smith Square, in Westminster, within sight of the river. Utterly content with the way things were working out I set off down Tottenham Court Road. I was still walking on air as I crossed Oxford Street and continued down Charing Cross Road, heading towards The Cambridge, a pub in Cambridge Circus, where I stopped for a drink, to deepen the intensity of the night, before completing the journey back to Clapham Common in the warm and magical orange nicotine-fug of the upper deck of a number 88 bus.

Come Monday my Edvarda stood me up. I waited at the foot of the steps outside the church until the last minute, and when I was certain she wouldn't be coming bought a ticket and went in anyway. A string quartet played something rhythmic by Haydn, and as the music raced forward I put aside my disappointment and followed it, rocking and swaying about in my chair. After a few minutes a middle-aged man sitting beside me tapped me on the shoulder and whispered something. I couldn't hear what he was saying. At that time I suffered from a kind of reverse paranoia in which I suspected total strangers of whispering kind words about me to each other, and plotting secretly to find ways of increasing my happiness. I dipped slightly towards him and half-raised a cupped hand to my ear to indicate I hadn't heard. I was probably expecting to hear something along the lines of how *good* it was to see someone so obviously *enjoying* the music. What I heard, as he leaned towards me, articulated as clearly as possible and almost audible above the music, was: *Stop joggling.*

It brought me right down to earth. I made a point of joggling even more energetically for the remainder of the movement, but it was joyless joggling, and well before the concert was over I realised that the steam had gone out of the whole thing. No doubt to her relief, I didn't try to see my Edvarda again. It turned out to have been just something I had to do. Having done it once I wouldn't have to do it again. But my dream of the cabin survived the death of the dream of love...

*

Now the priest had begun the unaccompanied chanting of the *Nattverdssalme*, the Communion Hymn. It was a sad and plaintive and austere sound, his voice swooping and twisting around the rafters and those Ten Commandments. It seemed to affect Alex too. From down inside the rucksack he raised up an eerie, howling response. No one minded, no one glared at me. Not even the priest. I was the only one, glaring at myself on behalf of the whole of institutionalised Christianity.

'I'll take him out,' I whispered to Nina. With forethought, I had taken a seat at the aisle end of the pew, and it was a simple matter to pick up the bag and carry a still wailing Alex the few steps that took us to the sanctuary of the function room behind the thick, partitioning curtain. Putting the rucksack down I unhooked my parka and shrugged it on, doubled the long woollen scarf around my neck, pulled the black woollen beanie down low over my forehead, hooked Alex up to his lead and stepped out into a blizzard.

Outside the parking area we turned right and headed down the cleared track towards Paul and Trine's cabin. It was just about visible through the driving snow. We passed a barrier that was always left up in the winter, to let the snowplough

through, then turned left up the sloping track that led past their cabin. Alex's ears streamed out behind him in the wind. Every now and then he stopped to describe a little map of Norway in the snow with his urine.

'*Flink gutt, Alex!*' I said to encourage him, leaning down towards his little grey bobbing head. 'Good boy!' I spoke mostly Norwegian to him, but then usually translated it. My wife caught me doing it once. I told her I wanted him to grow up bilingual.

Many aspects of becoming a dog-owner had taken me by surprise. Struck by the dog's gentleness, his decency, his strangely hesitant courtesy and his helpless submission to the demands of appetite, in one unguarded moment I had caught myself wondering whether he might not be the reincarnation of my late brother. In a tangential offshoot of this unexpected notion I had even sent off to Amazon for a copy of G. K. Chesterton's slender study of the life and work of St Francis of Assisi, but by the time it arrived I could scarcely even remember why I'd ordered it.

About fifty metres past Paul and Trine's cabin we turned left again, along another cleared track that passed five or six cabins in the woods on the right as it headed back parallel with the first track, pulling away from it just before it passed the church and dropping into a footpath through a small copse that was still just about navigable despite the snow, emerging via a small and slippery plank bridge onto the main track. On a rise directly opposite us stood the long narrow rectangle of the Veggli Fjellstue. In the distance I could hear the growling of a snowplough and as we headed down the track below the Fjellstue towards the sound it stopped. Dimly through the falling snow I saw the driver hop down from the cab, slide the headphones off his ears onto his neck and converse briefly with two people who were out walking. Alex stopped to pee again. Waiting, I looked around and saw that I was standing beside another of Norske Fjellhus's enigmatic signs:

### VI REALISERER HYTTEDRØMMEN DIN HER
*(We can make your cabin dream come true here)*

The walkers moved on. I stood there on the corner, still looking at the sign. The driver of the snowplough swung himself back up into the cab, pulled the headphones back over his ears, but then took them off again. Sliding the window to one side, he called out to me:

'Are you interested in a *hytta*?'

Was I interested in a *hytta*? It wasn't the far north of Norway. It was no more than a couple of hours by car from Oslo. There would be no endless days here, no dark and sunless winters. A cabin here would be a second-best dream. But when I looked across the valley at the jagged line of peaks dimming visibly behind the falling snow, it suddenly didn't seem to matter at all.

'Very interested,' I said.

He swung open the cab door, jumped down again, checked for traffic coming up around the corner and walked over to me. He introduced himself. Said his name was Jørgen. That he was the landowner. Turning, he pointed to a timber cabin about a hundred metres away up a turn-off higher up the track.

'You want to have a look at one? That belongs to my in-laws. I've got the key if you want to have a look round inside.'

'They're not there?'

'It's not finished yet. They're still working on the inside.'

'Okay.'

'I'll meet you up there.'

He crossed the track, climbed back up into the cab, started the engine and trundled off towards the cabin.

As I set off after him I heard faintly, in the distance, the sound of hymn-singing from the chapel.

# 3

## 8 January 1985

Visit to a cabin by the sea – party on an

island – conversation with Sverre – his

pursuit of the lucid dream – history of

Norwegian cabin culture – listening to

calls of shepherdesses in the Norwegian

mountains – internet at the cabin

'd had access to a Norwegian cabin before. Shared between my wife and her brother, Paul, it was a single-storey wooden building with a separate garage on a wooded promontory overlooking the Oslofjord, near a tiny settlement called Torød, just south of Tønsberg, on the Nøtterøy peninsula. Nina took me to see it one January day in the winter of 1985, not long after we met. It was snowing heavily. As I later learned, those first five winters I spent in Norway, between 1983 and 1988, were among the coldest and snowiest the country had known since the early 1940s and the years of the German occupation.

The drive from Oslo to Nøtterøy took about two hours. It was one of those journeys where the roads seem to get gradually narrower all the time, as though the car itself were having to concentrate ever more fiercely on reaching a tiny and obscure destination. After leaving the main E6 we passed through Tønsberg, then drove over the bridge to Nøtterøy. Tønsberg was a centre of the Norwegian whaling industry for much of the nineteenth and twentieth centuries and just out-side the village of Teie we passed a monument to Svend Foyn, inventor of the harpoon cannon. With the snow falling ever more heavily we entered a narrowing maze of lanes that finally brought us to Torød, with its single not-very-main street and small supermarket at the end. Beyond that the road turned into a track with a view of Vrengensund, actually a part of the extensive Oslofjord. Except for the small humps of snow-shrouded skerries and islands dotted about, the sea was hardly distinguishable from the sky.

'On a clear day you can see across to Sweden,' said Nina, changing down through the gears as the Polo followed the road up a small hill and past a few newish-looking apartment blocks built up the side of it, balconies jutting out like open drawers in a dresser. At the top she turned sharp right into a track that led through a stand of pines and continued along for about a hundred metres until the track ended in a small, cleared space. She stopped the car, pulled on the handbrake and turned off the engine.

'Are we there?'

'Yes,' she said. 'That's it up there.'

She leaned forward and pointed. At the top of the short, uphill drive on our left, through an obscuring fringe of white-coated branches, I saw my first Norwegian cabin. Or rather, I saw the draped form of it, sleeping beneath a dense white cocoon of snow. It looked like a Christo sculpture. A pine tree taller than the cabin itself leaned down towards a window through which the silver loop of a tap was just visible.

Ours was the only car there, and there were no lights showing in any of the four or five cabins I could now see, looking through the trees. A shower of powdery snow outside the passenger-side window drifted down from the branches of a pine. Looking up I saw a large magpie swaying clumsily about on a small ball of fat in a green net someone had hung out there.

The approach lane had been visited by snowploughs fairly recently, and you could still just about see the outlined tracks of the large tyres as the tractor shunted in and out of the parking space; but the snow on the driveway up to the cabin lay so thick that it would have been impossible to turn the car up there, and difficult even to walk the few metres. Perfectly cloaked in thick white soft snow, the cabin looked so poetic, so dreamlike, so perfect that I asked Nina the same question every foreigner probably asks when seeing a Norwegian cabin for the first time: why don't you live here all the time?

'You can't,' she replied. 'We close it down in the winter. The pipes are just half a metre below ground. We turn the water off at the mains or the pipes would freeze and burst.'

I was a little disappointed: 'So we can't go in?'

'We could, but there's no point. We couldn't even make a cup of coffee. I just wanted you to see it.'

We sat in the car eating sandwiches and drinking coffee from a thermos she had prepared and she told me the history of her family's association with the place. Her father had bought it from a local landowner in the early 1960s, and since the age of five she had spent every summer there with her mother and younger brother, from early July until the end of August. At weekends her father, who worked in shipping, would join the family, sailing up the fjord from Oslo every Friday with dozens of other working dads looking forward to seeing their wives and children again. For obvious reasons these special Friday evening ferry departures were known as *pappabåter* ('dad-boats'). She told me how a community built up among the other families with cabins on the hill, summer friendships, visits from relatives, weekend cruises at sea in the cabin cruiser that was moored for the summer at the jetty down in the bay. As she talked to me about it I began to be able to see it, she and her little brother playing hide and seek between the trees with the other children, always in their swimming costumes, the sun always shining, always in the background one or other of the Fred Olsen or DFDS ferries on its way to Denmark, or to Kiel in Germany, majestically slow and massively reassuring as they glided across the fjord in the half-distance, the view now and then obscured by floral baskets dripping with red petunias that hung from beam hooks on a sun terrace, which I could just see on the far side of the cabin, the seaview side. All of this I invested with a fabulous sense of timelessness and happiness, even knowing that, as we spoke, Nina's mother lay dying of cancer at the Oslo Radium Hospital, so doused in painkillers she scarcely recognised her own daughter when she visited.

After about half an hour we turned the car around and drove back to Oslo. The snow was so heavy it was often difficult to see where the side of the road was. Nina's Polo had the studded winter tyres that were standard on every Norwegian car in those days, before environmental concern for their effect on the air led to the more widespread use of studless tyres that were thicker and wider and gave better road-holding than summer tyres. Occasionally the car waltzed slightly as it came up out of the wear-pattern of waves and troughs ground into each side of the camber by the studs. It was a distinctly unnerving sensation and as we crossed the bridge that connects Nøtterøy with Tønsberg I remember wondering why she had gone to the trouble of making the long journey in such dreadful conditions. I think it was only later I realised that for her the trip contained an element of ritual of which I could have known nothing at that time, when the status and significance of the cabin in the life of the average Norwegian family were unknown to me: that the purpose of the drive was to tell herself – and me, had I but known it – that she was considering sharing her life with me. And that meant sharing her cabin.

### 28 April 2018

Less visible than the *skjærgårdsidyll** of the Swedes, less export-able than the social customs conveyed by terms like Swedish

---

* Cabin life on the Swedish skerries.

*lagom*,\* Danish *hygge*† and even Finnish *kälsarikännit*,‡ Norwegian *hytta* culture is more profoundly rooted than any of these in the history of the people. All of this was explained to me one evening by a man named Sverre Tangstad as we sat together in the stern of Ole's *snekke* and drank beer while we sailed along the Årøysund. We were on our way out to Ole's island cabin on Skrøslingen. There were ten or twelve on board, and a dozen more in another *snekke* belonging to Ole's brother-in-law, Iver, that was chugging along some fifty metres away on our starboard side. Boats are like cabins in Norway. They don't have anything to do with social class. Norway was historically a maritime culture, and for much of the twentieth century the Norwegian merchant marine was one of the largest in the world, a heritage that has persisted on into the twenty-first century in the form of a small-boat culture. Most of these will be some form or other of *snekke*. These are clinker-built boats with overlapping planks and an external rudder. For decades the wooden *snekke* was the most common type of boat you would see on and around the Oslofjord, although in recent years the plastic *snekke*, which requires less maintenance, has overtaken it in popularity. Ole's boat, named the *Gry Helene* after his wife, was the half-open type, with a protective windshield at the front behind which Ole was standing, the fingers of his right hand twinned around two spokes of the wheel, occasionally drinking from the tin of Pripps Blå beer he held in his other hand.

---

\* A word implying the pursuit of the happy medium in all things.
† A style of relaxation practised by middle-class Danes, usually involving candles and red wine.
‡ A very different style of relaxation practised by some Finns, often defined as 'drinking beer at home, alone and in your underpants and with no intention of going out'.

Ole and Gry Helene were throwing a party. A lot of other guests would be making their own way in boats out to the island. For us the evening had started with a concert at the little arts centre of Gamle Ormelet at Tjøme, further down the coast from Torød, where Odd Nordstugu played and sang with his guitar and his group. Odd is one of those singers who disdains the shot at world fame that singing in English might give him and goes on singing and composing in his own language. In his case the cultural loyalty is even more profound since he sings in *nynorsk* – New Norwegian – Norway's second official language. *Nynorsk* has had a special literary and patriotic status ever since it was codified as a written language from local dialects by Ivar Aasen in the nineteenth century. Aasen travelled the valleys and mountains of Norway in search of a language that was authentically Norwegian, and not the inherited 'status' language of the Dano-Norwegian (Bokmål) that was one legacy of Norway's more than four hundred years as a Danish colony, from the union of Kalmar in 1397 to the end of the Napoleonic wars. Performers like Odd have longer careers and are more likely to survive into old age as national treasures than the anglophone singers.

Sverre was an old friend of Ole's. I'd never met him before, but he had a melancholy seriousness about him that I found immediately attractive. In the course of our conversation I had mentioned to him that we had recently bought a plot of land – in Numedal, on the eastern rim of the Hardangervidda – and were having a cabin built on it. I had forgotten my own observation, that at the slightest opportunity a Norwegian will embark on an informative lecture on virtually any aspect of his or her culture in which a foreigner shows an interest, and with almost no preamble I found myself listening to what turned out to be a rather jaundiced lecture on the history of the Norwegian cabin tradition.

'You must understand,' said Sverre, 'that to a Norwegian, a cabin, whether by the sea or in the mountains, is so much more than just a piece of property or a possession. A cabin in the family is part of the soul of any Norwegian. It's a deep part of Norwegian national identity, one that is hidden and difficult to catch your eye on from the outside. It's to do with our roots. Norwegians are farming people, not really urban people. You know, at the start of the nineteen hundreds, there were about a hundred thousand cabins in the Norwegian mountains. *Sætre*, we call them. Summer mountain farms. I think you have them in Scotland, someone once told me the word...'

He fumbled in his jacket pockets, patting each one as though looking for the word there before bringing out a small round tin of chewing tobacco. He snapped open the lid, took out one of the little dark brown pellets, wedged it down onto the gums between his lower lip and front teeth with the tip of his middle finger. A lot of Norwegians still use snuff in this way. Often it's a habit acquired in the military while doing national service. Mechanically he offered me the open tin and when I rejected it with a shake of the head he snapped the lid back on and slipped it back into his pocket.

'Shielings?' I suggested.

He frowned and looked upwards.

'Yes, I think that was it. Places of work, not holiday homes. Summer farms, where the cattle and sheep and goats were driven up into the mountains in the summer to graze on the mountain pastures. A hundred thousand. Today there are maybe nine hundred of them that are still places of work.'

He stopped, adjusted the wad of chewing tobacco, folded his hands and said: 'Am I dreaming?'

The non sequitur came so suddenly that I turned in surprise. It was a starry evening, the moon was not yet up, and the stars shone bright and clear. In the faint green glow of the starboard light I saw that he was frowning. He caught me looking at him and seemed puzzled for an instant. Then, with a wry smile, he explained that it was a technique. He was reading a book about lucid dreaming. How to train yourself to have waking dreams in which you can control what happens. You can fly if you want to. Walk through walls. Breathe underwater – do anything you want, because it's all a dream. Every now and then, he said, you have to surprise yourself. In the middle of your ordinary life, even when you're awake. You have to ask yourself: *Am I dreaming?*

As though it were another part of the exercise or reality check or whatever it was, he reached out a hand and lightly touched my cheek. First my cheek, then his own.

'Don't you find it hard to tell whether you're dreaming or not? On a night such as this, for example? With other people, some you've never met before, some you see all the time, some you haven't seen for years. You're on the water, gliding past these little islands with the little cabins with the lights on. Through a lit window you catch a glimpse of two heads leaning across a table. They're talking. But out here it's dark. The stars are out. You're in a motor boat sailing towards Skrøslingen in Ole's boat. You've spent the evening at a concert at Gamle Ormelet. I mean, how would this be any different if you *were* dreaming? In Numedal, did you say?'

It was another unnervingly abrupt turn in his conversation.

'Yes,' I said. 'Do you know the area?'

'I should say so, I grew up there. My grandparents had a farm in Traaen, between Lampeland and Veggli, and they had a *sæter* up on the Hardangervidda. We used to spend our summers up there, my sister and brother and I, when I was a little child. Of course, it wasn't really a working *sæter* by then, my grandparents were too old, we were just on holiday there. That's what happened to most of the *sæter*, they were either abandoned or converted into holiday homes. And of course, the good thing about a cabin, being made of timber, you can take it apart and transport it wherever you like and put it up again. Fit it together like the pieces of a jigsaw puzzle. The same house, with the same knots in the wood. Even the same smell. My father moved it, when my great-grandmother died. We helped him, me and my brother and sister. Tell me about your cabin.'

'There's not a lot to tell. It's a Fjellstul 2.'

'*Hva behager?*'

'It's called a Fjellstul 2.'

'That's the name of it?'

'Yes.'

'Describe it to me.'

I described it to him. I told him it was a two-storey build-ing made of dimension stock, with notched and finger-jointed timbers on the ground floor, wood panelling on its upper floor. A gable roof overhung a front porch that was supported on three cinched pillars. I said that the builders had purposely included elements of the cabin architecture unique to the Numedal valley, such as these three pillars, and the characteris-tically oval face on both sides of the timbers. On a visit to the open-air Folkemuseum on the Bygdøy peninsula just outside Oslo, where you can walk around an artificial village of log cabins from all the different regions and periods, I told him, I had seen for myself, in the Numedal section of the museum, that these elements of our new cabin really did echo the charac-teristic building style of the region for much of the past three hundred years.

Sverre nodded sagely at this.

'I see,' he said. 'So you've bought yourself an IKEA cabin. I sincerely hope my directness does not offend you. What you're getting up there in the mountains – I hope you don't mind me saying this – it isn't really a proper Norwegian *hytta*. Let me tell you, something happened to our Norwegian culture after the oil came. It happened quickly. Almost overnight it felt like sometimes. You wake up one morning, everything's the same, but the world has changed. Do you know that feeling?'

I said I didn't think I did, but please continue.

'There's a narrative to the change, I've traced it. I thought tracing it might help. Go back to the 1950s, first point—'

He broke off, leaned forward and, rummaging inside the battered black rucksack wedged between his feet, pulled out another can of Heineken, snapped back the ring-pull, cursed under his breath, dabbed beer from around the opening with his finger and then sucked his fingertip before taking a long swig and resuming:

'First point – you need a car for mountain tourism. By the end of the 1950s, when wartime rationing came to an end, it meant a lot of Norwegians were suddenly able to afford cars. Where are they going to drive in these cars? To hotels. Big hotels in the mountains. That was the first entrepreneur dream of the Norwegian future. These big hotels that would spring up all over the mountainsides and in the valleys. But this, this was before feminism. Norwegian women didn't work any more, not like they did on the farms in the old days, like my great-grandmother did. They were housewives. That was their job. Working at home as housewives, doing the cooking, washing the children, cleaning the house with a vacuum cleaner. So all these hotels were supposed to be a great gift to the wives and mothers. No cooking for two weeks! No dishes to wash! No beds to make. No whatever it would be. Instead it would be just sitting in the hotel bar with a martini, going up into the local mountains for walks, going out for a drive while someone else makes your beds, cooks your meals, serves you drinks at these big mountain hotels.

'Like all rational attempts to predict the future, which are actually attempts to *create* the future, things didn't work out that way. You know, this is so typically Norwegian. We are always trying to *plan* the future, so that nothing can go wrong. No one believes in God any more, so now everyone believes in Reason. This is something that came over the border into this country after the Russian revolution. Social engineering. Plans. Five-year plans. Seven-year plans. The Labour Party had a three-year plan in the 1930s. Laws, plans everywhere you look. Laws for what you can and can't do, even in the mountains. The *naturvern* law in 1954.* The *friluftslov* in 1957.† And then the new laws for planning and building in 1965. The old building law from 1924 only applied to Norwegian towns; the new law applied everywhere. Not just to towns and cities but even to tiny little settlements far off in the mountains and the countryside. They took the Norwegian countryside from the farmers and the peasants and they sold it to the tourists and the cabin people.'

He stopped and studied his fingernail again, holding it up, moving it about, trying to catch it in the faint green glow of light from the starboard lamp mounted on the side of the cabin. He flapped his hand vigorously. I heard his knuckles.

'Where was I?'

'You were saying I've bought an IKEA cabin.'

---

\* Conservation law
† Outdoor recreation law

'Ah yes, that's right. Well, in the 1990s, the whole direction of this development changed. Why? Because for one, Norwegians had become rich. It takes time to realise it when you become rich. It took us twenty-five to thirty years before we understood we didn't *have* to stay in special hotels, we had enough money to build our very own little luxury hotels in the mountains. Luxury cabins, like yours for example. Another thing, Robert – what the hotel-building people never saw coming was the feminism of the 1970s and 1980s. Suddenly there were no housewives slaving over hot stoves any more. And besides, the husbands and fathers were tired of staying at hotels. Men travelled on business a lot in those days. My father did. He was always away in Germany, France, Italy when I was a child. When they were on holiday they didn't want to stay in hotels. People wanted all the home comforts, and they wanted them in the mountains. Now, with the oil, we could afford it. So since the 1990s we've had this explosion of people building new luxury homes in the mountains. We still call them cabins, but they're second homes. I suppose you're having Wi-Fi at your cabin?'

His look challenged me to deny it, and I didn't answer straightaway. Internet at the cabin was a sore point with me. Nina and I had discussed it at length, just as we had discussed whether or not to have underfloor heating in the hallway and bathroom. A third question on which we had not immediately seen eye to eye was the downlights she wanted installed in the living-room ceiling. They were dimmable, according to the electrician with whom we had discussed lighting and heating arrangements in the cabin. But I couldn't help feeling they would bring a sort of lift-like or hotel-like anonymity to the place. So I didn't really want Wi-Fi, or a pre-warmable cabin, or dimmable lift-lights embedded in the ceiling; but I had already travelled so far from my old, wooden dream that in the end I gave in.

'Yes, we are,' I finally said. 'But not television.'

Having conceded on all the other fronts, this remained my only real triumph. I saw Sverre nod and utter a small grunt of *I-knew-it* satisfaction as he turned away. We were passing under the slender arched bridge of the Årøysund. Ole, tall and thin, his back to us in the wheelhouse, turned the wheel over and we passed beneath the giant arches, the thrum of the motor briefly deafening, and then on into the open waters of the Oslofjord.

*

Ole had been in the same crowd as Nina in their teens and he and his wife, Gry Helene, had invited old friends from school days, university days and national service days to a reunion party at their cabin on Skrøslingen. The gathering was also to celebrate the fact that the cabin had been in the family's possession for fifty years. Thinking over the account Sverre had given me of the evolution of Norwegian cabin culture, I was reminded of something Ole had told me some years earlier, in the days when we still had the *hytta* in Nøtterøy, and Ole would sometimes call us up and suggest we meet down on the little concrete jetty in the bay at Torød and he would take us out to Skrøslingen, only a fifteen-minute sail away. We were out in his boat setting lobster pots when he told me that this idyllic and even paradisal second home had come into the family's possession all those decades ago by the merest chance. As a pre-testamentary gesture his great-aunt, the older of two sisters, had been given the choice: which would she prefer, the family's dishwasher or the cabin on the island? Without much hesitation, it seems, she had gone for the dishwasher. As Ole remarked, it's funny how things change; in the 1950s the dishwasher was a treasured labour-saving novelty and the island cabin a remote and infrequently used liability. Today the cabin was worth millions, and the marvellous machine had long ago rusted back into dust.

As the *snekke* chugged past the dark rise of the headland at Torød I realised we would be passing where Nina's old family cabin used to be. I tried to spot its exact location, but it was too dark, the wall of spiky pines across the hilltop too dense to see through. Memories of the many happy summers spent at that yellow-painted cabin flitted through my mind, a bright contrast to the soft darkness of the night at sea in Ole's motor boat, the tips of the small wavelets glinting white in the lights from the boat as it pushed through the water. Swimming back and forth across the little bay at Torød in the morning. Long sunlit afternoon hours lying in a striped hammock suspended between tall pines reading John le Carré, now and then resting the book pages-down on my chest to sip from a glass of cold white wine, the pleasurable slight sway of the hammock. Studying the tiny bubbles clinging to the inside of the glass as though doing so was a matter of the greatest consequence. The unpredictable moment when one of them suddenly let go and shot to the surface. The cries drifting up the hill of the children playing in the swimming pool Stokke had recently built in front of his cabin – an innovation that had baffled me, when the surging blue-black sea lay just a short ramble away down a narrow track bordered with grass and cornflowers and the early summer-flowering plant that the English call cow parsley, whose delicate little white flowers, Nina told me, Norwegians call *hundekjeks* ('dog biscuits').

Passing Torød we glided by the row of small, white wooden

houses known as *skipperhus* ('skipper's houses') at Årøysund, now bathed in the white light of the risen moon. For most of the way from Ormelet we had been sailing no more than a couple of hundred metres from the shore, but now Ole threaded the spokes of the wheel down through his hands and the *snekke* embarked on a long, slow curve that took us out to sea. I turned and looked back over my shoulder, hoping to catch a glimpse of the two white globes, like giant white golf balls waiting to be whacked off their tees, that stood on the brow of the hill on the opposite side of the bay at Torød from our old cabin. I had half-understood them to be listening stations erected by NATO during the 1950s. I couldn't locate them and asked Ole, who told me that they'd been taken down about five years earlier. Perhaps advancing military technology had rendered them obsolete. Or the Norwegians, in some typical gesture of unilateral trust, had just decided they didn't want them there any more.

*

Of the party itself I recall chiefly the incongruity of Sverre's thumbing through the menus on his iPhone in search of a recording he wanted to play me of his great-grandmother singing a *kulokk* (cattle-call) while people danced close by to a particularly raucous DumDum Boys track. He told me his great-grandmother had been a *budeie*, a mountain milk-maid or shepherdess. Over the centuries these women had developed a unique system of calling to their cattle or goats, and communicating with one another across the mountains and valleys. Aware that the tradition was dying out, collectors had travelled the country in the 1950s and 1960s, recording samples of these songs. A CD of the recordings, including one short sequence featuring his grandmother, which was the oldest in the whole collection, had recently been issued by the Norwegian National Library and Sverre had transferred it to his phone. He liked to listen to it, he said, because the sound of his great-grandmother's voice reminded him of the happy days of his childhood in the mountains above Flesberg in Numedal, where the family's converted *sæter* was.

It was past midnight. Most of the guests had left the candlelit intimacy of the narrow boathouse where we had been eating and drinking for the past two hours and had spilled out onto a short apron of grass that ran from the front door of Ole's cabin to a small, sandy beach cradled on each side in the arms of low, smooth, light-coloured rocks known as *skjærgård*. A sound system had been set up and people were dancing on the grass. We were sitting on a bench outside the boathouse. Sverre's wife, Tove, came up to us and Sverre introduced us. She was barefoot. With evident pride he told me she was a trained opera singer, so I was a little surprised when she took a packet of cigarettes from the top pocket of her denim jacket, shook one out and asked me for a light –

'No good asking him,' she said with a nod towards Sverre. 'He doesn't smoke. But you look as if you do.'

'Looks can be deceiving,' I said. 'I don't smoke either.'

She gave a little moue of disappointment and headed away towards a group of men who were sitting drinking beer on the rocks by the water. I saw her asking an Englishman I'd spoken to earlier. His name was Matt. He was in the oil business, working out a two-year contract for a Stavanger-based firm in their Oslo branch. He took out a lighter, flicked it open and she bent her head towards his cupped hands.

'I don't think I've ever met an opera singer before,' I said, turning to Sverre.

'She hasn't had an engagement for a while,' he said. 'Right now she's working as a supply teacher.'

He went back to thumbing through the menus on his phone, explaining to me at one point that it was a new one and he was still having trouble finding his way around it.

The mood of the music changed. 'Just my imagination', an old Temptations ballad, came on. I was getting bored waiting for Sverre to find this recording, and wondering if I should just get up and leave him to it. I glanced at my watch a couple of times. About to mutter some excuse and move away, I suddenly noticed the two people who were dancing in the sand by the water's edge, away from the main group of dancers on the grass closer to the cabin. In the bright moonlight I could see it was Tove. She was dancing with the Englishman. They were dancing in such an intimate and sensual way that I couldn't help glancing over at Sverre, to see if he had noticed; but he appeared completely bound up with locating the recording of his great-grandmother. Without losing the sensuous rhythm of the song she wriggled out of her denim jacket and tossed it behind her, onto the rocks. It landed with one sleeve just trailing in the water. She was wearing a tank top underneath, and a short white linen skirt that was almost luminous in the moonlight. As I watched, a pulse of waves from a passing launch broke against their knees. She laughed loudly, almost lost her balance and grabbed on to Matt's T-shirt.

At the sound of her laughter Sverre did look up. He stared down at the water for a long three seconds through half-closed eyes before returning to the screen. I carried on watching. The Englishman was wrapping and sliding his hands through the air around her, as though he were softly sculpting the outline of her body. The erotic charge between them was palpable and so strong that I fully expected Sverre to do something, I don't know what, interrupt in some way, put a stop to it. But he never did. Seemingly hypnotised, he held the rectangular, fog-white glow of the screen ever closer to his face, still tapping and swiping at it with the tip of his index finger. Then suddenly his face broke into a radiant smile and he turned to me:

'Here it is,' he said. 'Listen.'

He raised the phone and held it parallel to my left ear. Above the sensuous sounds of the Temptations I could just about hear a woman's voice, unaccompanied, harsh and high, coming from the phone's little speaker:

*Kitti Åla, kitti Killarros, kitti Grilå,*
*kitti Imå, kitti Grimå, kitti Hongje, kitti Flångje,*
*kitti Sylflidflångje*
*kitti venaste geita mina!*

There was a tinny and even slightly tortured quality to the sound and my first thought was that his great-grandmother sounded like an animal herself. Yet there was something beautiful about the voice. Frail and far off, as though some- how – and this was the distinct impression I had – as though somehow she was still up at the *sæter* in Numedal, singing as we sat there listening, and the sound of her voice only now reaching us from 1912, much as the light we see when looking at a star at night might have begun its journey millions of light years ago, and the star itself already be dead by the time the light reaches us.

'What does it mean?'

'Nothing. Åla, Killarros, Grimå, those are the names of the goats. She sings about how lovely they are.'

He pulled the phone away from my ear and slid it back

into the top pocket of his jacket. Draining the aquavit in his glass, he stood up.

'Want another?'

I held up my two-thirds-full glass of beer to show him I was okay. He nodded and disappeared through the dark doorway into the boathouse where the bar was set up. It was the last I saw of him that evening.

\*

Ole ferried Nina and me back to the mainland in the morning. She was due back at work in Oslo after the Easter break and we got into the car and drove straight through Nøtterøy and Tønsberg and onto the E6. We got held up for some minutes in Tønsberg as the bridge opened to let a ship through, and at the village of Stokke, a few miles outside Tønsberg, traffic was backed up for miles with cabin-owners heading back to Oslo after the break.

We turned off and took the country road that passes through Klevjerhagen. Klevjerhagen was a small, idyllically beautiful country village with predominantly old, white houses. The Norwegian countryside is full of them, but for me what rules them out as possible places to live is their uniform lack of a pub or small shop or any public gathering space. This was a feature I commented on several times to Norwegian friends, who would concur mournfully in my disappointment, sometimes adding that this lack of a social focus in country villages was one reason Norwegians travelling in England were so appreciative of the whole culture of the English country pub as a place of social connection.

The detour via Klevjerhagen added as much as forty minutes to our journey time back to Oslo, but at least it was forty minutes on the move through green, gently rolling countryside. There was something dreamlike about the landscape, and I was reminded of what Sverre had said during our conversation the previous evening, about how he was training himself to dream lucid dreams by asking himself 'Am I dreaming?' in the middle of his waking day. He had mentioned a dream he had had recently in which he had woken up in sleep to the fact that he was dreaming, and thereupon acted out all sorts of amusing impossibilities such as putting his hand straight through a closed door, speaking and breathing while walking fully clothed on the bed of the ocean, abruptly deciding to dance up to the top branches of a tall pine, flitting about between them, sometimes falling in a swift swoop towards the ground – like a man bungee jumping, as he described it – and leisurely pulling out of his dive moments before he hit. From somewhere Sverre had discovered that the writer Robert Louis Stevenson was similarly fascinated with the pursuit of the waking dream and he told me he had even adopted a piece of advice he had come across in Stevenson, that by settling to sleep with arms stretched out above the head the sleeper could heighten the chances of such a dream occurring. As we slowed to navigate the zebra-striped and almost pyramidal metal speed bumps through Klevjerhagen, I remembered the only occasion on which I had ever had what I suppose Sverre meant by a lucid dream. It involved flying too. By comparison with his oneironautics, mine was a strangely low-key adventure in which I found myself able to swim through the air by dint of a strenuous breaststroke that kept me suspended a few inches above the worn carpets of what seemed to be an old hotel or mansion. I was able to make my way around corners and through open doorways, but conscious most of the time of the enormous and exhausting effort involved, and aware that even a momentary lapse of concentration would lead to a belly-flop onto the floor.

★

It seems that Sverre's life was more dream-like than most. Several weeks after the gathering on Skrøslingen I arranged to meet Ole in Oslo for lunch and to pick up a green woollen hat of which I was particularly fond and which I had left on his boat. We ate at Justisen, on Møllergata, not far from the IT place where Ole worked as a programmer. Justisen is a rambling and crannied restaurant and beer hall that meanders over two floors with long wooden balconies over-hanging a central inner courtyard. As the weather was fine we sat up on one of these. We both had the day's special – meatballs, potatoes and cabbage – and afterwards sat over a beer. In due course our conversation turned to the reunion over the Easter weekend.

At one point I asked him how his friend Sverre was, adding that it wasn't every day you met someone who was married to an opera singer, and especially one who smoked. I had thought about Sverre several times since that evening on the island. He had become one of those people you meet only briefly but who arouse in you a curiosity about their life and fate. In part it must have been his fascination with the subject of lucid dreaming that made him stick so vividly in my mind. That, and a kind of impersonal sympathy I felt for him each time I recalled the way his wife had danced with the Englishman. The way he had watched them for a few seconds before averting his eyes. I couldn't fathom his lack of a reaction, but in the light of what Ole then told me it made a sort of sense.

Four years ago, he said, his friend had developed testicular cancer. It had resisted all forms of treatment, and finally he had accepted that it could only be dealt with by chemical castration. He can't have sex any more, said Ole. But Tove's quite a bit younger than him, she's in her late thirties, eleven or twelve years I think is the difference. And they came to an agreement about it. He lets her have boyfriends, and as long as it's nothing permanent Sverre looks the other way.

I said how terrible it must be to have something like that erupt into your life.

Ole nodded his agreement. 'In the beginning he took it very badly,' he said. 'In fact, I'll tell you something. In complete confidence?'

He looked over his beer at me with raised eyebrows. I nodded my assent.

He put the glass down.

'Sverre and I are members of the same kayak club, on Kalvøya. You know, where the rock festival used to be? That's how I got to know him. A few weeks after the treatment was over we arranged to meet there. It was a Saturday morning. We were supposed to be going out in my boat for a couple of hours, but at the last moment he said he wasn't feeling up to it and I should go alone. Well, what happened was that while I was away he walked off with a coil of rope and a plastic bucket and he went into the woods and hanged himself from the branch of a tree.'

Ole broke off and studied a fly that had landed on his wrist and was making its way up the back of his sun-browned thumb. He flicked at it but it buzzed away. I waited for him to go on, and when he didn't I said:

'So what happened?'

'Well, the branch broke. He told me about it afterwards. He said as soon as he kicked the bucket away and put his full weight on it, the branch snapped. He laughed when he told me.'

'Did he try again?'

'Not that I know of. I suppose he thought once was enough, if you know what I mean. He was very depressed at the time. He said he was tired of his life and he wanted his old life back. He called it his black and white life. His acoustic life. From the days before rock 'n' roll.'

Ole drank up the rest of his beer and we parted company outside on the pavement. Ole headed back to his office and I turned left onto Møllergata and then left again through the July 22 Information Centre, past the government buildings shattered by Breivik's bomb back in 2011, emerging by the enormous concrete roadblocks that now limit traffic access between the centre of town and Akersgata. I turned down Apotekergata, past the only slightly larger than life-size statue of a businessman and publisher named Tinius Nagell-Erichsen, sculpted with typically low-key Norwegian modesty in a lounge suit, with walking stick, briefcase and spectacles, and waited at the end of the street outside Hansen and Dyvik's interior shop on Pilestredet for a number 19 tram that would take me back up to Majorstua. We would need a complete new set of bed linen for our cabin and I saw in the window they had an offer of 30 per cent off all duvets. I wondered briefly whether I had time to go in and check them out, but a glance up at the electronic arrivals board told me the tram was due in two minutes. As I waited I was thinking about the cabin, and about Sverre, and what seemed to me his addiction to the past. I felt for him, so harshly rejected by the present, knocking and knocking on the door of a past into which he could see so clearly, but to which he could never gain readmittance. I could sympathise with that almost painful nostalgia. I'd suffered from it once myself.

The long, sky-blue concertina-tram rumbled round the corner from Grensen and into Pilestredet, blocking the view across to the Herr Nilsen jazz club as it came to a halt. Boarding through the central doors, I was thinking that hanging was a strangely old-fashioned way to try to kill yourself but that, all other things being equal, it would probably never go out of fashion. The tram was packed and as I made my way to the centre and found a strap to hold on to I couldn't help wondering if Sverre had remembered to ask himself, as the branch broke, 'Am I dreaming?'

# 4

## 5 May 2018

Thoughts on the nature of dreams – a

second-hand bookshop – Malcolm Lowry

and Nordahl Grieg – translation problems

– street life around Majorstua – 'Your cabin

is being delivered today' – the drive through

the Numedal valley – the petrol station at

Lampeland – we meet the builders –

I resolve to find out more about wood

as a building material

'The discussion of making all things equal', the second chapter of the fourth-century BC Taoist text *Chuang Tzu*, ends with a description of a dream in which Chuang Tzu dreamed he was a butterfly. He had no idea he was Chuang Tzu until he woke up. Thinking about it afterwards, it occurred to him that he couldn't be sure whether he was a man named Chuang Tzu who had dreamed he was a butterfly, or a butterfly dreaming he was a man named Chuang Tzu. For many years I had enjoyed thinking about the implications of this dream, that the distinction between what is real and what is dream can never be known for certain. But as the number 11 hummed along Pilestredet and up past the old Frydenlund brewery building, with traces of my conversation with Ole about Sverre lingering on, I was suddenly struck by the realisation that I had never had a dream in which I was anything or anyone but myself, and that to dream one belonged to another species was not merely unlikely but probably impossible. That dream of flying Sverre had described to me, and even my own fustian version of it: we weren't birds or butterflies in those dreams, we were human. Otherwise, where were the feathers? Where were the gossamer wings?

These sceptical mutterings troubled me. As the tram trundled up past the Natural History Museum on Tullinløkka I impulsively pushed the bell and jumped out at the next stop, in the shadow of the towering SAS hotel in Holbergs plass. My intention was to walk the rest of the way home up Bogstadveien and dispose of these objections along the way.

There is a second-hand shop directly behind the tram stop, one of the small chain of Galleri Normisjon shops run by the mission church in Norway to support its work. Glancing into the shop window I recalled that my wife had asked me to look at a particular rose-painted cabinet she had seen there. She thought it might look nice on one of the cabin walls. I could see the cupboard through the window. It was standing on a low wooden table. It was about a metre high, and both its black-painted sides and the front of the door were decorated in garlands of once-bright but now faded traditional Norwegian *rosemaling*, a pattern of interlocking painted roses and scrolls.

I pushed open the glass door of the shop and stepped down inside to take a closer look, unlocking and opening the cupboard door. Almost at once I noticed a distinctive carbolic smell, and made a mental note to refer to this when describing the visit to Nina, as a way of showing that I had given the matter of buying it considerable thought. Surely, I was thinking as I bent to peer at the back of the cupboard in search of the tell-tale pin-prick marks of woodworm, surely if a man was going to dream he was someone or something other than himself he would only ever dream he was another man? And that being the case, wouldn't he dream of being a man who was in some way *better* than himself?

Locking and closing the cupboard door again to leave the display as I had found it, I then made my way around the cluster of sofas and armchairs that occupied the centre of the shop to the rear wall, which was shelved from wall to wall with second-hand books. On a number of occasions since we had bought the plot in Numedal I had visited Oslo's antiquarian booksellers, including Nordli's just down the road, opposite the National Gallery in Universitetsgata, in search of the five-volume *Rollag Bygdebok: Ætt og gard og grend* ('Rollag County History: ancestries, farms and hamlets'). I knew from the copies in the Reference Section of the National Library in Solli plass that the second volume contained several pages on the history of Veggli, including details of emigration to the United States from the area in the late nineteenth century – something I hoped to make use of in this book. A bare and pitiful footnote describing a brother and sister being executed for incest had also attracted my attention, as do all brief references to personal tragedy.

It was a long shot that a Galleri Normisjon shop would have copies of the Rollag history, and once I had established it wasn't there I looked around to see what they did have on their bookshelves. Almost at once I came upon a Norwegian translation of Malcolm Lowry's *Under the Volcano*, done for Gyldendal Norsk Forlag back in 1949 by Peter Magnus. Ever since moving to Norway in 1983 I had been in the habit of reading in Norwegian translation books that I had already read in English. Originally I did this as a way of trying to improve my grasp of the language, but I enjoyed the dislocating oddity of the experience and continued the habit even after I became fluent. The distinction is difficult to describe. It's the same book, but in some subtle way it's also a different book.

*Under the Volcano* had been significant for me in a number of different ways ever since I first read it in my early twenties. One was the thrill of sharing with Lowry a fascination with Norway and even the idea of *being Norwegian*. Opening the translation at random I came across the passage in which Geoffrey Firmin's brother Hugh arrives to visit him in Cuernavaca in Mexico, on his way back from the Spanish Civil War. From Douglas Day's biography of Lowry I knew that Lowry's model for Hugh was the Norwegian novelist and playwright

Nordahl Grieg, a distant relative of the composer, and that this Grieg had been a war correspondent in Spain during the Civil War in the 1930s.

Like me, Lowry's fascination with Norway had originally been excited by a novel. In his case it was Nordahl Grieg's *Skibet går videre*, translated as *The Ship Sails On* by A. G. Chater in 1927, when Lowry was eighteen years old. He felt a bond with Grieg: both were the sons of wealthy fathers; both had been keen to see the world and attend what used to be called the 'university of life', both had gone to sea on long voyages and made novels out of their experiences.

In his biography Day describes a trip Lowry made to Norway as a deckhand aboard a Norwegian-registered merchant ship called the S.S. *Fagervik*, bound for Ålesund on the western coast. Lowry jumped ship or signed off when the *Fagervik* docked and took the train east. By his own account he had no idea where Grieg lived, only that it was somewhere in Oslo. After registering at the Parkheimen Hotel on Bygdøy allé, the long tree-lined avenue that stretches from the National Library in Solli plass all the way down to the roundabout by the Bygdøy peninsula, he went out into the street and asked the first person he met if he knew, by any chance, where the famous young writer lived? The man replied that he did indeed, it was just a little further down Bygdøy allé, at number 68 – he was headed that way himself, would Lowry care to accompany him?

Lowry goes on to describe how he took the lift up to Grieg's apartment, how Grieg opened the door to him looking distracted and dishevelled (he had just returned from a walking trip in the mountains), but gave him a friendly greeting and invited him in. Grieg was struggling to finish a play commissioned by the National Theatre and Lowry quickly realised that he had disturbed his hero at work. Although invited to sit down he did not remove his overcoat, and stayed only long enough to down a couple of whiskies with Grieg and to tell him how much he had liked and admired *The Ship Sails On*. It seems he suggested that Grieg dramatise the novel for the stage. Grieg himself was not interested, but he encouraged Lowry to go ahead and make the attempt if he wanted to.

They had lunch together the next day at Jacques Bagatelle on Bygdøy allé, visited the Viking ship museum, and dined at the Red Mill in the Grønland district of Oslo. Lowry then spent a few days exploring Oslo on his own, taking long walks through the city streets, and a metro ride up to Frognersæter, the magnificent old restaurant perched high above the city from which, on a clear day, you can see up the fjord almost as far as Drøbak. He also visited the cemetery at Trefoldighets-kirken, halfway up St Hanshaugen. Lowry's main purpose was probably to visit Henrik Ibsen's grave, an austere black slab with a simple carving of a miner's hammer on it. In his wanderings through the cemetery, however, he came across the grave of the Hilliot family and duly renamed the hero of his novel *Ultramarine* 'Dana Hilliot', turned him into a young man 'born of Viking blood', and even provided him with a 'brief education in Oslo'.

For a few moments I stood there, turning Lowry's novel over in my hands and wondering whether to buy it, but decided not to and slipped it back onto the shelf. You never know; in my early days here, still trying to improve my grasp of Norwegian, I bought a translation of J. D. Salinger's short story collection *For Esmé – With Love and Squalor* at a Steiner school jumble sale. There's a scene in the title story where the narrator, a US serviceman stationed in England during the Second World War, glances through the windows of a Red Cross recreation room. He decides against going in because he sees soldiers standing there 'two and three deep at the coffee counter'. Salinger's Norwegian translator* rendered these words as *i dype tanker ved kaffebaren*, meaning 'deep in thought at the coffee bar' and making it sound like some weird abandoned sketch for Hopper's *Nighthawks*.

On my way out of the Normisjon shop I stopped and took three or four pictures of the cabinet. There was no accompanying card with details, only a price tag (a hefty nine thousand kroner) and I had no idea whether the stylised flowers and scrolls and tendrils were typical of Numedal or not. When we bought the land, and once the contract was signed, Jørgen had presented us with an illustrated book on the subject of Numedal's 'rosemaling' and I guessed that consulting this in conjunction with the photographs might give us an answer. It hardly mattered to me whether the pattern was local, but I felt that if it were, hanging it on the wall would bring a valuable touch of authenticity to what Sverre had described as our '*IKEA-hytta*'. Although even there, something in me resisted: what is it anyway, this longing for an authenticity that almost always turns out to be in some way compromised? What is this enduring and even awed respect we feel for the past? All this wandering in and out of junk shops and flea-markets and second-hand bookshops, in search of what? The artefacts of the dead. Their rubbish.

---

* Checking this reference recently I noticed to my surprise that the translator was Torstein Hilt. Hilt was an adventurous and popular man whose subsequent career included playing the part of Jappe Nilsen in Peter Watkins' film *Edvard Munch*, and founding Hilt og Hansteen, a small but successful publisher of Mind, Body and Spirit books, where my wife worked with him for a number of years. After selling the company, Hilt emigrated to Colombia to start a new life. In 2018 he was robbed and murdered by an unknown assailant in the town of Minca, in the north of Colombia.

But with people it's different. The dead we love don't die to us. Leaving the Normisjon shop on Holbergs gate* I crossed Tullinløkka and walked through the old university buildings in the centre and took a 31 bus up Drammensveien. Although there were vacant seats, I remained standing so that I could follow the numbering as the bus turned into Bygdøy allé, looking out for number 68, all the while half-expecting to see Lowry slouching down the road in his overcoat. Just past the junction with Thomas Heftyes gate I spotted it. I got off at the next stop and walked back up the road a few metres.

Opening the door, I stood in the stairwell. There was a lift with a black metal door and brass-rimmed porthole, and a floor-dial set into a brass plate on the wall beside it. By the look of it, it was the same one the young Lowry rode to the top floor of the building to meet Nordahl Grieg eighty-six years previously. Nordahl Grieg was the man Lowry dreamed of being, the man of action, the idealist, a writer who dedicated his life and work to the pursuit of social justice for all. Grieg died young, his RAAF Lancaster shot down during a bombing raid over Berlin in December 1943, his body never recovered. In the days after the Breivik murders in 2011 his 1936 poem 'Til ung-dommen' ('To the Young') became an anthem of solace to the relatives and a moving tribute to all of Breivik's young victims.

That was all. I just stood in the lobby for a minute, sensing the presence of these two dead men, hearing the sound of their voices as they stepped out of the lift and walked past me towards the door, talking energetically about the paper Grieg was writing on the poet Rupert Brooke. I watched as

---

* The suffix 'gate' means street or road in Norwegian. A number of street names in York, such as Coppergate, are historical reminders of the city's existence as a Viking kingdom in the ninth and tenth centuries.

they headed up the rise towards Solli plass, in the direction of Jacques Bagatelle, and when I could no longer see them I set off, walking up Thomas Heftyes gate. At Frogner plass, at the top, I crossed to the park side of the road and headed up Kirke-gata. It was hot. The playground next to the wrought-iron entrance gates to Vigelands park was teeming with children, laughing, crying, swarming about on the rigging of the big wooden schooner at its centre. Turning into Slemdalsveien I stopped for a coffee at Baker Hansen's, a café where the back-ground music was always jazz. As I took my mug of flat white outside to the pavement seat with its unimpeded view of the pedestrian crossing, Charlie Parker's version of 'Just Friends', from the album *Charlie Parker with Strings*, fluttered light and breezy from the overhead speaker.

I sat there so regularly at this time of day that I had become familiar with certain sights: the young couple who always crossed the road together, stopping to kiss outside the entrance to the Metro and then going their separate ways, the young woman to board a train, her boyfriend mounting his bicycle and riding off down the pavement in the direction of the park; the tall, bald-headed barber standing smoking outside the door of his shop thirty metres up the road from the café, often talking on the phone at the same time – I noticed that he'd lost some weight and made a mental note to mention it next time I went in for a haircut; the woman with cerebral palsy, always with a wine-red rucksack and wearing black cotton trousers that showed the upper few inches of her backside. She was a librarian at the main Deichmanske library. She'd once helped me get hold of a recording of *On the Heights*, Delius's setting of one of Henrik Ibsen's greatest poems, *Paa vidderne* ('On the heights'), but I could tell she didn't remember me.

I watched her slow, tortured progress over the crossing and up the slope to the side entrance of the metro station. Each dragging step she took in the hot sun cost her a huge effort. Charlie Parker's serene alto glided across the blue sky. How could such airy lightness and beauty have survived the booze and heroin-shot awfulness of his personal life? He died at the age of only thirty-four, but the doctor who signed the death certificate estimated his age at 'between fifty and sixty'. I thought of his incarceration at the Bellevue mental hospital in New York. And all the other great jazz musicians who spent time there – Thelonious Monk, Tadd Dameron, Bud Powell, Charlie Mingus – maybe every last one of them would have swapped their genius for a life of ordinary and unspectacular happiness. I recalled that Lowry had spent a few weeks there too, an experience he describes with hallucinating clarity in 'Lunar Caustic', one of the early sketches for *Under the Volcano*. For most of the six years he spent writing that book he lived in a simple cabin by the waterfront in Dollarton, Canada. He wrote about the experience with a bewildered and loving warmth in 'The Forest Path to the Spring', a short story in which his intention had been, he said later, 'to write of human happiness in terms of the enthusiasm and high serious-ness usually reserved for catastrophe and tragedy'.

The phone vibrated in my jacket pocket and I took it out and checked the email. It was from Ståle, our contact at Norske Fjellhus in Kongsberg: *Hytta blir kjørt ut i dag*, it said: 'Your cabin is being delivered today.'

So it *was* an IKEA cabin after all, I said to myself as I drank the last of the flat white and slid the phone back into my pocket. Maybe I had been missing something here. Maybe we were supposed to assemble the cabin ourselves, with one of those little L-shaped metal keys?

★

When Nina returned from work that evening we discussed Ståle's news. It was exciting, and even though we didn't expect to see much we decided to drive up to Veggli at the weekend to take a look. It might only be a pile of timbers, but at least it would be *our* pile of timbers. As she headed out into the kitchen she asked if I'd had a chance to look at the cupboard in the Normisjon shop and I told her I had, and that I had liked what I saw. I said it might be interesting if we could find out precisely where in Norway the cupboard was from. I suggested we check in the book Jørgen had given us, but it turned out she had lent it to a friend at work.

Later, after we'd eaten, I pulled up the photos of the cupboard I'd taken on my phone and we did an internet search of *rosemaling* sites that showed examples of the different regional styles. It wasn't easy, especially as the pattern on the cupboard was faded and my photographs a little out of focus. After about twenty inconclusive minutes the dog appeared in front of us, announcing his presence with an all-body shake then walking to the hallway and staring fixedly at the array of leads, halters and collars hanging from the hooks on the wall.

'I'll take him,' said Nina. 'I feel like a walk anyway. You'll keep looking?'

She fastened the click-on halter around his chest, stuffed a roll of black plastic waste bags into one pocket of her parka and a bag of treats into the other – 'Grass Fed Lamb', I noticed it said on the packet – and as they headed off down the stairs I closed the door behind them and went back to the living room to resume the internet search. Very quickly I became distracted from the immediate goal and found myself engrossed in an article on the general history of rose-painting, from which I learned that the fashion for decorating interior walls and ceilings and furniture with bright flowers in primary colours developed in the eighteenth century, that its centre was the country of Telemark and the surrounding regions of south central Norway, including Numedal, and that the art only became possible once the smokey central hearths of the old houses were replaced by the enclosed chimneys of modern, iron wood-burning stoves. It was, wrote the author of the article, a way Norwegians had developed of cheering themselves up during the long and dark winter days with the memory of bright summer days gone by, and the promise of summers to come. Well off track by this time, I then clicked more or less at random on a link and came across a reference to the fact that, as early as the 1890s, at least two Norwegian firms had been in business selling prefabricated cabins for export around the country. It brought a strange relief to realise that Sverre had been wrong, and that there was nothing disappointingly modern and mass-produced about the arrangements we had made with Norske Fjellhus. On reflection it made sense, for the great advantage of a timber house over a building made of stone is that it can be dismantled with the same ease as it was assembled and moved to another location, where it can be rebuilt in exactly the same way, as Sverre had told me his father had done with the old mountain *sæter* that was now their family's summer cabin.

After about forty minutes Nina returned with Alex. As she knelt to unhook his halter she asked if I had managed to find the location of the rose-painting pattern, and seemed slightly annoyed when I confessed that I had allowed myself to be distracted. In my own defence I pointed out that it seemed to me a waste of money to buy organic dog treats made from

'Grass Fed Lambs' that cost over a kroner each, and on that stalemate I closed down the laptop and we went to bed.

\*

Early on Saturday we set off for Veggli, enoying the unusually quiet drive out of Oslo on a weekend morning. We were beginning to get used to the pleasures of the journey. Once the rather dull stretch of E18 motorway between Oslo and Drammen is out of the way, you follow the Rv 134 along the southern bank of the Drammenselva (Drammen River), through Mjøndalen and Darbu to Kongsberg. There it crosses the Numedalslågen river on a graceful, arced bridge, which gives a thrilling view of the great river as it comes rolling down the valley from the Hardangervidda and bursts exuberantly into a wide white waterfall before hurrying on towards Larvik and the Skagerrak. In winter the drifting ice can freeze the fall into the most fantastical shapes and sculptures, but on a summer morning like this the waters pulsed calmly below us as we crossed the bridge and then turned right off the roundabout and joined the Fv 40 into Numedal.

The local tourist information office promotes the valley as *Middelalderdalen*, the Medieval Valley, for its numerous old wooden farm buildings, and in particular the many well-preserved *stabbur* or *loft* that you pass on both sides of the road with such frequency you almost forget to appreciate their strangeness and sheer architectural beauty. In former times the *stabbur* was the farm's storehouse and, as such, its treasure house. As a tribute to its importance the facades are often decorated with the most intricate and beautiful designs.

Past Kongsberg the road becomes ever more narrow and twisting as it passes through first Flesberg and then Svene

before reaching Lampeland. Lampeland is a settlement of fewer than four hundred inhabitants, but it has a petrol station and small conference hotel. We pulled in, and while I took the dog for a short walk Nina headed off to the petrol station shop to buy two coffees and two *pølser med lompa*. This is a classic Norwegian street-snack consisting of Frankfurters in mustard and ketchup rolled in a flat potato cake. We ate them seated on a bench behind the conference hotel facing a grassy area with a small and rather forlorn playground. After a couple of minutes a small boy wearing a Neymar football shirt emerged from one of the crescent of houses on the far side of the grass, approached a faded red plastic rocking horse and stood eyeing it dubiously for a few moments, as though weighing up the risks involved, before deciding against a ride and returning to the house.

Presumably in tribute to its name, the street lights in Lampe-land are an unusual feature of the village, strikingly large and rust-red. Having finished my sausage, I googled 'Lampeland' and found that its origins were both more ancient than electric street lighting and more prosaic. The name turns out to be a corruption of a fifteenth-century reference to the settlement as 'Landbu land', meaning 'land belonging to the archbishop in Oslo', an explanation that made a cartographic corruption to 'Lampeland' easy to understand. In the same Wikipedia entry I read that the village's modest claim to fame was that it had been home to the father of an astronomer named Carl Otto Lampland who, like so many Norwegian emigrants, had adopted the name of his native village after emigrating to America in the nineteenth century. Two craters, one on the moon and one on Mars, are named after Carl Otto.

I had to go to the toilet before we drove on and went back to the petrol station shop and headed for the narrow spiral staircase that leads down to the toilets. The staircase is next to an area at the back of the shop reserved for gamblers who follow *trav*, a type of horse-racing in which small jockeys ride in tiny lightweight wagons drawn by horses that are constrained, by the rules of the sport, to proceed around a circular track in a sort of tormented and high-stepping near-run. *Trav* is especially popular among men in rural parts of Norway, though on this occasion there was no one at either of the two round tables strewn with coupons and the discarded pink sports pages of *VG** and *Dagbladet*, and the two television screens, permanently tuned to a channel showing nothing but *trav*, carried on unobserved.

On my way back out of the shop I stopped briefly to watch the last stages of a race, which, I gathered from the Swedish

---

* Originally published as *Verdens Gang* but now universally referred to by its initials.

commentator, was taking place in Sweden. As I did so I felt, as I always used to feel when watching competitive skiing in the early days, after I first came to Norway, that the act of over-taking – such an important part of the attraction of any kind of race for those watching – was more or less impossible in the case of this sport. The beauties of *trav* have never revealed themselves to me, though in time I came to appreciate the subtle excitements involved in watching competitive *langrenn* ('cross-country skiing'), the skill in the timing of a crucial lane-change, the sudden injection of pace by a Bjørn Dæhlie, a Petter Northug or a Johannes Høsflot Klæbo that leaves opponents for dead.

*

As we turned off the Fv 40 at the roundabout just past the petrol station and the road began to climb up the side of Vegglifjell, I could feel my excitement mounting. I had been looking forward so much to following the building process, from its beginnings here today to the scarcely imaginable moment of its completion at some point in a distant but hope-fully not-too-distant future. A whole house made of wood, with windows through which one could see, on fine days, at least three and sometimes as many as five *blåninger*, a lovely Norwegian word used to describe the slate-blue waves of successively fainter mountain ranges visible on a horizon. I recalled the bitterly cold February morning five months earlier when we had driven up to meet Ståle and Reidar, the builders' foreman, to discuss exactly where the cabin should stand, and at what angle to the landscape. Certain restrictions had to be taken into account. All new cabins had to follow the natural contours of the mountainside, and there should be at least four metres between any of the walls and the edge of the plot. External dish aerials were prohibited, and there were stipulations governing the range of colours that could be used when the time came to paint the cabin. All of it was within a band of black, browns and near-browns designed to ensure the cabin merged with the natural colours of the mountain.

We had parked on a bend in the road, and waded through thigh-deep snow to where Reidar, Ståle and two other men stood waiting for us. They were gathered beneath a stand of tall pine trees. Reidar was holding a pole about two metres tall, hooked at the top like a giant walking stick. He introduced the two other men. Odd was the digger-driver, he would be clearing and levelling the site. Marek was the firm's Polish chargehand.

To my untrained eye, the angle of the slope we were standing on looked to be not far off forty-five degrees, and on that freezing and overcast February day, with so much snow and so many tall pines laying what looked like irrefutable claim to the land, I remember thinking it inconceivable that one man, with a digger, would not only manage to clear and level the rugged terrain but that on some clear, blue, warm day in the summer a team of men would be able to build a cabin there. According to the contract we had signed a couple of weeks previously, the handover was in the first week of July, weather and other unforeseen hazards permitting.

I had always taken the inclusion of that 'unforeseen hazards' to mean that things would very certainly be delayed, for the idea that a cabin could be built and ready for habitation in a matter of a few short weeks seemed out of the question. But we had Ståle's almost brutally prosaic email to confirm that work was about to start: *hytta blir kjørt ut i dag*. For all these reasons I was expecting, as I looked northwards and upwards from the final bend in the track, to see nothing much more than a pile of logs to one side of a cleared rectangle of mountain dirt. I intended to take pictures of it, to document how my dream of a cabin in the Norwegian mountains was about to come true, however late in the day, and however far it might be from the dream I had started out with so many, many years earlier. I intended to touch the logs, to sit down on them and drink instant coffee from the thermos we had brought with us. I looked forward to meditating on how these sticks, these timbers, these old bits of tree would, at some indeterminate future time, magically spin themselves up into the shape of a home, a place where my wife and I could cook, eat, talk, sleep and wash.

Instead of a pile of mythopoeic timbers, what I actually saw was the entire structure of the first floor of the cabin, already in place atop a rectangular foundation of concrete, whitely glowing in the May sunshine. A sixty-metre access road – our driveway – had been cut into the land, and we left the car at the head of it and started walking.

Four men were hard at work. One was standing on a ladder behind a wall of pale yellow logs wedging a lintel log above a door-opening into position. Like some troll from Asbjørnsen and Moe's collection of Norwegian fairy tales, a second man was standing below him holding a thick, wooden mallet in his two hands. A third man was at work behind them. The fourth man was preparing to feed a plank into a bench saw. As we approached he leaned the plank up against the bench, walked towards the open door of the dust-grimed old Fiat parked close by, knelt on the passenger seat and turned down the car radio. I reached into my jacket pocket, took out my phone and started taking photographs of the scene.

None of them had given any sign that they had seen us

approaching. The man who had turned off the radio stepped back up onto the concrete foundation and disappeared behind one of the walls. I thought it strange that they ignored our presence so completely; were we making them feel uncomfortable? They didn't look up from their work, not even when we walked right up to the building. The man who had disappeared behind a wall now reappeared with a length of bright orange webbing in his hand. He passed it up to the man with the mallet, who fastened one end of it over the top of the wall, then fed it back down to his workmate, who slid it under the bottom timber and set about tensioning it. As I glanced across at the car I noticed the number plate on the Fiat was Latvian, and suddenly their unease made sense to me.

'I think they're wondering if we're from STAMI,' I whispered to Nina.

STAMI is the state's *arbeidsmiljøinstitutt*, Norway's National Institute of Occupational Health. The institute deals with 'all aspects of Norwegian working life'. It pays special attention to health and safety practices and often visits workplaces to check that these are being properly observed. This concern for the health and safety of workers is a cornerstone of Norwegian social democracy, but it's one reason why things cost so much in this country, and as a principle it is under constant threat as people look around or through its prescriptions for ways of getting a job done well, cheaply and quickly. In the earliest years of immigration from countries like Poland and Latvia the workers brought the added bonus, from a Norwegian perspective, of a 1950s work ethic that predated concerns about health and safety at work. Polish and Latvian workers would put up with a great deal for the chance to earn something approaching Norwegian wages. Some fifteen years ago the flat next to ours was sold after our neighbour, old Kåre Falkenberg, died at the age of eighty-six. He and his wife had lived there all their married life, and raised a family of four. A Norwegian builder bought it, and for a few weeks housed a team of eight Polish workers in it. We never heard a sound from them. Never a raised voice, never a midnight blast from a record player. The only sign of their presence was the pile of black work boots propped against the wall outside the front door each evening, and the smell of cigarette smoke that drifted into our bedroom through the wooden walls. Once we were woken by an enormous crash at about two in the morning. I got up, put on my dressing gown and opened the front door to see what had happened. Four men were standing outside, looking into the space where the door to their flat had been. The door itself lay on the floor inside the flat.

'What's going on?' I asked in English.

One of them turned. He raised his arm, pressed his fingertips together and gave a quick twist of the wrist.

'No key.'

No key, so someone had just kicked the door in. By next morning, though, it was back in place as though nothing had happened, and the only sign of the night's disturbance was the starburst of splintered cracks in the pale blue paint at the foot of the door where the metal toecap of a Polish boot had struck with the precision of a karate blow.

Speaking English, I told the Latvians working on the cabin who we were, that this was our cabin they were building. I said I was very surprised at how quickly it had gone up and complimented them: they must have worked very hard.

For a while they just looked at me. Then the one sitting on high with the mallet rested it on the topmost timber and jabbed his finger upwards.

'Maybe roof tomorrow,' he said.

'I don't believe it,' I said, turning to Nina. 'This thing is going to be up and complete in seven days' time. It's bloody biblical.'

We wandered around for another fifteen minutes, took a few more photographs, took the dog for a quick walk and then set off back to Oslo. *Maybe roof tomorrow*. Unbelievable. I realised that I had understood nothing about cabin-building in twenty-first-century Norway. As per the contract, it really was going to be ready for us by July. I realised then that I had sleepwalked into this whole cabin business. Over the years I had picked up a lot of superficial knowledge about the status of cabins, why they mattered so much to the Norwegians; but of the heart of the matter I knew nothing.

And the heart of the matter was wood.

'I'm going to study log cabins,' I told Nina. 'I'm going to

find out everything I can about them. In six months' time I'll be able to build one myself.'

Easy, confident dreaming of this kind is something I've done a lot of. Offhand I can recall a resolution to become fluent in Chinese so that I could read the *Tao Te Ching* and make up my own mind what it means, and an intention to walk from Land's End to John O'Groats. As proof of the reality of these plans I still had a small library of Chinese grammars, dictionaries and readers as well as two recordings in Chinese of the *Tao Te Ching*; and three paperbacks written by men who had done the walk from John O'Groats to Land's End. I had realised neither goal and come to terms with the fact that I probably never would, at least not until I was dead, and at last had time to concentrate, as the great Swedish poet Tomas Tranströmer once put it. Compared to those unrealised aspirations, the plan to find out more about wood and about cabins seemed distinctly feasible.

# 5

## 23 June 2018

Midsummer's Eve party near Oslo – the

spirit of *dugnad* – the curious phenomenon

of *Norgesvenner* ('Friends of Norway') – an

argument concerning Bob Dylan and the

Beatles – on translating *Norwegian Wood*

into English – on wood as a building material

– differences between *loft* and *stabbur* –

courting customs related to the *loft* – a case

of mistaken identity – the drive home

By the time of Hanne and Petter Næss's annual Midsummer's Eve party, however, I had more or less forgotten my resolution to try to learn something more about wood. I was reminded of it in an unexpected way that night, in the course of a heated discussion that arose about the relative merits of the Beatles' song 'Norwegian Wood' and Bob Dylan's '4th Time Around'. In the historical Christian calendar Jonsok (John's wake) commemorates the death of St John, but it's actually a pre-Christian feast celebrating the summer solstice throughout Scandinavia with bonfires, when people stayed up all night drinking and celebrating life, and the gathering up at Hanne and Petter's was more in the spirit of this original feast. The Næsses actually always held their party on the Saturday nearest 23 June. In the early years of what had become a traditional gathering up at Siljuseter, a mountaintop farm Petter and Hanne bought back in the 1990s – when he was working as information officer at the American Embassy in Oslo and she was at Statoil – there would always be a bonfire at midnight of piled branches at the edge of the cleared ground surrounding their house, until some years back the local fire brigade put a stop to it, claiming the risk of a forest fire was too great. That meant the focus of the evening was entirely on the spit-roasted lamb that was slowly turned on a rusted and industrial-size trolley they brought out once a year and moored on the outskirts of the lawn in front of the house. The brown fleece jacket I was wearing that night carried a souvenir of the days of the fire in the shape of a seared black scar the size of a thumbprint on the left breast where some flaming scrap of debris had settled.

There were usually thirty or forty guests at these Siljuseter gatherings. A hard core of Petter and Hanne's friends and colleagues from work could be relied on each year to make the half-hour drive out from Oslo, with the rest a changing corpus of temporary acquaintances, often visiting Americans Petter came into contact with through his job, or people on temporary placement at Statoil whom Hanne invited along. Siljuseter is a difficult place to get to, even with a map. You have to know when to turn off the country road that passes through Mehren at Sjåstad church, which is set back on the left on a bend in the road, and after that you take a forestry track that twists and turns its way up through the pines of the Merenmarka, crossing sheep grids and passing farms on its way up.

Petter and Hanne's home is where the track runs out at the top of the hill. It's a one-storey timber house built in the style of a Swiss chalet. Once it was a smallholding, so there's a large red barn and a henhouse built on to the back of what used to be a small milking parlour. In the early days, when the Næsses ran it as a part-time smallholding, they had a dozen sheep grazing up there, as well as an old retired horse called Ramona who lived out her days in meditative solitude, grazing on the long grass around the back and along the sides of the log cabin.

The party was always held on the cleared carpet of lawn directly in front of the house, which was built on a slight rise. Each year, seven or eight tables would be arranged out there for the guests at the Jonsok gathering. The roast lamb was the main course, and each year guests would be asked to bring a bowl of salad, or a dessert or a cake, and these would be laid out on two tables on the covered terrace of the house. People didn't have to be told to bring their own drink.

We were never the first to arrive. By the time we had parked down by the barn and started walking up the grassy slope towards the house there would be a score of people already there, standing around between the tables, glass of wine or can of beer in hand, talking and swapping news in the friendly but slightly formal way of people who know each other only quite well and have not yet lost their inhibitions for the evening. There were always a number of young children there, very often belonging to families who were staying the night, the parents busy pitching their green or blue or orange tents on the edge of the lawn with the children already crawling in and out of them. They laughed excitedly at the prospect of the night ahead, some of them kicking a plastic football around, breaking off as if at some secret signal to rush across to where a slack rope was tied between two small apple trees at the bottom of the lawn, to see how far along it they could walk, screaming and waving their arms with delight, apart from the occasional girl or boy who took it with a deadly seriousness, already blighted by self-consciousness, already feeling that all eyes were upon them, following their least move and judging them.

Nina and I had been guests at these Jonsok gatherings for most of the past twenty years and we always knew at least a dozen other guests by sight and often, though not always, by name. I was especially bad at remembering their names. Among Hanne's regular guests were a group of women who, as far as I understood it, had become friendly while playing in the same football team. They always sat together at the same table and, as sometimes happens with tightly knit groups, it was not easy for an outsider to be completely sure which name belonged to which face. Even after all these years, I still have trouble with Norwegian personal names. On an almost daily basis, either in personal encounters or in the newspapers or on television, I seem to come across names I've never encountered before, and the problem of remembering them is made worse by the fact that so many of the first names are doubled, often in combinations that are highly unpredictable. It endows them with a kind of exoticism, which has not diminished for me over time, and which reminds me of something I am in increasing danger of forgetting, which is that I am not Norwegian myself, nor ever will be.

Over the years, I had got to know the husbands of these football wives, and at a certain point in the evening all of us would find ourselves sitting together round a table. Our conversations tended to revolve around football and the rock groups of the 1960s. Occasionally, if a youngster in his forties was sitting with us, we might reach as far as Blur, Oasis and Coldplay. Sølveig's third husband, young Kjell, was especially fond of Joy Division, and I remember late one evening he gave a memorable rendition of 'Love Will Tear Us Apart', accompanying himself on Petter's guitar, an instrument more used in its owner's hands to interpreting the music of seventeenth-century composers for lute such as John Dowland or Johannes Kapsberger. In general, though, our greybeard wisdom would always be that these later groups lacked originality, and could only be judged on how well they carried on the traditions established by the Beatles and the Stones.

It was on this particular June night in 2017 that the conversation about 'Norwegian Wood' and '4th Time Around' took place. On my left was Beate's husband Per, a man with an encyclopedic knowledge of the Beatles and their songs; opposite me was Bjarne, whose knowledge of Bob Dylan was almost but not quite exceeded by his Mastermind-like grasp of the life and career of Frank Sinatra. It was a combination of tastes I respected but did not share. At the other end of the table, out of reach of the conversation, sat a white-bearded man whose name I think was Bjørn. Each time I looked in his direction, he seemed to be concentrating deeply on the act of hand-rolling a cigarette. Next to him was a woman in a pink fleece jacket whom I recognised as a weather forecaster for NRK, the Norwegian Broadcasting Corporation. Although nothing came of it on this occasion, I remember making a mental note to try to have a word with her later on that evening. I wanted to ask her about the habit NRK's forecasters all had of referring to Norway as *vårt land* ('our country') as they slowly waltzed about the screen in front of the weather map. Was it policy? I wanted to ask her. Because they all did it. Each time I heard this modest but firm expression of pride in ownership I felt a sense of regret at not being Norwegian myself.

At times the feeling was so strong that I seriously considered applying for Norwegian citizenship. All that held me back was the certainty that it wouldn't make any difference. A child of ten born here is more deeply Norwegian than I could ever be, even after more than thirty years residence. Belonging to a small country with a language understood by few outside its borders shapes the mind in a way that has nothing to do with passports. At a trivial level it might involve, for example, the existence of a clutch of Norwegian celebrities whose very celebrity will always be a source of quiet wonder to a foreigner who can't actually *feel* their celebrity. This modest pantheon depends for its successful functioning on an agreement between star and admirers that keeps it well below the level of the hysterical adulation you get in larger societies. The bass guitarist in one of Norway's biggest and most enduring rock bands, CC Cowboys, lives in our block in Oslo. Everyone

in the block knows who he is; nobody pesters him for his auto-
graph when they meet him coming and going, carrying plastic
bags of shopping from the local Coop supermarket, on his
way to the gym, or to pick up his daughter from the airport.
Sometimes, at the height of the concert season, in the summer and around Christmas and the New Year, you'll see him
emerging through the front door looking rock-musician sharp
in his tight black jeans and snakeskin boots and black jacket
with silver buttons, his hair freshly dyed jet black. Then you'll
know the CC Cowboys are playing a gig somewhere that
night, or maybe tomorrow night, in some far-off Norwegian
town. But he's always there in his old cord jeans when the
annual spring *dugnad* comes around. In the context of our
block, this almost untranslatable word* refers to the day when
the tenants meet up on the central grass enclosure to weed the
flower beds, prune the shrubs, plant flowers, hose down the
bike stands, carry the furniture dumped in the lofts by previous tenants down four flights of stairs and toss it into one of
the rented containers standing at each end of the driveway,
and afterwards mingle on the grass for an hour or so, talking
and drinking strong black coffee and eating Cecilia's homemade waffles. The *dugnad* spirit is one of the most attractive
expressions of the Norwegian communal imperative, and
one of the strongest reminders of the country's working-class
roots.[†]

---

* *Riksmåls Ordbok* defines the word (in Norwegian) as 'voluntary and
unpaid work done by neighbours, club members etc in carrying out a
specific project'.

† In a letter to a Swedish aristocrat, Henrik Ibsen once described the
relationship between the three Scandinavian peoples in terms of social
class: 'We three peoples have all the qualities needed to form a spiritually
united single nation. Sweden provides our spiritual aristocracy, Denmark
our spiritual bourgeoisie, and Norway our spiritual working class.'

Even here though, I begin to notice the erosion of affluence. For the first twenty years in which I lived in this country, tenants of each flat would take their turn at washing the staircases and corridors according to a weekly rota. This was never taken lightly. It encouraged a sense of responsibility for the general tidiness and cleanliness of one's own immediate environment. Now the cleaning is done by external agencies, largely run by Eastern Europeans. It is only a matter of time before the culture of the *dugnad* goes the same way: for many years our tenants' association in Oslo levied a fine of 300 kroner (about £30) on tenants who failed to participate in the *dugnad*. In 2018 this modest fine was dropped and the monthly rent raised by twenty-five kroner to cover the expected fall in income. In effect it means there is no fine, and the slight but entirely salutary sense of shame one always felt if, for some reason, one couldn't make it, or simply didn't feel like it one year, will inevitably disappear.

It was about ten o'clock and still bright enough to read the labels on the tins of beer on the table in front of us. But it was cold in that special clear, late June evening way. There was a faint breath of heat from the roaster-trolley with what remained of the headless, tailless quadruped, but not enough to stave off the chill. Bjarne sat with an enormous black woollen scarf wrapped twice around his neck like a boa constrictor. Per's padded orange puffer jacket was zipped up to the neck and he had a black beanie pulled down over his forehead to keep his shaven head warm. I had stepped inside the house and borrowed a thick Icelandic pullover from Petter, dragging it on over the fleece jacket. He had opened up Spotify on the outdoor speakers and had been amusing himself by playing a selection of music featuring that band of entertainers known as *Norgesvenner* ('Friends of Norway').

It's a self-deprecating term used to describe a handful of pop and rock acts whose flame has continued to burn brightly in Norway sometimes decades after it went out in their native lands. As a phenomenon it's almost extinct now, its eccentric charms unable to survive the globalisation of all cultures, and the current generation of *Norgesvenner* will surely be the last. But it was an art in itself, knowing exactly who belonged to this exclusive club and who didn't. We'd already had Smokie's 'Living Next Door to Alice', Mungo Jerry's 'In the Summertime', Dr. Hook's 'Sylvia's Mother', and now Petter was playing Bonnie Tyler's 'It's a Heartache'. I had begun to run out of guesses as to what might come next. Nazareth's 'Love Hurts' maybe? Nazareth were lifelong members. The last time we stopped at the petrol station in Lampeland I saw a CD of their greatest hits displayed right next to the cash register. Or maybe something by Johnny Logan. I couldn't see him playing Leonard Cohen, even though Cohen had been a *Norgesvenn* throughout the years of polite recognition that preceded his sudden rise to superstardom in his seventies. It was a loyalty built on 'So Long, Marianne', a song that turned out to be about a Norwegian girl Cohen had stolen from her Norwegian partner, the novelist Axel Jensen, when all three of them were part of a literary-hippy commune living together on a Greek island sometime in the 1960s. But you can't belong to the world *and* be a *Norgesvenn*, and I knew we wouldn't be hearing from Leonard Cohen.

It was strange, listening to those songs. I could remember disliking most of them first time around, but with the years they had transcended the boundaries of taste and become a part of my own personal Norwegian history. Now I actually enjoyed listening to them. I knew of old that taste is an enigma; I remember one night at the age of about eleven simply deciding to like Paul Anka, even though I knew I didn't enjoy the sound of his voice, which I thought too nasal. But as an experiment, as the first notes of 'You Are My Destiny' emerged, budgerigar-faint, from the speaker of the tiny transistor radio under the pillow as I lay in bed, I had decided to see if I could like Paul Anka *as an act of will*. I succeeded with an ease that was almost frightening, and that can still make me uneasy when I think back on it, for what sort of shallowness did it reveal about me as a person?

As the acoustic guitar figure that opens the Beatles' 'Norwegian Wood' waltzed out across the chilly night air, I realised Petter had either got bored or run out of *Norgesvenner*. Per at once put down his beer can, closed his eyes in bliss, and held out his hands, palms downwards, in a plea for silence. His head was tilted back and his new beard jutted out over the table. It was one of those braided Viking beards about a foot long, like a stub of rope. He must have been growing it all year. The rest of us humoured him for the two minutes plus of the song, and as the last strains of the sitar died away he announced that the Beatles, as ever, were the originators; they had started everything; nothing had happened in popular music since then, and the best proof of it was 'Norwegian Wood', because this little song had started the whole sixties school of raga-rock.

'That's crap,' said Bjarne. 'You don't know what you're talking about. There was never any *school of raga-rock*. I was there, I would've noticed. Listen, if it hadn't been for Bob Dylan the Beatles would still have been banging on about she loves you yeah yeah yeah yeah. He made it okay to be intelligent.'

Per took the bait. 'The Beatles copying Bob Dylan? Excuse me. I presume you know "4th Time Around"? It's a complete rip-off of "Norwegian Wood". Waltz-time, storyline, everything.'

Bjarne tried to claim that the Bob Dylan song came first,

and when Per triumphantly read him the Wikipedia entry on '4th Time Around' to prove his point, Bjarne didn't back down but instead claimed that, in that case, it was highly likely that Bob Dylan had sung his song to the Beatles *before* he recorded it, or sent them a tape of it. Bob Dylan was a poet. He deserved to win the Nobel Prize for Literature. The Beatles were just a pop act.

'Å *vær så snill*,' Per said with a groan. 'Please – a poet? What's that line from "Hattie Carroll"? "Lay slain with a cane". And what's that he sings in "Blowin' in the Wind": "How many ears must one man have before he can hear people cry"? How many *ears*?'

He grabbed hold of the tips of his ears and pulled at them.

'Two, Bob, same as everybody else,' he crowed.

'It's not "ears",' Bjarne said angrily, 'it's "years".' But he looked unsure of himself, and decided it was best to go on the attack again, denigrating the Beatles in general and in particular John Lennon. According to Bjarne, John Lennon was a talentless big-head whose one great break was bumping into Paul McCartney.

As I recalled from the conversations of previous years, Lennon was a special hero of Per's. To my surprise he didn't respond. But when I looked at him I saw the blood darken in his eyes and suddenly realised that these two middle-aged men were on the verge of coming to blows over this quite trivial matter.

Petter, always an impeccable but discreet host, seemed to sense that something was up at our table. Standing in the centre of the lawn he now clapped his hands together loudly, and when the conversation died down informed us all that he had recently returned from a trip to Sweden where he had purchased a Canadian Red Shaver. It was a kind of chicken, apparently very rare. If anyone wanted to see it now was the time, because he was heading down to the hen coop right now to put the birds to bed for the night. He strolled off down the slope, clicking his fingers, his black labradoodle, Oskar, bouncing along at his side. About a dozen of us stood up and set off in a ragged train behind him. Bjarne clambered up from the bench but then gave me a wink and whispered he was going up to the house to see if he couldn't find some Bob Dylan records to play.

From the jut of his beard and his profound silence I could tell Per was still very angry, and in an attempt to develop the conversational theme of wood without actually resuming it I told him, as we made our way across the grass towards the chickens, that I had recently finished translating Lars Mytting's book *Hel ved* for a British publisher, and described to him the difficulties I had encountered with the title.

'"*Hel ved*" in English means "all wood". If you say someone you know is "*hel ved*" it means you like them, you admire them, you trust them.'

'I know that,' he said irritably.

'I'm sure you do. But my point is that it's simply untranslatable into English. As a matter of fact, it was quite a hard book to translate. It's full of technical terms involving wood-burning stoves and types of wood and chainsaws that you just don't find in ordinary English dictionaries. I kept having to trudge all the way over to Blindern to use the specialist dictionaries at the Treteknisk Institutt. It was very annoying because, even if I did find the right translations, I never imagined anyone in England would actually *buy* the book. But the title was the biggest problem of all. And then one day, walking back from the Treteknisk Institutt, I suddenly knew what it would be called: *Norwegian Logbook*.'

'That's very good,' Per mused. '*Norwegian Logbook*. I like that.'

'Me too. I was very pleased with myself. I sent the translation in and told them that was the title. I heard nothing until a few weeks later when I saw a copy of the publisher's catalogue with Mytting's book in it: *Norwegian Wood: Chopping, Stacking and Drying Wood the Scandinavian Way*.'

'So it wasn't your title?'

'No. Of course "Norwegian Wood" had occurred to me almost at once as the obvious title. But then I thought, it's already been used as a song title by the Beatles, as the title of a novel by Murakami, and even a third time as the title of a book about Norwegian architecture. How could you use it a fourth time? Where's the dignity? Where's the pride?'

'Ignorant bastards,' Per grunted sympathetically, from which I knew that in relating the tale of my own trials and defeats I had successfully lightened his mood.

A tall, bespectacled man, who had been walking just behind us in silence, now leaned forward.

'You're English,' he stated. 'What does it mean in the song when they sing "Isn't it good, Norwegian wood?" How is that about Norwegian wood?'

'I think it just means pine,' I replied. 'But in Lancashire where I grew up people called it "plain deal". It was the cheapest wood you could get. Then IKEA came along and made it fashionable. Now let me ask you something: why did Mytting's book sell so well here? It's fun, it's well-written, but when all's said and done it's just a book about chopping and stacking wood and the best kind of chainsaw to buy.'

'It's not "just about wood",' he said. 'Well, actually, yes it is. But you have to know the true significance of wood to Norwegians. Wood is one of the deepest things you can know about our country. In the south of the world, in countries like Spain and Greece, they have stone cultures. That's because the sun is hot down there, it shines all day, even at night it's hot, the people need houses that are cool and dark so they build with stone. Up here in Norway we have a wood culture. It's dark and cold, so we need houses that are warm and light.

'Wood is the fundamental environmental fact of our lives. We grow up in houses with wooden walls and wooden roofs. We play with wooden toys on wooden floors. Until not long ago even our skis were made of wood. Do you know that there are over ten thousand million trees in Norway? That's about two thousand trees to each person living here. It's a far greater wealth to have than the oil-fund. Pines, firs, birches...' He gestured vaguely towards the dark pines that rimmed the smallholding, piercing the sky like the points of a crown. Only now did he seem to recall that he was carrying a half-full bottle of white wine and without breaking stride raised it to his lips and took a long swig.

I took a sly look, trying to place him. I had heard someone address him as Christian: was it Roy's brother Christian? Roy was my dentist and a good friend. Both had the same pronounced twist in their noses. And if it was him, then I knew he worked as a repairman for Canon or Xerox, driving around to service and repair photocopy-machines onsite at offices in the Østfold region.

We were gathered around the chicken wire of the henhouse. The grass around the edges of the compound was long and I could feel a wetness penetrating the instep of my trainers. Petter went into the barn behind the shack to turn on the lights. Oskar made a sudden dart up onto the far side of the driveway and began rushing and diving about, burying his nose in the grass. It was long now, but in the early days of these midsummer eve gatherings, at a time when Petter and Hanne kept sheep, part of the deal was that guests would cut and rake and shake the grass before hanging it to dry on long strands of wire stretched between a line of crossed poles. It was an old country technique called *hesjing*. They didn't have any farm machinery so we used scythes to cut the grass. It was two hours of hard work, raking the cut grass into piles and folding it in armfuls across the wire where it would be left to dry in the wind and sun for a few days before being gathered in as winter feed for the sheep. It felt good to walk away from the piled grass, wash your face and hands and comb your hair free of grass, and sit down afterwards for the first beer of the evening, feeling tired but content at the honourable simplicity of the task you had carried out. Later on in the evening, just after the sun had set, when there was still enough light lingering in the dip of cleared land, you could look up the slope at your work and in the flowing grey dimness the shaped lines of hay might seem alive, a caravan of mysterious, yak-like beasts ambling silently across the grass. Each time I saw them I was reminded of a painting by Theodor Kittelsen, an artist who specialised in themes from Norwegian folklore and whose pictures conveyed so well the now almost forgotten sense that every last thing in creation is alive, everything is sensate, everything can be enrolled into the world of human imagination. 'Pine and fir make up ninety per cent of those ten thousand million trees,' Christian continued. 'Right up until the end of the nineteenth century, with very few exceptions, wood was all Norwegians ever used for buildings. Norwegian builders knew all about wood. They knew it had qualities like elasticity and strength that stone and brick don't have. They built using a very precise knowledge

of the behaviour of wood, how it ages, how it weathers, how to make use of its natural shape and form. There were two main building techniques used in building with wood. One was stave construction. You must have seen stave churches in your travels around Norway?'

I said I had, but I had never before thought to wonder why they were referred to as stave churches.

'Stave is like your English word "staff". It means "upright". The timbers of a stave church stand upright. The same technique was used to build longhouses in the Viking Age. Vertical timbers and planks driven straight into the ground, with no supporting frame. They used less timber than log houses, so for areas that weren't as rich in timber, like the coastal regions in the west of Norway, the technique persisted for centuries; but with the walls being thinner they couldn't retain heat in the same way. With the discovery of the *laft* technique things changed. You've been to the Viking ship museum on Bygdøy?'

I said I had, many times. It was probably my favourite Norwegian museum.

'Remember the Gokstad ship? The burial chamber where the chieftain's remains were laid? You can see the *lafteteknikk* there. Not on the ship itself, that was built with strakes, a continuous line of planking from stem to stern of the boat. But from that burial chamber you can see how at least a thousand years ago Norwegians knew how to interlock timbers to create strength and stability. Some unknown genius of an architect realised that if you cut notches at the corners of the logs, and stacked them horizontally on top of one another, you would get a house with strength, stability, elasticity as well as a high degree of insulation against the wind and the cold. From then on everything changed. For one thing buildings became lower and shorter, because the horizontal extent of the walls was dictated by the size of the log, because think how simple the whole thing is: your principal unit of building is a tree trunk. In place of the old Viking longhouses, a single building big enough to house everyone, even the animals, you got a lot of small houses on the farm, built together for warmth and protection against the elements, but each with its own separate function. You couldn't build a better, stronger house. They had found the perfect way to build. So they never changed it. Houses were built to the same simple plan for centuries. The stave method of building lived on in the western coastal regions of the country, where timber was scarce; but everywhere else in Norway they used the *laft* technique. Did you know that up until the early part of the nineteenth century, there were only twenty cities in Norway?'

I said I hadn't known that. He called them cities, but I presumed he meant towns. Even today, there aren't twenty places you would call cities in Norway.

'Twenty cities,' he repeated. 'With less than ten per cent of the population living in them. And because variety within unity is the secret of all art, within the rigid format of this building tradition a fashion arose for making decorative and quite exquisite refinements to the fronts and doors and windows of these buildings, so that within the great basic similarity no two houses or *stabbur* are ever quite alike. What's that in English, *stabbur*?'

'I don't think there's an exact equivalent,' I said. 'In Numedal I think they call them *lofts*. There's dozens of them, literally, once you've passed through Kongsberg and you're headed out along the Fv 40. There's so many of them they call Numedal "Middelalderdalen" in the tourist books. In English *stabbur* means something like a pantry or a larder. It's a place where people used to store food, and...'

'Actually it isn't quite the same thing, a *loft* is not the same as *stabbur*,' said Christian, declining to let me finish. 'They're quite similar, but a *loft* always had two floors and an external staircase. The staircase ran up to the *svalgang*, which is a kind of covered balcony that runs round the front and sides of the building. You also get *svalgang* in stave churches. In a *stabbur*, on the other hand, the stairs are inside, to protect the grain store and the smoked meat and salted meat from the rats and mice. People lived in *lofts,* they didn't live in *stabbur*. Any unmarried girls on the farm used to be moved out to live and sleep there for the summer. It was to get them out of the way of the grown-ups, so they could flirt with the local boys without disturbing their parents. And on Saturday nights, the boys from the other farms would come round. They'd shout and carry on and make a lot of noise outside her window. She'd let them in, offer them some *hjemmebrent* (home-brewed alcohol) and cakes and biscuits. The boys would start showing

off in front of her, doing arm-wrestling or thumb-wrestling, things like that, to show her who was the strongest. The champion was allowed to sit on the bed beside her. That was the prize. Not *in* the bed with her, of course.

'Then the gang would head for the next girl in the next *loft*. After a while a girl might pick a boy she liked better than the rest, and that was it for the rest of the gang, they couldn't come back. Her favourite would go back alone and call up to the girl and plead with her to let him in. That was *nattefrieri* (night-courtship). In Bø in Telemark, where I come from...'

His phone was buzzing and he reached into his back pocket, turned away and took the call. It left me thinking about *nattefrieri*. It seemed so simple and direct. Actually, I thought, give or take a few details, it wasn't so different from the way we used to do things back where I grew up in Lancashire. What I didn't like the sound of were the arm-wrestling and the trials of strength. That could only end with the same boy winning every time. And I didn't really believe that, even back then, girls could have been so easy to impress.

Petter came back with the news that there was a problem with the light switch and we'd have to see the Canadian Red Shaver another time. A woman gave a shriek of disappointment and pretended to start crying. Everybody laughed. Petter then lifted up a flap cut into the chicken wire and stepped inside the enclosure. Bending low he began clapping his hands and making upward, whooshing motions with his palms to urge the five or six chickens that had still not gone up the *hønsetrapp* to roost inside to do so. Bjarne, his resolution to take charge of the music forgotten, had joined us by now and vociferously demanded to see the Scottish Pink Floyd, insisted he wasn't leaving until he'd seen the Scottish Pink Floyd. Someone said Petter had just stepped on it in the dark. Someone else said it was already inside, resting after the long journey from Sweden. No one seemed to mind that the main purpose of the excursion had been defeated, and in groups of twos and threes, muttering and chatting and laughing, we headed back up the grassy slope towards the tables and the flickering candlelight.

Both pleased and intimidated to have come across someone so knowledgeable about matters of which I knew so little, and vaguely recalling that I had made a firm resolution to do something about my ignorance, it now occurred to me to show Christian photographs I had taken of the partially built *hytta*, to see if he could identify some of the joints being used and give me their technical names – those heavy, interlocking 'finger-joints', as I thought of them, which looked as if they ran all the way along the interfaces of the horizontally stacked logs and were only visible at the ends, outside the cabin and at three junction points within it.

We sat down at the table again. I was drinking Aass that evening and offered him a tin. It's a beer brewed locally at Drammen, pleasant enough when chilled, but for an Englishman a Norwegian beer is always just a lager, and I've never been able to taste the difference between them. Christian declined anyway, preferring to carry on swigging from his bottle of white wine.

'These are full-round logs,' he said as he studied the glowing image on the phone. 'But they've been slightly dressed on both sides. That was a seventeenth-century innovation. It's very typical of Numedal architecture. The logs look oval, but next time you go up to your cabin, take a closer look at them. You'll see there are actually six surfaces, it's not a perfect oval. Although actually,' he corrected himself, holding the screen closer to his face, 'you won't. In the days when wood was dressed by hand, with an axe, you would. These logs are milled. But the pillars are beautiful. That's genuine Numedal architecture. All of it – the pillars, the turf roof, these small log-heads here, the lock-and-stop notching – it's all characteristic of Numedal.'

He handed the phone back to me and said something about how wood architecture developed in a different way in Sweden, how the Swedes had developed a greater interest in the aesthetics of the corner notches, often choosing a refined and detailed end-treatment that would have looked out of place on Norwegian wood.

Aud-Marit, whom I knew from previous gatherings to be the most literarily inclined of the footballers, had joined our table after the visit to the hen coop. She was sitting at the end, at the periphery of three intense conversations, and when she overheard Christian's words she jumped in and began enthusing about Murakami's novel. As I had never read the novel I was sidelined for the rest of the conversation, although in the course of it I did learn the answer to something that had vaguely puzzled me over the years, namely, the exact nature of the connection between the Beatles song and the title of Murakami's novel: according to Per, it was the main character's favourite song.

It was gone midnight by now. It had been Nina's turn to drink alcohol-free Munkholm beer that evening, and looking around in my sudden conversational idleness I saw her sitting two tables away from me. I knew she would be worrying about the dog, and sure enough she at once sent me a 'shall-we-go-now' lift of her eyebrows. I hadn't seen anyone else leave yet, and there was still a faint sliver of apricot-coloured light above the pines in the west, and for the briefest of moments I considered pretending not to have seen her signal. But at some point over the last couple of years the old fear of missing something unforgettable by leaving a party early had disappeared. It was time to go and I knew it. I stood up and began pulling my legs up over the bench. As a way of winding things up, and in acknowledgement and recognition of our conversation, from which I felt I had learned a lot, I turned to Christian and asked him how the photocopying-machine business was doing.

He looked up at me, his eyebrows raised in mild surprise.

'I've no idea,' he said. 'Do they even still have them?'

'I thought you worked with them.'

'Me? With photocopying machines?'

'Yes. Don't you?'

'No. I'm an architect.'

Without another word I bounded up the two steps to the house and removed the pullover I had borrowed from Petter and tossed it onto the sofa. I got my coat and woollen hat from the cloakroom, Nina and I said goodbye to Hanne and Petter and whoever else's eye we caught, and we walked down the slope to the car. As we drove back down the forestry track I told her about the case of mistaken identity. I had assumed she would focus on the strangeness of the misunderstanding, but instead she began asking a series of questions clearly designed to work out how such a misunderstanding could possibly have arisen in the first place. This aspect of the story didn't interest me at all, and rather than laboriously trying to trace the cause of the mix-up I changed the subject, asking her whether she knew that, as of the present moment, eighty per cent of Norwegians were city-dwellers, and that this represented a massive and near-complete reinvention of Norway as a rural country? It was a statistic I had picked up from Christian's conversation.

She didn't answer. I glanced across at her, and in the pale glow of the dashboard digitalia saw that she was sitting unnaturally upright in her seat, fingers gripping the steering wheel fiercely as she peered at the night through the windscreen, concentrating hard on navigating the sharp bends in the forestry track as it twisted downwards, light from the headlamps flashing in a series of vanishing and reappearing arcs across the dense wall of dark pines. Loath to disturb her intense concentration, I continued the conversation inwardly with myself, now thinking of Knut Hamsun's famous novel *Markens Grøde* (*The Growth of the Soil*), for which he won the Nobel Prize for Literature in 1920, and of how he articulated in that novel a dream of a world in which people would of their own choosing turn their backs on urbanisation and return to the simpler ways of the past. To a Europe still reeling from the horrors of the 1914–18 war and wondering how on earth to make a fresh start, and whether it was even worth trying, that book must have seemed like the most beautiful beacon of hope. But then how quickly that dream became bound up with the violent *völkisch* nationalism of the Nazis in the 1930s. I recalled the penultimate chapter of the *Tao Te Ching* and its calm disdain for the invention of all labour-saving devices, its vision of a world of small societies living in easy and incurious isolation, so content with their lives that the urge to travel never troubles them. The neighbouring village is so close they can hear the dogs bark and cocks crow, yet they live out their whole lives without ever visiting it. Not for the first time I found myself wondering how I could find that vision so appealing, for on its own terms I had not only visited the neighbouring village but stayed there, and looked like spending the rest of my life there.

# 6

## 14 July 2018

We pick up the key to the cabin – fault-finding tour –

painting the cabin – different ways of thinking

about mountains – Ibsen the collector of folk tales –

Carpelan's mountain painting trip – Olsen's auction

of *Scream* – secret fears of working up a ladder –

W. C. Slingsby and Therese Bertheau climbing 'Storen' –

Norwegians adopt mountaineering as a sport –

Johannes Heftye – Emanuel Mohn's unpatriotic

failings – Amundsen's dogs

We picked up the key from Norske Fjellhus' head office in Kongsberg on the drive up. I had no idea what my reaction would be on entering the completed cabin for the first time. As we opened the front door, painted in darkly beautiful 'Røros red', we entered a dim hallway paved in dark grey flagstone. There was a *hønsetrapp* ('hen-ladder') staircase leading up to the two bedrooms on the first floor. Stepping past this we stood in the combination living room and kitchen. Sunlight flooded the room through the four windowpanes on the far wall and my first thought at the sight of all that radiantly warm blonde wood was that I did not want to sully it by the application of even a single brush-stroke of paint, never mind the intrusion of a roomful of furniture.

As we waited for the builders to arrive we made a brief, fault-finding tour of the cabin. I was so thrilled by the beauty of all the wood I was not really minded to dwell on the small but palpable imperfections: the bedroom door that didn't quite close; the work-surface top that angled slightly inward on its way from the kitchen sink to the fridge; the glimpse of bare wood from the small gash low down on the shed door; and the dishwasher having been installed in the wrong place, two cupboard sections away from the sink and the water supply.

'There's a draught here.'

Nina was squatting in a corner of the main room, moving the back of her hand up and down against the wall. Squatting beside her, I made a fist of my right hand and held it up to the spot. I felt a steady stream of quick cold air blowing across the back of my hand. I stood up. It was like a warning. A whispered resolution from the mountain to take back and reclaim these few acres of terrain we had had the temerity to appropriate.

Reidar, the builder, was a tall young man. He looked to be in his mid-thirties but had an authoritative way about him that made him seem older. He spoke the simple but good English necessary to communicate with the largely foreign workforce whom Norske Fjellhus employed to carry out their building projects. At about two in the afternoon he arrived with Marek, whom we had met several times previously, and a Latvian, who was not introduced and whose name we never learned.

Almost alone of the imperfections on our list, the draught had made me uneasy, and this was the first thing we drew to Reidar's attention. He bent down, held the back of his hand to the joint where the timber from the living room and the bedroom intersected, then stood up and told the Latvian to take some sheep's wool, dip it in something that sounded like *tirilolje*, and wedge it into the gap on the outside.

*Tirilolje* was the only Norwegian word in the whole exchange. Otherwise they had spoken in English. I had no idea what it meant. While the Latvian was outside I took out my phone and surreptitiously googled it. But no matter how I spelled it, Google couldn't answer. At the point at which it tried to introduce me to the singing of an Albanian named Tiri Gjoci I almost gave up, but then hit the jackpot when I tried spelling it *tyriolje*, and learned that it means 'pine tar', a substance long used in Scandinavia as a preservative for wood exposed to harsh conditions.

And then the little party of builders was gone, and the place was ours, and for the next ten weekends we made the three-hour drive up from Oslo every Friday evening, spent all day

Saturday and Sunday painting, slept over at Paul and Trine's cabin, and drove back to Oslo on Sunday night. The paint we chose came from a Maxbo concertina catalogue that offered up to thirty different shades of brown, each described individually, each with its own unique name. We had spent long hours pondering these entries but, try as I might, I could see no significant differences between them. They seemed so similar to me that an act of choice was hardly called for, but in the end I had voted emphatically for a shade called 'Lys Varde', meaning 'light cairn'.

We spoke of it as 'paint', but a voice within me longed to call it *creosote*. It was brown, and thinner than ordinary paint, and I had distant memories of applying something very like it to garden fences while working as a builder's labourer on a house-refurbishing project done by Laings on a council estate in the Elephant and Castle in South London in the 1970s. On trying to discover a suitable translation for the Norwegian term for the paint I was using (*beis*), I discovered that creosote was now an illegal substance in the United Kingdom, apparently on health or environmental grounds, or both. I googled 'creosote', hoping to discover exactly why it had become illegal, and came upon a promising discussion of the matter; but with the strange rapidity typical of internet groups the discussion descended into an exchange of abuse and I abandoned my search.

★

We began working indoors, and downstairs, where the main bedroom was. The idea was that once we were finished and began work on the outside we would be able to sleep in our own cabin.

For the most part it was monotonous and straightforward work. Nina likes to talk as she works, while I prefer to sink into a deep and seemingly morose silence when involved in any project such as this. I was working on the long, east-facing wall, working around the two windows. I began to notice for the very first time how the staining of the wood revealed certain beauties in it of which, in my devotion to work and to the practice of a free and easy mental wandering, I had not previously been aware. Sitting back on my haunches I suddenly found myself savouring the dragonfly-like beauty of the 'branched knot', in which two splayed or spiked knots appear to originate from the same central source; or the mysterious lens-shaped hollow of a resin pocket, like a lenticular galaxy glimpsed at the remote limits of the Hubble telescope; I noticed the 'heart shakes' on the stacked ends of the supporting quarter-walls that marked the division between kitchen area and living-room area; fissures; end shakes, radiating from the pith; the way the staining process enhanced the delicate lines of the undulating grain in tight and irregular curves.

All of these esoteric observations, I now realised, were vestigial memories from the time spent translating Mytting's book into English, a task that had quite incidentally furnished me with a degree of knowledge about timber that I would never have acquired in the normal course of events.

The work was hard on the back, and hard on the hips, and presently I stood up to stretch. Idly looking through the windows, I saw the jagged line of the seven peaks on the Blefjell range. My thoughts rambled off in their direction, and I found myself thinking about the Norwegian mountains, and the changing ways Norwegians have looked at them over the centuries. To Norwegian heathens the world was a flat circle divided into three distinct regions, each with its own characteristic set of inhabitants, and sharing a common centre. The innermost world was Asgard, where the gods, known as the *Aesir*, lived, each in his or her own home. Odin lived in Valhalla, Thor in Thrudheim, Freyja in Folkvang. Odin's work was to inspire poets, wage war and give fighting men courage in battle. Thor was responsible for natural phenomena such as wind, rain, thunder and lightning. Beyond this inner region was Midgard, the domain of the humans. The word meant 'home in the middle' and conveyed clearly the humans' sense of being located midway between the gods in Asgard and the giants of Utgard – the outer rim of their discworld, an untamed region of mountains and plateaus inhabited by elemental beings associated with wildness, danger and chaos.

The vertical axis of the flat, round world was an ash tree named Yggdrasil, connected to the sky at its crown, and at its roots penetrating to a subterranean realm that included a well, known as Urd's Well, where the gods held their assembly meetings and where three female beings, known as the Norns, spun out the destinies of humans and gods alike. Yggdrasil represented an assurance to the inhabitants of Midgard that there was indeed a centre to the world, and that all things were connected, despite appearances to the contrary, despite the ceaseless struggle between a will to order, represented by the gods of Asgard, and the entropic lure of chaos, represented by the giants and creatures of the mountainous Utgard. And although Utgard was a threatening and frightening place to be, even for the gods, it was understood that in the chaos within its borders lay the raw materials necessary for the learning of new skills and the creation of valuable treasures, which the Aesir could hand on to the inhabitants of Midgard. The story of how Odin forced the secrets of the art of writing runes from the reluctant terrain of this mental region is a dramatic illustration of the view that learning, knowledge and progress had to be fought for and suffered for.

There were, I reflected, echoes of this idea of the mountains as fearful, threatening but also valuable in the folk tales that survived in oral form until well into the middle of the nineteenth century, when Peter Christen Asbjørnsen and Jørgen Moe produced their collection of Norwegian Folk Tales, the fruits of trips through the Norwegian mountains and countryside in the summers of 1843 and 1844. In 1862 a hard-up Henrik Ibsen applied for and was given a government grant to make a folk-tale collecting trip in the Hardanger and Sogn regions of the country, a task for which this taciturn and introverted man proved ill-suited, requiring as it did someone with a friendly and sociable personality able to persuade storytellers to relax and open up to him. Indeed, it seems the roles were reversed: 'The visitor was silent and unapproachable,' one potential source recalled, 'and all our efforts to get him to open up were in vain.'

In the end Ibsen departed with a ready-made collection

offered to him by a local man named Peder Fylling, and once he got back to Kristiania he boldly offered several tales as the fruits of his own labours in the pages of the magazine *Illustreret Nyhedsblad*, without so much as a mention of the man who had done the actual collecting. The stories also hugely enriched *Peer Gynt*, which Ibsen wrote some five years later. Nina and I had recently attended a performance of *Peer Gynt* at the Oslo Nye Teater, in an adaptation built around and for Toralv Maurstad, the greatest Norwegian actor of his generation, then in his ninety-first year. For many native Norwegians Ibsen is as uninteresting a phenomenon as Shakespeare is to the average Englishman, and the sheer size of his reputation a bore. But of late Nina had evinced an interest in *Peer Gynt*, prompted by Peer's dialogue with the Button Moulder on the subject of reincarnation. The Nye Teater production turned out to be a 'best-of' *Peer Gynt,* with twelve different actors playing Peer at various times of his life under the largely silent scrutiny of a very old Peer, as played by Maurstad. The decision picked up nicely Ibsen's image of a human being as an onion, to the heart of which no amount of peeling and stripping of the outer layers will ever penetrate.

As usual when I visit the theatre I drifted in and out of attention. On one particular occasion, with eight or nine Peer Gynts crowding the stage, I found myself recalling an out-door performance of *Peer Gynt* on the shores of Lake Gålå that Nina and I attended in the autumn, during which ice-cold rain fell unremittingly for the entire three hours the performance lasted. It was not far off midnight by the time the performance ended, pitch dark and still pouring with rain. The hotel we were staying at was a forty-minute drive away in the coach. There was nothing to see through the windows, and after about fifteen minutes I tried to start a conversation with the man sitting beside me, and asked what he thought of the way old and young Peer had been played by two actors who were father and son, Nils Per and Jakob Oftebro? For a few moments he stared at me in dazed bewilderment, then he smiled and, with a note of triumph in his voice, pointed out that Peer's claim to have encountered a flock of seagulls while flying down the Besseggen scree on the back of a goat was wrong, because you don't get seagulls in the mountains. He said it showed how little Henrik Ibsen actually knew about the mountains. I enjoyed the non-academic nature of the objection, but suggested an alternative explanation: wasn't it possible that the reference might have been deliberate, and an example of Ibsen's talented slyness in undermining the credibility of Peer's tale? He said he supposed it was possible, and then turned and stared fixedly out of the window, leaving me alone with the further thought that what Ibsen really knew about mountains was empathic, and derived from the perspective not of the climber but of the miner, with whose labours, toiling deep underground in darkness to bring riches into the light of day, he could identify as a writer and explorer of the shadows and hidden depths of the human soul. It was a perspective brilliantly summoned in *Bergmanden* ('The miner'), written in 1851 when Ibsen was only twenty-three:*

Rock-face, crack and boom and go
Crashing to my hammer-blow;
I must clear a way down yonder
To the goal I dare but ponder.

---

* The poem was published at a time when Ibsen was still using the pseudonym Brynjolf Bjarme.

Deep within the fell's still night
Treasures rich and rare invite,
Precious stones and diamonds blazing
Midst the gold's resplendent mazing.

In the depths here all is peace,
Peace and night that never cease; –
Soon earth's very heart shall clamour
To the smiting of my hammer.          (tr. John Northam)

The identification with stone ran deep; for much of his life Ibsen lived in fear of a kind of self-petrification, clearly expressed in the long early poem *På viddene* (On the heights), where he writes of a feeling of turning to stone in the vault of his chest. Oddly enough it is in that same poem that he coined the word *friluftsliv* ('outdoor life'), which has become the standard term used by Norwegians to convey the idea of the mountains and the Vidda as positive and liberating places, arenas in which to soar temporarily free from the trivia of everyday life.

But rather than the poets and the collectors of folk tales, it was the painters – men like the Danish-born Johannes Flintoe, and native Norwegian masters like J. C. Dahl, Hans Gude, Peder Balke and Thomas Fearnley, with their working expeditions into the Jotunheimen mountain region, Hurrungane, the Hardangervidda and the mountains of northern Norway in the early years of the nineteenth century – who announced the end of the fearful fantasising about 'Utgard'. They replaced 'fear' with an aesthetic response that was at times ecstatic and almost religious in its nature. One of the earliest of these aesthetic explorers, the Finnish-Swedish adjutant and painter Wilhelm Maximilian Carpelan, crossed the interior of Norway twice, from Christiania to Bergen, in 1819. As the cataclysm of the Napoleonic wars drew to an end, the Swedish crown had acquired Norway in a personal union, by the terms of the treaty of Kiel in 1814. Carpelan's brief was to ensure that the route across the mountains was navigable for the Swedish king's newly appointed governor-general August Sandels, who planned to make the trip to find out more about exactly what it was the king had acquired. The route traversed central southern Norway, via Valdres and the mountainous region of Filefjell to the village of Lærdalsøyri, and continued by boat along Sognefjord, Norway's longest and deepest fjord, and south towards Bergen. There had been major flooding in the spring of that year, and rumours that the road via Lærdal had been swept away. The immediate purpose of Carpelan's first trip was to ascertain whether this was in fact the case. Once he was able to confirm that the route was navigable, the main party set out for the inland crossing. It was in the course of this trip that Carpelan produced a number of watercolour sketches and drawings of the Norwegian mountains for which his status as a pioneer of the new genre has long been recognised.

The experiences of that summer made an unforgettable impression on him. He recalled how, on Midsummer's Day 1819, in the early morning, he climbed Filefjell:

Midsummer's Day 1819, in the early morning, I climbed this peak for the first time. Before I reached the highest point on the track, the sun had risen in all its majestic glory behind the Hurrungane peaks, spreading a light of shifting colours across their desolate vastness. The air was cool and rather damp, as it is in early April in the central parts of Sweden. Just a few wisps of clouds floated in the sky, soon dispersed by the rays of the sun. At my feet, beside the glinting waters of Lake Uttra,

Nystuen was still in shadow. The mountains on the far side of the valley, with Stugu the highest among them, stood like dark phantoms flecked by bright patches of snow. In a blue-tinged declivity lay the valley of Skougstad, where the masses of the mountains to the east meet. Below the Hurrungane a layer of mist hung, seeming to rise from the waters of Bydin lake.

After his tour of duty ended Carpelan returned to Stockholm, where his experience of the aesthetic power of the Norwegian mountains continued to haunt his imagination. Between 1821 and 1823 he published *Voyage pittoresque aux alpes norvégiennes*, a set of aquatints based on the sketches from 1819, and continued to produce work based on that magical summer until his death in 1830, in Stockholm, at the age of forty-three. Tuberculosis, a common killer at the time, was suggested as the cause of death. His contemporary, Johannes Flintoe, was of a different opinion: 'While he carefully

monitored its corrosive effect on the copper plate, the nitric acid, including dispersed copper, inhaled in quantity, did its morbid work – all the while his fascination with the artistic product was enough to drive all thought of the poison and its fatal consequences from his mind.' It was clear to him that Carpelan's fascinated addiction to the aquatint process, through which he refined and reiterated his love of the Norwegian mountains, was the true cause of his death, as surely as if he had lost his footing and tumbled from the top of Filefjell.

One of the finest examples of Carpelan's hand-coloured aquatint, 'Skutshorn ved Vangsmjøsa', is a depiction of a mountain that is little known among Norwegians themselves, but remarkable among connoisseurs of the mysterious for a phenomenon that has given the mountain its name: at intervals Skutshorn emits a series of shot-like booms or groans, accompanied by a vertically slanting jet of steam. These phenomena may, it occurred to me, be understood as a reminder of the persistence of *danger* to be associated with mountains, no matter how many times we paint them, no matter how easily we may fly across them and burrow through them. It seemed to me – as I reached the south-eastern corner of the living-room wall and stood to stretch my back for a few moments, noticing, as I did so, that the faint hints of grey in the *beis* that now showed subtly through in the afternoon sunlight slanting in through the terrace windows went some way towards justifying the poetic name given the shade by its manufacturers – that Skutshorn's shot-like groans might conceivably be understood as a kind of warning on the dangers of taking mountains for granted; indeed, that our fear of mountains was something better left intact, and that our appalling and requisitioning arrogance, the idea that all of this is somehow *ours*, somehow just for us, for our convenience and use, has led inevitably to a diminished respect, which might possibly provoke a catastrophe the real dimensions of which have not yet become apparent to us, so that as soon as possible we should return to the attitude of devotional respect epitomised by the ninth-century Icelandic chieftain Thorolf Mostrarskjegg who, the *Landnámabok* ('The Book of the Settlements') tells us, named the only mountain on his farm 'Helgafell', meaning Holy Mountain, and who in the strangely touching intensity of his devotion insisted that no one might look upon it with an unwashed face.

Perhaps we should not even look on mountains at all, or we may yet experience the fate of the homunculus depicted in Edvard Munch's painting *Skrik – Scream –* and hear so acutely as to be unable to blank out the anguished howl of the landscape. Over the years Munch wrote several different versions of the experience that led to the painting, but the gist of them was always the same. Making his way on foot into Kristiania (Oslo) down the Ekeberg hill, 'the sun set and suddenly the sky turned into blood. My friends continued walking. I stopped by the fence, deathly tired. Over the cold blue fjord and city was a flaming reddish yellow, and I felt a great scream pass through nature.'

Returning to the task of painting the cabin, as I moved the paint-pot onto a new bed of newspapers I saw in an old number of *Aftenposten* from 2012, in an item about the sale at Sotheby's in New York of one of the five more or less identical versions of *Scream* that Munch made of the image, that a version of this point had in fact been raised by the seller of the painting, the Norwegian philanthropist and idealist Petter Olsen. At a press conference after the sale he spoke to the world's journalists. Expecting to hear what it 'felt like' now that he no longer owned the painting, now that he was a hundred and twenty million dollars richer than he had been yesterday, they were instead treated to a halting address by a man in a suit slightly too big for him who urged upon the world a new understanding of Munch's painting as a visionary cry of pain and a warning. Almost incidentally, as he did so, he corrected a widespread misconception concerning this painting, that it is the creature that is doing the screaming, for as Munch's captions to the picture consistently make clear, the creature raises its paws to its ears to block out the terrifying sound being made by the landscape. In our anthropocentric lunacy it is we humans, said Olsen, with our shrugging indifference to the frailty of all forms of life on Earth, who are responsible for this scream of pain, and for which we must now take responsibility.

Olsen's was an interesting interpretation. It seemed to me, as I loaded up my brush and resumed my long, crouched, sideways shuffle along the timbers below the terrace windows, that it came close to a secular form of the belief in Original Sin that holds our presence and activities here on Earth to be essentially malign. In doing so it also suggested a nostalgia for the oppressive and yet bracing power vested in that ancient conception. Better far to accept that as humans we are born bad and that our first great challenge is not to become worse, and our second to improve.

At this point, realising I had forgotten to protect the white sashes of the terrace windows, I stood up and began applying strips of masking tape along their edges, lulled by the simplicity of the task into permitting myself a few moments in satisfied contemplation of the sheer extent of timber I had now stained, almost without my having noticed it. I was, however, quickly brought down to earth by the sight of the massive gable overhang, supported on three large and heavy cinched pillars that defined the outer limit of the planked terrace that extended along the entire length of the front of the cabin and outwards for about two metres, and the knowledge that at some point that gable would have to be painted. Dimly I realised that in a not-too-distant future I would need to climb all the way to the top of a fully extended sliding ladder, bearing with me as I did so the open pot of wood stain and two brushes of different widths, in order to paint the weatherboards nailed horizontally along the peak of the gable.

Already this gable had begun to haunt my dreams. Frequently, before falling asleep at night, I would spend what felt like an hour but was probably ten minutes imagining ways of painting it that would totally eliminate any and every possibility of my falling from the top of the fully extended ladder, either directly backwards, or in slow motion sideways as I leaned over to extend the reach of my brush as far as possible. Most of these ideas involved coils of rope threaded around and through the rungs and sides of the ladder, anchored in some way to the central pillar or to the network of supports that connected each pillar to the front wall of the cabin.

As these imaginings progressed, what started out as a simple anchoring strategy might gradually develop into a fantastic web of criss-crossing ropes connecting the ladder, all three pillars, the cross-pillars, even entering the cabin itself through the open window of the *hems* (loft or first floor) and like some Jules Verne monster flailing about the walls and floor and ceiling in search of the ultimate fail-safe anchorage. I spent an entire evening on YouTube watching short videos showing how easy it was for one man to handle a fully extended sliding ladder. In one, which seemed to be an American fire-brigade training video, the instructor trained recruits to shout verbal warnings to themselves. I latched on to 'NO OVERHEAD OBSTRUCTIONS' and fell asleep whispering it repeatedly to myself, as though it were a mantra guaranteeing my safety.

It was in the middle of one of these fitful half-dreams of falling that I saw again a photograph I had come across recently in a book about the early history of mountaineering in Norway. As the old ambiguity towards the mountains and Vidda as predominantly places of work and fear died away, and following the work of collectors like Asbjørnsen and Jørgen Moe and the aestheticisation of the mountains by painters like Carpelan, Balke, Flintoe, Tidemand and Gude, who found beauty and magnificence there, a third phase in Norwegians' relationship towards their mountains began with the advent of mountaineering as a sport.

The photograph I saw in my mind's eye seemed in its way to encapsulate the emerging history of this development, and I was struck once again by the way in which this too was tied, as so much of the understanding of modern Norway is tied, to that unique brand of nationalism practised by Norwegians in which a ferocious patriotism is soundly underpinned by a remarkable sense of – for want of a better word – decency.

Two of those in the

photograph are Norwegians. Leading on the rope is the local guide, a farmer named Per Berge; behind him, wearing a skirt and hat, is Therese Bertheau, the first lady of Norwegian climbing; the third member of the party is a Yorkshireman named William Cecil Slingsby.

The photograph is from an ascent made in 1900 of Store Skagastølstind, commonly known as 'Storen' ('The big one'), a peak in the Jotunheimen and the third highest mountain in Norway. Twenty-five years earlier, in 1876, Slingsby had made the first ascent of what has sometimes been described as 'the Norwegian Matterhorn'. In 1894 Bertheau had made the first ascent of the mountain by a woman. Slingsby, a man free of many of the most common prejudices concerning women, who had on several of his climbing expeditions in Norway been accompanied by both his sister and his wife, practised a great courtesy in all his dealings with the Norwegians of both sexes whom he came across, and held Ms Bertheau in particular regard; in the preface to his memoirs *Norway: the Northern Playground*, she is the only mountaineer whom he thanks by name. It was at his specific request that Bertheau agreed to join him in what was self-consciously a celebration of their joint individual achievements as the first man and woman to reach the top of the mountain. In a second famous picture, Bertheau and Berge can be seen standing on the top and helping Slingsby up the final few yards. In both photographs it is Bertheau, in her skirt and tall, brimmed hat with its bright decorative band, who compels our attention. It looks as if the climb were undertaken on a whim one day after work (she was a schoolmistress in Kristiania) and, for a reason I cannot quite fathom, the hat makes it look as if the whole thing was somehow easier for her than it was for Berge and Slingsby.

Her triumphs, and her status as the first lady of Norwegian

mountaineering, are beyond question. But it was Slingsby, as a serial conqueror of peaks previously thought to be unclimbable, on the twenty-one visits he made to Norway between 1872 and 1921, and by his introduction of what were, to Norwegians, useful novelties like the ice axe and climbing boots with nails in their soles, who was most intimately bound up with the third great change in the attitude towards mountains, the conquest phase that succeeded the fearful respect of the Middle Ages and the aestheticising of the Norwegian mountain landscape by painters and poets. His status in this respect remains unquestioned by Norwegians, and his maiden ascent of Store Skagastølstinde in 1876 is universally regarded as the beginning of mountaineering as a sport in Norway. He remains an important figure in the recent history of the country, his name and its association so familiar to Norwegians that Bergans, one of Norway's largest manufacturers of outdoor clothing and equipment, when launching a new range of high-performance jackets in 2018, called it 'the Slingsby Collection'.

For much of the first part of his ascent Slingsby was accompanied by two Norwegians. One was an urbane philologist and schoolteacher, a native of Bergen named Emanuel Mohn, whom he had met in 1874 on a steamboat on its way to Bergen.

Mohn had already climbed a number of peaks in Jotunheimen and knew the region so well he described himself as a 'jotunologist'. The second man was Knut Lykken, a farmer, reindeer hunter and their guide. Mohn was a tireless advocate of the mental and physical benefits of mountaineering and the outdoor life and in his writings extolled the virtues of climbing and rambling that remain such an intrinsic part of the Norwegian self-image. Mountaineering adventures, he wrote, were 'the Viking expeditions of our own times', offering as they did the same opportunities to exercise 'manly courage and strength'. But like the Englishman Slingsby he urged women, too, to discover and share with the men the joys and benefits of mountaineering.

Knut Lykken took a different and more traditional view of their enterprise. For him the mountains remained the Utgard of pre-Christian mythology, a hard and dangerous workplace. The idea of a mountain peak as something to be climbed for its own sake was quite foreign to him. Mohn recalled Lykken telling them, as they stamped their way across the Galdebergsbreen glacier, that it was one of his best fields for reindeer hunting, but that though he had often in the course of the chase been to the upper edge of the glacier, with the summit of the Galdeberget mountain a mere three hundred feet above him and easily climbable within fifteen minutes, the thought of doing so had never occurred to him. Here, in this collision of attitudes, the peasant working-class past of Norway met its urban, middle-class future.

Basing the belief on certain passages in Snorri Sturluson's *History of the Norwegian Kings*, Slingsby shared Mohn's view that in climbing to the tops of mountains as an end in itself they were reviving a pastime that had first been enjoyed a thousand years earlier, in Viking times. In the ensuing centuries its pleasures had been forgotten, and not been seriously revived in any way until 1820, when the geologist Professor Baltazar Keilhau and a botanist and doctor named Christian Boeck scaled Falkenebbe (Falcon's Beak), later renamed Falketind (Falcon Peak), and made a brave but unsuccessful attempt to scale Skagastølstind, the most northerly of the Skagastøl peaks. Slingsby relates that, on one of Keilhau and Boeck's expeditions, one member of the party was almost killed when caught in an avalanche, his life saved only by a large and solidly constructed barometer strapped to his back, which protected him from a falling stone that would otherwise have broken his spine.

On their way into the Hurrangane peaks of which Storen forms the most majestic part, Slingsby, Mohn and Lykken followed the route into Jotunheimen taken by Keilhau and Boeck in 1820. Bad weather delayed their start for several days but, when they finally set out, during the next five days they made five maiden ascents. Slingsby describes the ascent of the great mountain in gripping detail; how Mohn declined to join him for the final and most dangerous part of the ascent, pleading exhaustion, and Lykken refused to go any higher on the grounds that it was too dangerous, leaving him to climb the final five hundred and eighteen feet alone and without ropes, using tiny ledges no wider than his hand, which first had to be chipped free of the layers of ice that covered them all with his axe. Reaching what they had thought from below to be the summit, Slingsby found there to be a knife-edged ridge some sixty yards long leading to the actual top, with three peaklets and a notch that obliged him for the first time to trust to an overhanging and loose rocky ledge. When at last he reached the summit, 'a rock table four feet by three', he abandoned himself to the pleasures of the experience, mingling the triumphs of conquest with the aesthetic ecstasies now revealed spread out to him on all sides. 'But in such a place, alone, out of sight of every living creature,' he writes, 'one of the greatest desires of my heart granted to me, it will be easily understood, when I say that a feeling of silent worship and reverence was more suitable than the jotting down of memoranda in a notebook. The scene was too overwhelming for my notes. I longed to have my trusty friend Mohn by my side, and his absence was a bitter disappointment.' Later, after a drink of cold tea, some goat's milk cheese and a few prunes, he built a small cairn and wedged his khaki handkerchief into the side of it before making his way down to rejoin his companions.

★

Norway was still, at the time of Slingsby's conquest of Store Skagastølstind, a property of the crown of Sweden; but in retrospect there is an overwhelming sense of inevitability about the three decades that preceded 1905 and the achievement of full independence. Ibsen was already conquering the literary world on behalf of his countrymen, but there was always a feeling that the identity of the nearly-nation was intimately bound up not so much with its literature and its fine arts (though in addition to Ibsen the Norwegian contribution to world culture over these decades includes Edvard Grieg, Knut Hamsun and Edvard Munch) but to something more directly connected to the unique landscape of the country and the deeply rural heritage that all Norwegians shared.

Rumours that Store Skagastølstind had finally been conquered preceded Slingsby and Mohn as they made their way back to civilisation, Knut Lykken having returned to his farm at Øystre Slidre in Valdres. It was said that Mohn and Lykken had reached the top, but not the foreigner; then that it was the foreigner who had reached the top alone; then that the hero of the hour was Knut Lykken. When at last Slingsby and Mohn arrived at the small tourist hotel at Røisheim and the truth was made known, Slingsby observes, though the congratulations and celebrations were warm and sincere, disappointment that the honour had not been claimed by a Norwegian was palpable. And, with the innocence of a true enthusiast, Slingsby continued to gobble up first ascents of some of the highest peaks in Norway on his subsequent trips.

Perhaps unwisely, in a lecture on the ascent given later in the summer at the Norwegian Students Union in Kristiania, Mohn expressed the view that the sport of mountaineering in Norway was not as yet developed enough to produce Norwegian climbers capable of the ascent of a mountain like Store Skagastølstind. Provoked by this assertion, a young landscape painter named Harald Petersen made the second ascent of Storen in 1878, and the first by a Norwegian, claiming that he had done so solely to refute Mohn's assertion and demonstrate that Norwegians were quite capable of such feats. As proof of his ascent he sent Slingsby the khaki handkerchief the Englishman had left behind at the summit, leaving behind his own red one, and a tobacco pouch containing a medicine bottle with his name on it and a few coins.

Another who was stung by what he interpreted as Slingsby's act of proto-cultural appropriation was a wealthy Norwegian lawyer and landowner named Johannes Heftye. The summer before Slingsby's sensational solo climb, Heftye had made the first ascent of Knutsholstind, another peak in the Jotunheimen and at that time believed by many to be the highest in Norway. He took Slingsby's triumph as a personal affront. Absolutely convinced that his own achievement was of greater significance, and that the ascent of 'Storen' was hardly comparable, he climbed the mountain himself in August 1880, with two others. Intending to follow Slingsby's route, he lost his way slightly and inadvertently discovered a 'chimney' up which he was able to make the last part of the climb. This was dubbed 'Heftye's Chimney'. It remains to this day one of the most popular routes to the top, so much so that climbers proposing to make the ascent are advised that there may be a queue and a long wait at the entrance to it.

Heftye had made the ascent only to prove how easy it was compared to his own ascent of Knutsholstind, and he made his point clear in a booklet published the following year, in 1881. Slingsby's response was to climb Knutsholstind himself, with Johannes Vigdal and a *budeie* from Gjendebu named Marie Sølfestsdatter. In describing the climb afterwards he added, perhaps a trifle unnecessarily, that in the course of the climb they had hardly needed to use their hands at all.

Heftye was a short-tempered man. Some years later, in a dispute with local people whom he found trespassing on his estate on Christmas Day 1899, he shot and killed a twenty-four-year-old fisherman with his revolver. He was duly arrested but released even before the young man's body was in the ground, the court finding that he had acted in self-defence, and the newspapers lamenting the lack of respect for property laws among the uneducated of the countryside. It was the second human life Heftye had, or didn't have, on his conscience; in 1881 a man named Henning Bødtker Tønsberg, having read Heftye's booklet and been impressed by his misleading account of the ease with which Store Skagastølstind could be conquered, set out on the climb and fell to his death.

Responding to Slingsby's account, Heftye wrote a newspaper article in which he censured Slingsby most especially for having invited 'a defenceless woman' along with him on such a 'dangerous expedition', and expressed the fervent hope that the liberation of women would never reach a stage at which the ascent of Knutsholstind would become some kind of rite of initiation for women. Heftye continued to attack Slingsby in further newspaper articles, accusing him of being largely motivated in all he did by the wish to diminish his own achievement in being the first man to climb Knutsholstinden. He wouldn't tolerate it, he wrote, especially not from a foreigner.

Mohn's failure to have made the top of Storen with Slingsby was not forgotten. In the late summer of 1876 he became the target of a number of hostile articles in *Morgenbladet*, in which he was accused of cowardice for allowing a foreigner to be the first conqueror of a national icon like Storen. 'We are a mountain people,' he was told. 'It does not look good for us when foreigners beat us to the tops of our own mountains.' He was advised that in future a man like him should avoid embarking on more trips with foreigners, 'if in any doubt at all about one's own courage and capacities'. Norwegian nationalism, nowadays such a notably benign, inclusive and child-centred phenomenon, was much harsher in these crucial decades, where every public act a man performed was reckoned up against its contribution to the creation of a Norwegian national identity, in accordance with an understanding that until this was demonstrably in place for all the world to see, only then would the demand for independence be irrefutable.

So Emanuel Mohn had let the side down. He had failed to realise that 'on such occasions' he had become, whether he liked it or not, a 'self-appointed representative of his nation'. Replying to the attacks he expressed indignation and bewilderment at the criticism, and rejected completely any notion that he, a private person on a private venture with an Englishman whom he considered a friend, was responsible to anyone but himself. To him the whole week they had spent climbing together in Jotunheimen was quite free of 'irrelevant national jealousies', and he expressed his astonishment at the way the question of national honour had been introduced into the discussion. Later on, Knut Lykken came in for criticism too, for his failure to have been something more and greater than a Norwegian working man whose view of the mountains was as a place of employment rather than an arena for the display of pride in his nationality. Young Henning Tønsberg, whose father had been Støren's first victim, informed him that his reluctance on two occasions – with Slingsby and thereafter with Petersen – to continue to the top of the mountain was not, as he himself might have thought, a simple desire not to risk his life in an enterprise that had no interest for him, but the result of a typically peasant lack of imagination and initiative: 'It's worth noting', wrote Tønsberg, 'that this mountain farmer, this hunter, regarded the venture as a sort of blasphemy, a result of the view of mountaintops among that type of person as something ugly, forbidding and dangerous.' Norway, although without an aristocracy since the abolition of titles of privilege in 1821, nevertheless preserved, as it does to this day, a subtle but distinct class system, and Tønsberg's expressed contempt for the cautious farmer–hunter Knut Lykken was one example of it. So was the fact that Johannes Heftye's killing of the trespassing young fisherman went unpunished.

But maybe there is another, kinder way of looking at it, I thought. Here, in these heated debates and discussions of national identity, of what it means to be Norwegian and what it *should* mean to be Norwegian, are we not on the cusp of modernity, the watershed that divides old, rural Norway from the Norway of the industrial revolution and after, manifest in this urgent desire to lay claim to all of Norway in this very literal sense, by clambering to all of its highest points? Could this not be seen as the last gesture of a rural people, asserting its final triumph over a landscape that had for so long over-awed them, before leaving it permanently behind and settling in cities and towns?

Indeed, was it possible, I asked myself – noting at the same time the almost facial beauty of certain clusters of knots that seemed often to occur in triangular groups of three, in which the upper two together suggested the sad scrutiny of some dog-like animal gazing darkly out from within a parallel uni-verse that passed through the wood – might it be possible to relate all of this to what is probably the most dramatic manifestation of Norwegian national identity, as an out-door people, a people of mountain and ice, in the careers of Fridtjof Nansen and his protégé, Roald Amundsen? I thought of the cabin Nansen and Hjalmar Johansen built and lived in for six months during their heroically failed attempt to reach the North Pole in 1896; of how Nansen became a

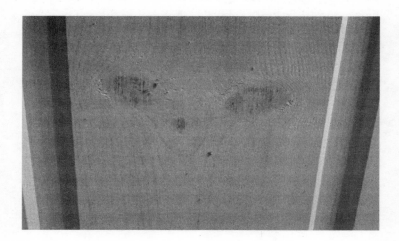

hero and a role model to a whole generation of young Norwegian men. Concerning Amundsen, something of the same may be said. Perhaps it was boyhood memories of those expressions of national disappointments verging on humiliation associated with Mohn, Lykken and Slingsby that had enabled Amundsen to lie so cold-bloodedly about the true goal of his expedition to the South Pole in 1912, knowing as he did that the Englishman Robert Scott was also planning an expedition? Did being first seem to Amundsen a matter of such consequence, both to him as an individual and to a newly independent Norway – the country was just six years old at the time of his triumph – that subterfuge and lying were justified in establishing once and for all in the eyes of the world that Norwegians were kings and queens of the snowy and icy regions of the world? That this was *their* world, in a way it could never be the world of the Englishman? Was the cruel and harshly personal nature of the attacks on Emanuel Mohn a sign of how desperately important it was, this ambition for a terrain that psychologically and physically belonged to them, and them alone? Did Mohn's shocked realisation that he was somehow not a 'proper' Norwegian, that in his insufficiently communal sense of being a Norwegian before he was an individual he had 'let the side down' in a fundamental way he could never do anything to correct – did all of that have anything to do with his suicide on 26 April 1891, jumping overboard from a ferry on its way from Bergen to Utne, leaving behind only his hat, floating on the waters above him? A detail from *Risen som ikke hadde noe hjerte på seg*, 'The Giant Who Had No Heart', one of the folk-tales collected by Asbjørnsen and Moe in the early 1840s, now imposed itself on me. The tale concerns a king's son named Ash who sets out to find what happened to seven brothers who failed to return from a journey made in search of seven wives. The brothers took all the best horses with them so Ash must use the only one left in the stables, a broken-down old nag. It serves his purpose well, until he meets a starving wolf who begs him for something to eat. In return he promises to come to Ash's aid whenever he might have need of it. Ash can't imagine a situation in which he might need a wolf's help but nevertheless agrees and *gives the wolf his own horse to eat*: in all its bleak realism, its utter lack of sentimentality, did this detail not shed light on the mind and character of Roald Amundsen, who used his own huskies as food, eating them one by one as the journey progressed, until in the end only one was left standing, and then that too was killed and eaten? And what of the Andes survivors, I thought, jabbing my loaded brush furiously into the shadowed joints at the end of the terrace wall, the ones left alive after their plane crashed in the mountains, who survived for seventy-two days by eating the bodies of dead friends and relatives? The wolf and the horse, Amundsen and his dogs, the Andes survivors – surely some spiritual truth must link these dark stories? And perhaps it did. But as I discharged my brush into the last of the joints I stood up and called out my wife's name, suddenly filled with the longing to hear her voice, to turn and see her standing in the doorway of the room by the staircase, wearing her white paper overalls and suggesting we break for tea.

# 7

## Early September 2018

Walkers' cabins in the mountains – on

using a tent – a triangular walk in the west

of the Hardangervidda – Haukeliseter cabin

– first night out – petrified trees – footpath

marking – Hellevassbu – losing the way –

up into Slettedalen – blood on the snow –

Amundsen nearly freezes to death –

the descent to Haukeliseter – how

memory edits experience

By the end of August we had finished painting most of the inside of the cabin. We had driven up from Oslo almost every available weekend since taking over the cabin early in July, sleeping over at Paul and Trine's cabin, happy to crash out on their big sofa and, on the rare occasions when I was able to combine the two remote controls successfully, watching their giant, wall-mounted television. If I was feeling particularly lively I might chase the dog around the square wooden coffee table a couple of times. The dog would walk, I would run.

A series of deep and critical sniffing sessions in the living room and the bedroom convinced us that the sharp smell of wood stain had cleared enough for us finally to spend the night in our own cabin, but when we did so it felt like a slight anticlimax. Although we had talked a lot about the kind of furniture we were going to buy, we were still eating off the small, rickety wooden table we had bought twenty years earlier at a school jumble sale in Abildsø. And when we broke off from painting we didn't have a sofa to stretch out on but instead sank into two yellow folding nylon chairs with their seats about a foot off the ground. Nina had draped a sheepskin over the back of each one, presents from the time when Hanne and Petter kept sheep up on their smallholding at Siljuseter. But even with the addition of these pelts, the chairs didn't provide much comfort when our legs and arms were aching from the repetitive and monotonous exercises of the day's painting.

The one permanent item of furniture already in place was the bed. This was a black wooden-framed IKEA bed with two storage drawers underneath on each side. The dog, still only a few months old and disturbed by the succession of different venues in which our nights were now being spent, sometimes at home in Oslo, sometimes at Paul and Trine's cabin, now here at our own cabin, crept in between us and hardly stirred all night. Drifting off to sleep, I tried to itemise the main jobs we still had to do. There was the outside of the cabin to paint. And sometime within the next two weeks we were expecting the arrival of our *levende tak*, literally a 'living roof', consisting of grass and wildflowers and anything else that fancied its chances of surviving up there. Driving up through Numedal I had seen small trees and bushes sprouting from the roofs of cabins and *stabbur*, and I was looking forward hugely to the day our own 'living roof' arrived. Until it was in place, and the black, glistening membrane that was currently keeping the weather out covered up, the cabin would not be a *hytta*.

While waiting for it to arrive, and before starting work on painting the outside, which would have to be done before the first snow fell, we both felt the need of a break. Nina arranged to spend a week in the Languedoc with a like-minded friend on the trail of the Knights Templar and the Cathars, and rather than just hanging around the flat in Oslo and watching repeats of *Bonanza* I decided it would be a good time for me to explore the western side of the Hardangervidda, which I hardly knew at all. I would get to know the terrain by spending a few days hiking there.

Over the years Nina and I had been on many walking trips in the Norwegian mountains. We had explored Jotunheimen, Espedalen, Rondane, Aurland, the northern and eastern parts of the Hardangervidda, but never the west of the great mountain plain. These walks of ours, normally lasting between three and five days, had become sources of great joy to me. I discovered in them the most powerful sense of solace, peace, and most of all, relief from that endless and anxious background questioning of the purpose of it all, all this frantic activity, all these jobs and tasks, all these obligations, these dreams and ambitions to pursue and fulfil before we die, as though we were born with a set of binding instructions in our pockets.

My wife shared my joy in all this. Where we differed was over the use of a tent. She was very happy with the level of comfort provided by the network of cabins provided by the Norwegian Trekking Association (Den Norske Turistforening or DNT) stretching across the length and breadth of the country, and simply refused to entertain the idea of sleeping out in a tent. As there are 540 of these cabins, it was hard to muster purely practical arguments against her preference. But I longed for the independence and privacy that nights spent camping in the open would bring, and, as though engaging in a magical act, I had bought as many as four different tents to offer her over the years, including three- and two-person varieties. Finally, once all hope was gone, I acquired a one-person tent. It was as though I believed the mere possession of these, and their presence in the loft, might be enough to make her change her mind. But it didn't, and so we had always followed the network of paths that wandered between DNT's members' cabins, following the red 'T' with which DNT volunteers marked the way, and had done so very enjoyably and successfully.

But I still longed to embark on a more independent type of trip, something that required a greater degree of self-sufficiency, and this autumn break seemed to offer an ideal opportunity to do so. I would need to be back at Veggli on the Friday, when we had been told the turf roof would be delivered. That gave me four days and nights in which to take a look at the more mountainous and less-travelled south-western corner of the Hardangervidda. Simen and Helene, neighbours of ours in Oslo and dog-owners themselves, kindly agreed to look after Alex for the time I would be away, and early on Tuesday morning I took the Metro down to the bus station in central Oslo and boarded the 945 for the five-hour drive to Haukeliseter.

I spent part of the journey going over my plans. Using Map 1414 IV, I had decided on a triangular route that would take me northwards from Haukeliseter towards Hellevassbu, then westward following the trail to Middalsbu, and then back south-east to return to my starting point at Haukeliseter. I had my map, and the brief route descriptions provided in DNT's own compendious handbook of marked trails. From the pastel innocence of the map I could see no particular difficulties to take note of. My only unease concerned the final leg of the journey back to Haukeliseter. After the track came down off the mountains to meet the Fv 11 at a place called Fentadokki, there appeared to be a five-kilometre walk along the side of this narrow but fairly busy highway back to the cabin at Haukeliseter.

The first section of the bus journey, through the Numedal valley, was by now familiar to me from the many times we had driven between Oslo and Veggli. It was years since I had last made a long-distance bus journey and I had been looking forward to the drive, but once we had passed through Kongsberg I fell asleep and did not wake up until shortly before the bus pulled in off the Fv 11 at Haukeliseter in the late afternoon.

I jumped down, the driver raised the side of the bus and I bent down and dragged my green rucksack from the storage bay beneath the bus. I watched as it drove away, then shouldered the rucksack and headed for the nearest bench. Because of its easy accessibility by road and its situation halfway between the east and the west of central-southern Norway that gives access to trails in all directions across the Vidda, Haukeliseter is a popular starting and stopping point for walkers, both those walking north to south and east to west. There is a sizeable restaurant, and before setting out I decided I needed a cup of coffee and the dish of the day, which today was *reinsdyrgryte* (reindeer stew).

I carried the tray with my plate and cup to a seat by a north-facing window, which gave me a view of what would be the first leg of my walk. It involved crossing the road and then following a steep and twisting path that disappeared over the top, where the walk proper would begin. It looked like a ten- or fifteen-minute climb. Every few minutes hikers would appear on that upper horizon and make their way down the twisting track towards Haukeliseter. A burst of late sunshine hit the track and made it glisten like silver, from which I deduced that it was muddy and that it must have been raining a lot recently. Even as I was watching two women make the descent, one of them lost her footing and slipped. As quickly as it had brightened, the sky grew dark again. Sated and comfortable from the stew and the coffee I was briefly tempted to book a bed for the night and postpone my start until the morning. That would be a good idea, wouldn't it? A fresh start, bright and early, with the whole day before me? What time was it now? Four-thirty? A bit late to be starting, surely? Suddenly a flock of goats passed the window, moving purposefully between the timber buildings on either side of the courtyard. One climbed to the top of a flight of steps outside a cabin and watched. He seemed almost to be counting them as they went by, to make sure none were missing. Then when the last animal had passed

by he jumped down and the herd continued its way into the rough fields below the little complex of buildings, spreading out as they went.

Bad idea, I told myself firmly. Standing up, I shouldered my rucksack, clumped out of the restaurant and slowly plodded in between two of the dormitory cabins to a gap in the fence where a waymark post pointed the way up. I crossed the road, navigated carefully around the puddled and boot-muddied junction of about six different paths, then bent my back and headed up towards the first of the red 'T's that would guide me on my way to Hellevassbu.

My fully packed rucksack weighed twenty kilos. I knew this because I had weighed it at home, dangling it from a digital suitcase weight. I'd also tested the feel of the full pack at home, walking around in the living room, the bedroom, and the kitchen. It sat very comfortably on my back. The big difference between this and previous mountain-walk packs was that I was walking alone, with no one to share the weight, and I was carrying a tent, a sleeping bag, a full set of cooking equipment, and the food – all the things that spending nights in DNT cabins rendered unnecessary. I had packed the biggest of my tents, a three-person Rondane 3 that weighed four kilos. For cooking I carried a single-burner gas stove and canister, a small aluminium saucepan and kettle, and several packets of dried meals in containers, which, once water was added, could be heated directly on the stove. It was September now, and the nights might be chilly, so I had packed two woollen pullovers and an extra set of warm, full-length underwear. In the identical zippered pouches on either side of the main body of the rucksack were two plastic litre bottles of water. Add the weight of the raingear and the extra pair of lighter walking shoes I had packed, and it made for a heavier pack than I had ever walked with.

The track turned out to be considerably steeper than it had looked from my window seat in the restaurant, and every bit as slippery as that brief burst of sunshine had suggested. Within five minutes I had stopped, exhausted, and was bent double, hands resting on my knees as I heaved to get my breath back. You should have known, I told myself, recalling my subjective observation that the first moments of any departure from a DNT cabin always seem to involve a brutal, twenty-minute near-vertical ascent in which you find yourself wondering which bastard filled your rucksack with stones while you were innocently sleeping. But then, I recalled, if you just keep going, quite suddenly, like a reward, the track flattens out, you rise to an upright position, the view opens out, and you realise you are indeed in the Norwegian mountains, and there is no more beautiful place on Earth to be than this. So I ploughed on upwards. Sure enough, after a succession of three illusory tops had flattened out momentarily only to reveal yet another, a fourth turned out to be the real end of the climb.

I stood up straight. Suddenly the rucksack didn't seem so heavy after all. Peering through the dusk, I traced the line of the path stretching out ahead of me, dipping between and around mountains rather than over them. In the middle distance, in the shadow of a tall dark mountain, I saw a lake and decided to pitch the tent there. I left the marked trail and walked for a further ten minutes until I found a firm, grassy site not far from a small stream that fed into the lake.

That night was the first time in years I had slept out. The utter remoteness of the site on which I had pitched, on a grass-strewn patch of sandy ground, made me feel as though I was the only human being on Earth. Before settling for the night, before zipping up the tent and climbing into my Egyptian mummy-shaped sleeping bag, I gave in to a strong impulse to take off all my clothes and stroll as far as the water's edge. In perfect certainty that no one would come by, I walked around completely naked for some fifteen minutes, bending now and then to part the leaves of the dense thickets of dwarf birch, kneeling to scrape a track through the dark yellow lichen on a boulder with my fingernail, touching the pale dust to my lips to taste it.

I made my way over to a rock about a hundred metres away from the tent. It was about three metres high and turned out to have an opening on one side large enough to slip inside. Once inside it was obvious to me that it must have been used as a storm-shelter. There was room enough to sit and even stand, but not to lie down. Peering through the gloom, I noticed something pale on the floor. Bending to pick it up, I took it outside into the light. It was a rectangular tin can, rusted close to extinction. The words 'Delito' and 'Sardines' were still just legible on it. From the lettering it looked as though it had lain there since at least the 1950s, and possibly even before that. The Hardangervidda, beyond the powers of the Germans to monitor its vastness, had been a favoured gathering place for members of the Norwegian resistance during the years of the occupation. The British had used the region for parachute drops: perhaps this was a relic from the war years?

Or perhaps not. In obedience to some half-sincere sense of reverence I put the tin can back where I had found it and strolled back down to the lakeside. If I had had pockets in my skin I believe my hands would have been in them, so relaxed and free and easy did my wandering feel. The clouds had cleared and the sky was full of stars. I looked up. There was tall Perseus, the little triangle of stars like a pointed hat on his head, a string of jewels dangling from his left hand as he danced into the face of Auriga the Charioteer, whose bright eye Capella glared at him in disapproval. Over there was the Great Bear, with the two Hunting Dogs poised to strike at his throat. The majestic Swan skimmed down the Milky Way heading straight for the Eagle, with the Northern Cross and Dolphin in the shallows on the side of the pale river watching to see what would happen when they met, and Vega in the Lyre on the other side looking on with cold blue indifference. I lowered my gaze and on the unruffled surface of the water saw Polaris in the Little Bear trailing a crescent of stars, all reflected so close I could have bent down and scooped them up in the palm of my hand.

I slept heavily and well and after a breakfast of hot porridge and coffee I was on my way again by nine the next morning. A look at the map told me I had spent the night on the southern shore of Loftsdokktjønn. The terrain ahead for the next few kilometres looked undemanding, and my spirits were high as

I set out beneath a cloudless blue sky. The temperature was mild, a gentle breeze wafted me along from behind. I had the map hanging in front of me in a clear plastic folder and periodically stopped to consult it. The track was now at 1320 metres above sea level, well above the treeline. That peak in the east was undoubtedly Vesle Nup, 1510 metres above sea level. Even when following a marked trail, I noticed, there is real pleasure to be had in locating oneself exactly on a map. After about an hour the track ran down and along the shore of Mannevatn, a large lake guarded in the west by the brooding heights of Mannevasstoppen.

From there the track ran more or less straight ahead, meandering very slightly as it passed a mountain called Klingenberg. Here I stopped to rest on a large, flat white rock I had had in my sights for the last twenty minutes. As I was brewing up coffee, a woman with a dog came up the track in the opposite direction. She had the dog on a leash, which surprised me. Even though the general rule is that dogs should be kept on a leash in the mountains, to stop them chasing after sheep or goats or reindeer, many walkers allow them to run free if there appears to be no immediate sign of any such temptations.

We stopped to chat. She looked about forty, with dark eyes and round, nut-brown cheeks. I complimented her on her dog, a beautiful Irish Setter with a glossy, deep-rust coat. I asked her if she kept him on a leash all the time, even out there in the wilds, and she surprised me by telling me she had to, as the animal was blind.

'Blind?'

'Yes. He lost his sight when he was a year old. First one eye, then the other.'

'It must be hard work looking after him. He's lucky to have you.'

'No,' she said with a diffident smile. 'I'm the lucky one.'

I asked her if she wanted a cup of coffee but she said no, they'd had a stop just a half hour ago. I watched them as they walked off. Her pack looked bigger and heavier than mine, and she had a fishing rod strapped to one side of it. She was walking the *vidda* north to south, she told me, from Finse in the north to Haukeliseter in the south, camping at night with her blind dog and fishing for food along the way.

After another hour's walking the track rose up the side of a peak, crossing a scree slope of small and slippery rocks that became steeper as it approached the top. For some hours I had been able to forget about my pack, but now I felt its dead weight bearing down on my shoulders as I bent double to scrabble upwards, often having to use my hands to steady myself. From previous experience I knew the best plan was not to look ahead when negotiating steeply rising terrain but to try to keep your eyes fixed on the ground beneath your feet. Near the top the track began to level out, and I began to feel a sensation of pleasurable relief at the thought of soon being able to rest. My anticipation came a little early, however. Before reaching the top the track encountered an almost smooth wall of rock just over head height. I looked around, hoping I might have made a mistake and come off the track somewhere. But a red 'T' visible on a stone set back to one side at the top of the ledge ruled out any possibility of that.

I stood for at least a minute, staring at that wall of rock. Standing on tiptoe, I could just get my fingertips onto its flat top. On examining the surface closely I now saw that there were indeed ledges on the wall – small, but large enough to be used for toeholds, and sloping the right way, inwards, towards the centre of the mountain. It was technically possible to climb. But what about the rucksack? Should I remove it and toss it up on top first? Should I take it off, make the climb, then somehow find a way to hoist it up after me? Throwing it up first seemed the most sensible choice. But it was heavy, and in my mind's eye I saw it just failing to clear the top, ricocheting off the ledge and bouncing away down the mountainside.

There was always the option of turning back, but I knew once I left the marked trail I would be lost. There was nothing for it but to make the climb, and to get it over with as quickly as possible. I tightened the pack until the straps felt as if they were biting into my flesh, raised my left hand to the first handhold I had spotted and my right leg to the first toehold. As my left leg then left the ground and looked for the second toehold, I swung my right arm up as high as I could and clutched for a purchase on top of the ledge. For a nauseating instant I felt the rucksack swing me out over the drop, and then my fingertips gripped on to the rock. The ledge sloped down almost immediately at the top and once I had my left elbow securely wedged over it I was able to haul myself the rest of the way up.

I lay motionless for the next five minutes, with my eyes closed. Once I had recovered I unbuckled the rucksack and took out the gas canister and the two black cloth bags, one containing the burner with its foldaway legs and the other the little aluminium kettle. I opened the lid of the kettle and took out the plastic bag with the mixture of instant coffee, sugar and powdered milk, unzipped the side pocket and slid out the blue plastic water bottle, lit the gas and sat cross-legged and listened and watched the water boil and looked out over the fabulous landscape spread out below me. Layered and misty blue horizons in all directions, with here and there the silvery splashes of lakes and rivers. I took out my other-wise redundant mobile phone, opened the music player and navigated to Geirr Tveitt's *Concerto for Hardanger fiddle and orchestra* and lay back and enjoyed this extraordinary composition. The *Hardingfele*, or Hardanger fiddle, is a native variant on the violin of European classical tradition. A four-stringed instrument with a variable number of drone strings, it has been used at dances and on social occasions since at least the seventeenth century. Hardanger fiddles and their cases were often ornately decorated with *rosemaling*. More than any other instrument, its wild and mournful sounds conjure up for me the soul of the Norwegian mountain landscape.

About twenty minutes later I stood up and cleaned out the green folding plastic cup with grass, packed away the stove, dried the inside of the kettle and put the bag of coffee mixture back inside. For the first time since leaving Haukeliseter, I felt my bowels move. Watched only by a curious crow, head turned to one side on a smooth rock some two metres away from me, I squatted down behind what I took to be a section of fallen tree trunk.

I buried the evidence of my passing presence beneath a small pile of stones then subjected the tree trunk to a closer examination. It was ridged along the sides, rather like a stick of coltsfoot rock. Ever since leaving Haukeliseter I had been walking above the treeline; so what was a tree trunk doing up here? And it wasn't the only one. Scanning the plateau I saw several other of these light brown, log-like objects scattered about. Walking over to examine one more closely, I knelt beside it. I tapped the bole with my knuckles. It was rock hard. In fact, it *was* rock. From a book I had read on the geology of the *vidda* I knew that it had once been covered in forest; was it possible that I was standing among the remains of a petrified forest?

The onward track had no visible presence on a surface

that was entirely rock, and the longer I failed to pick it up the more uneasy I felt. I was no Lars Monsen, Norway's favourite television adventurer, who lives out in the wilds for weeks on end with just his dogs for company; nor was I a hunter like Lieutenant Glahn who could tell the time by the lay of the grass beneath his feet. I had, moreover, been without a signal on my mobile phone since leaving Haukeliseter. My wife was not even aware that I had decided, on a whim, to take these few days walking in the mountains; if I should fall, or even simply twist my ankle, I realised for the first time, I might find myself in real trouble. I had already developed an almost religious devotion to the sight of these red 'T's in the landscape, and rather than ramble on in a more or less straight line – for what logic would ever suggest that the path ahead ran in a straight line? – I spent a full five minutes minutely systematically scrutinising the terrain ahead for any sign of them.

These 'T's are deliberately marked to intrude as little as possible on the landscape. Almost invariably they are either found on wooden signposts, or on stones or boulders. Only very rarely, and where there is no alternative, are they painted directly onto surface rock. Waymarking the Hardangervidda presents particular difficulties. The land is high, and through-out the year – but especially in winter – it is exposed to extreme weather conditions. The markings are often on small cairns, but the terrain is littered with cairns that mark other, older routes across the *vidda*. Cairns can collapse. And in the kind of rocky landscape I was now traversing it is all too easy to mistake a natural pile of stones for a constructed cairn. On the heights, after a run of two or three harsh winters, a once-radiant red marking might have been toned down to a pock-marked remnant hardly visible more than twenty yards away. Red lichen too can play tricks, luring the wanderer onwards until he suddenly realises he has lost contact with the last reliable waymark.

The trails are marked by volunteers, and for obvious reasons their efforts are concentrated on the most popular tracks; in the more remote and less-travelled wilderness of the south-western *vidda*, the wanderer must place a greater reliance on a combination of waymarks, maps, compass and GPS finders. Finally, however, I spotted my next T, slashed across a triangular slab of rock that had slid from the top of its cairn and come to rest at a slight angle to the track. I set it back up on top and walked on.

After descending from the plateau the track wound slowly down into the wide open spaces of Dyredokk, covered in huge rafts of smokey-white arctic cotton grass. The terrain was boggy and marshy, although somehow the track always just managed to find the firm ground. At the far end of Dyredokk I encountered a stream in full spate that was impossible to ford, and had to make a detour of about a kilometre before reaching a wide, shallow crossing that I could wade across ankle deep, my boots tied together by the laces around my neck, my trousers rolled up, the ice-cold water biting and nipping at my ankles.

For the next two hours I had the DNT cabin at Helle-vassbu in view as the track twisted west around the foot of Simletind and slowly approached it. There was a bridge across the Nekko, the river that links upper and lower lake Hellevatnet, and the last stretch of the track to the self-service cabin followed the eastern shore of the upper Hellevatnet. Only now did I find the leisure to enjoy the unobtrusively lovely flowers that murmured alongside the track, the white mountain avens with their mustard yellow hearts, the lemon yellow flowers of the alpine cinquefoil and the pale purple

spikes of milkvetch. The hardiness of these tiny forms of life is breathtaking. The lichen that one sees everywhere on the *vidda*, sometimes in the form of a flat, velvety growth clinging to the surfaces of rocks and bare mountainsides, sometimes growing close to the ground like tiny, perfectly formed trees, are the staple diet of the vast herds of reindeer that wander the *vidda* and without which they could not survive. The cost of their power to endure everything from drought to frost, from freezing, whirling snowstorms to summer heatwaves, is an infinitesimally slow rate of growth, in some cases as little as a tenth of a millimetre per year.

Walkers who want to use the facilities are allowed, for a small fee, to pitch a tent close to one of the DNT cabins, although as I came to the cabin itself there were no tents nor any others signs of life. July and August are the favoured months for walking in the mountains; September was late. The weather was still settled, however, the temperature warm and the sky blue, with no indication of a change on the way, and after a brief rest on a plank bench supported by two round stones and a trip down to the stream to fill my water bottles I shouldered my rucksack and continued northwards along the track, following a sign for Litlos and keeping my eyes open for the split in the route that would take me west towards Middalsbu. My plan was to pitch the tent shortly after the split. It turned out to be further than I had imagined, and it was approaching seven by the time I joined the track going west towards Middalsbu, the site of another DNT cabin and the end of the second side of my triangular walk.

The terrain changed character as the path ran between the steep west side of a mountain and a lake called Vassdalsvatnet. It was closer to the water than the mountainside, grassy and soft and a pleasure to walk along, for my feet were feeling tender after the rather stony surfaces of much of the route so far; but it was narrow and for the next hour I scanned the landscape in search of a suitable place to camp but failed to spot one. By about nine o'clock it was getting dark. A strong wind had risen and I decided to camp along the track itself, feeling fairly confident that no one else would come by at that time of night. The wind continued to rise, pulling and tugging at the canvas for most of the night. I didn't get much sleep and after waking for about the fourth time and noticing that it was light outside I decided to break camp early.

I followed the track as it continued to head west, passing high above the watery region around Vassdalsegga before heading down into the Middalen valley, at the foot of which was the Middalsbu cabin. As at Hellevassbu, there was no sign that anyone had spent the night there, and after another brief rest I walked on.

Within a couple of hours the track was once again below

the treeline and I was walking through landscape much less stern and forbidding than on the previous two days. After crossing a farm lane at the northern end of Valldalsvatnet, an enormous lake, the map showed a continuation of the path down its eastern side, to a point about halfway down it where the river Kvesso flowed into it from the east. I must have spent fifteen minutes trying to find this path but saw no red 'T's anywhere. The very fact that this was the easiest terrain so far made my failure to pick up the next section of the walk particularly unnerving. In the end, I decided to continue in the direction shown by the dotted line on my map, but without the reassurance of the red lettering to guide my way. So I crossed the farm lane and set off south, picking my way along the rocky boulders of the inclined bank of Valldalsvatnet.

I walked on, all the time keeping my eyes peeled for the T that would confirm I was on the right track. It never came. Instead, the side of the lake banked ever more steeply. It dropped straight into the deep, dark water, and in mortal fear of losing my balance from the cursed weight of that rucksack and rolling helplessly down into the water I presently adopted a strategy of clambering in simian or crab-like manner from rock to rock on all fours. Any glance ahead only confirmed that there was no relief to come; the dizzying band of grey rock continued round every bend in the shoreline, as far as the eye could see. *Why the hell hadn't they marked the track?*

At times, in a stolen glance upwards, towards the dense line of dwarf birch that followed the outline of the lake, I saw what looked like a suitable patch of ground on which to pitch a tent for the night; but on closer inspection these areas turned out to be either too short, or too narrow, or too sloping. Finally, high up on the bank, some two or three metres below the wall of trees, I found somewhere.

I swung the rucksack off my shoulder, and within ten minutes the tent was up and I was lying on my back alongside it. The sun had slipped behind the mountains in the west, and though the sky was still high and blue the strong wind that had risen in the afternoon seemed suddenly much colder. My head was resting on the rucksack and I stared up into the sky in vacant exhaustion. Clouds formed and dispersed with a dizzying rapidity. With what seemed to me a peculiar and malevolent creativity, the wind ripped them into pieces and flung the fragments into the furthest corners of the sky. Every shattered wisp of cloud, even the tiniest, took on recognisable shape. I saw a lamb up there, a bus, a hearse, an open newspaper with a turning page. I saw the face of my dead brother, a rocking horse, a toothbrush, a hedgehog. It was unbraining, intolerable. I stood up and crawled inside the tent, zipped it closed behind me.

When I felt sufficiently composed I rigged up the stove in the storage space between the outer and inner tents, out of the way of the wind. As the wind bucked and snapped at the canvas I felt glad of the extra space, for the only time on that trip glad that I had chosen to take the biggest tent. I had brought a packet of bacon and I fried every rasher in it, washing it down with three cups of coffee. There was an element of compulsion about it, no doubt. What Norwegians call *trøstespising*, eating to mask your distress.

The work of tearing up the clouds seemed to have exhausted the wind and by eight o'clock the canvas had stopped flapping. Brimming with optimism from the bacon and the coffee, I decided it would be a good idea to undertake a modest exploration of my surroundings. Unzipping the outer tent I poked my head out and looked up. In the east I saw Orion taking his first giant step into the sky above the lake. I strolled a couple of metres up behind the tent, stepping over the black ruins of a campfire a previous tenant of the site must have built, and slipped, high-stepping over gorse and scrub, between the slender trunks of two birch trees. Starlight can be remarkably bright in the mountains, and even through the canopy of trees there was enough of it to make out the narrow, twisting outline of a well-defined dirt track running at my feet. On the other side of it a solitary stone stood looking up at me, impishly displaying the enormous 'T' outlined on its chest.

Aha.

I had been walking parallel to the marked track. Throughout the afternoon's travails I had probably never been more than ten metres away from it. Had I extended my initial search at the top of the lake by a mere ten paces, I would have found it. The prospect of yet another day clambering and crawling along those brutal rocks had already started weighing on my mind. Now, feeling as though God had taken pity on me, I walked back to the tent, pulled off my boots and slipped into my sleeping bag in a state of relieved elation. Wrapping my scarf around my neck and pulling a woollen hat down over my ears, I zipped it up and within seconds was sleeping like a stone.

At eight o'clock next morning I set out in bright sunlight. For the first half hour the track, though muddy, was all downhill as it passed through a spacious wood of deciduous trees, mainly oak and birch. Presently the track slipped down closer to the water's edge and entered a series of fields that were lush with long green grass, and boggy, so that by the time I reached the other side and clambered over a stile onto a hard-surfaced brown track my boots were soaked. But at least it was still all downhill.

At a bridge on the left-hand side of the lane, where the

Kvesso joined Valldalsvatnet, a wooden fingerpost directed me to cross the water by a small humped wooden bridge. I rested for a few minutes on a grassy slope overlooking the river, munching an apple and a handful of nuts. Then it was on with the rucksack and up again.

The onward path rose steeply, spiralling ceaselessly as it looped around the trees of a spacious pine forest. Very soon I was stopping after every ten paces to rest in breathless exhaustion, bending double, both hands resting on my knees. I must have made fifty such timed stops before the terrain gradually levelled out. The pines gave way to a straggling line of mountain birches, and then I was back above the treeline and gazing into a wide, upward-sloping stony valley, the stones almost dazzling in their sun-splashed whiteness. Fifty metres to my left the young Kvesso leaped and danced in its bank on its way down the mountain. Huge jagged peaks looked down on either side. I stood taking in the cold and austere beauty of this view for several minutes. It was as though I couldn't quite believe my eyes.

On the climb up, the map had driven me almost to distraction, swinging and swaying idiotically around my neck in its plastic holder and making the walk *twice as difficult*. Halfway I had stopped, unhooked it from my neck and banished it to the top pocket of the rucksack. Now I sat down on a flat rock, unzipped the top pocket, and unfolding it discovered that I was walking through a valley called Slettedalen. It means something like 'Desolation Valley'.

For the next hour I made my way slowly up the rock-strewn floor of the wide valley. With every step I took I was aware of the bleak loveliness of the landscape I was passing through, and of the fact that in some absolute sense I was failing to appreciate something I would probably never be offered the chance to appreciate again. I cursed myself for being old, for having ludicrously overpacked, for failing to understand that a walk through terrain such as this, for an amateur walker such as myself, at my age, was too much and I was going to die. Then, when I got tired of that monologue, I walked over to the river, took off all my clothes, laid them in a pile, then slid down from the bank and submerged myself in the clean and sparkling water.

Loneliness began to nag at me. Apart from the woman with her blind dog, I had met no one, spoken to no one for three days. The feeling took me by surprise. I had never expected to experience a need for someone else up there. But I did now. I would have given anything to have someone to talk to.

I talked to myself instead. Fixing my gaze on a rock perhaps a hundred metres further up the track I might say, *Now, once you get there, you can stop and have some coffee, I promise.* And as I made my way towards the chosen spot I would utter words of encouragement to myself – *You're nearly there, not far now, just keep going, soon there, soon there. Here. Here. Now you can stop and sit down and rest.*

And sitting there, sipping from the little green plastic cup, the hot, oversweet coffee would seem like the most sublime drink imaginable. Looking around at the jagged peaks rising up on either side of the valley, the rushing torrent of the Kvesso the only sound, filling the air, I would imagine myself resting in a shimmering, sun-white paradise. Someone would come along sooner or later. *You can't stay here,* she would say. *The snow will come any day now, you must walk on.* And like Bartleby the Scrivener, the hero of Herman Melville's strange novella, I would look up at her and reply: *I would prefer not to.* I would be a man frozen inside his own mistake, unable to go on, unwilling to go back.

A large snowfield covered the saddle where the valley rose up to meet the mountains. I knew my track crossed it, but the sunlight bouncing off it with such dazzling brilliance made it hard to look at directly. The snowfield seemed to draw me on. Everything in that desolate valley was compelling in the same dangerous, tempting way. *Just make it as far as that snowfield. Then you can take off your rucksack and lie down and go to sleep. Don't worry. Everything will be all right.* Seductive and attractive and dangerous thoughts. But then, out of nowhere, and restoring me to my senses, a memory came to me of reading Roald Amundsen's account of the adventure that had so nearly ended his life when he and his brother spent the Christmas of 1896 attempting to cross the *vidda* on skis. They had planned to start from a little mountain farm called Mogen, the last outpost of civilisation in the east, and follow a diagonal across to the Hardangerfjord. The trip was no more than a hundred kilometres. Both expert skiers, they had expected to make the crossing in under two days and provisioned themselves accordingly with a few biscuits, chocolate and butter. They didn't pack a tent, just a sleeping bag each.

Mountaineering for the sake of it had struck men like Knut Lykken, Slingsby's Norwegian guide in the Jotunheimen, as a puzzling eccentricity. Similarly, skiing for fun, rather than as a way of getting from A to B across snow-covered terrain, was something upper-class urbanites did that baffled the average Norwegian peasant. The family at Mogen regarded the Amundsen brothers as insane, or suicidal, and probably both, but willingly offered them sleeping space on the floor by the fire on the night of their arrival.

The weather turned during the night and a raging snowstorm delayed their departure from Mogen for eight days. It also rendered the landscape more or less unrecognisable from their maps once they were able to set out.

For the next three days it continued to snow heavily, at the same time as the temperature rose from the minus twelve in which they had started out. Sleeping out on the third night, their clothing and sleeping bags soaked through, Amundsen had the bright idea that a swig of kerosene from the lamp might improve his circulation. They had wrapped it along with their provisions in a bag and marked the spot with a ski pole, but in the dark he was unable to locate it. A search of the area in daylight failed to locate it either. They began to fear for their own survival, and pushed on westwards, hoping to reach their destination before nightfall. Once again a blinding snowstorm descended on them. Now on their fifth day out, with their map in sodden tatters and the compass useless without visible reference points, they decided the better option was to turn back and try to return to Mogen, their point of departure. When darkness fell they still had no idea where they were. An icy wind whipped them as they prepared to spend yet another night out in the snow. Amundsen decided to dig a narrow tunnel into the snow, wriggled inside with his sleeping bag and fell asleep. While he was sleeping the temperature rose, and then it fell. The wet snow froze, closing off the entrance to his tunnel. In the middle of the night he woke up. His right hand was over his eyes, palm upward, as though trying to block out light. He couldn't move it. In terror he realised he was entombed in ice.

Amundsen began shouting for help, but there was no hope of being heard. He passed out, and when he came to again he heard the faint sounds of his brother Leon calling his name. Leon, too exhausted to dig a shelter himself, had awoken to find himself alone in the freezing white desert. Feverishly he looked around for any sign of what might have become of his brother. By an extraordinary stroke of luck, a few hairs from Roald's reindeer-hide sleeping bag were still visible at the site where the entrance to his tunnel had been sealed. Using his bare hands and a ski pole, it took Leon three hours to dig his brother out. Recalling the experience many years later, Amundsen wrote that its dangers and tribulations were the equal of anything he experienced later on his expeditions to the polar regions. The memory of Amundsen's vivid account of his Poe-like experiences on the Hardangervidda was enough to jolt me out of the wretched mental terrain into which I had wandered.

For some time before reaching the snowfield I had noticed a pinkish-red staining across the snow. At first I took it to be the site of a killing, somewhere a fox had ended the life of a linnet or a plover. Getting closer, I saw that it was more extensive than that. I wondered briefly whether this was the site of the mass death of a flock of over three hundred reindeer in a lightning storm the previous year. From the point at which the lightning struck, the bolt had run out along the drenched ground and up through their hooves, stopping their hearts and killing them instantly.

When I eventually stepped onto the snow, however, and was able to examine the markings closely, I discovered with a sense of relief that they weren't blood at all but the dramatic staining of snow algae.

After the snowfield the path followed the southern bank of Lake Nupstjørn, where the Kvesso rose, and then turned on up to Nupsredet, the ridge connecting Slettedalen and Nupsdalen. The map showed what looked like a dramatically sharp descent towards the first and smaller of the two lakes in Nupsdalen. Once again I lost the way, and for the next twenty minutes walked back and forth on the cliff top, making a detour to an adjacent height and looking back at where I had come from in hopes of spotting it, but to no avail. According to the map it led more or less straight down the cliff face, but it took a long time before I eventually located it, craning my head over the edge of the bluff and looking sharply down and to the right, and was able cautiously to make my way down. I thanked God the weather was fine, for in even slightly wet conditions so sharp were the angles of the corkscrew descent, so loose and stony the surface, that I would not have fancied my chances of making it on my feet. On my arse, maybe.

A long grassy descent now lay before me, leading in the far distance to the road. I saw cars passing along it in a steady stream and already I dreaded the last leg of the walk, the five kilometres along the roadside back to Haukeliseter. I passed sheep grazing. The last hour seemed interminable, but finally I crossed a stile onto a small track that led from a farm onto the Fv 11. One effect of the adventure had been to make me stoic, and as I headed for the small road bridge that led to the main road I was mentally prepared to accept the last hike along the side of the Fv 11 as a just punishment and a sort of final – and actually quite unnecessary – warning to me never again to attempt such a trip with so little preparation and forethought.

In the farmyard I saw a small Hyundai truck pull round a corn silo and turn onto the road behind me. I stepped to the side of the road, without turning round. The truck stopped beside me, the engine still running. Through the open window a young farmer in a check shirt asked if I wanted a lift to Haukeliseter. When I said I did he told me to throw my rucksack into the back and climb into the cab beside him.

Half an hour later, fresh from a hot shower, I was seated at the same window as the day I started out, but now facing the opposite way, looking south across the waters of Lake Ståvatn, with a plate of the day's special (reindeer stew again), and an ice-cold half-litre of Hansa beer in front of me. Two little girls and a boy were climbing on the wooden roof of the sauna down by the lake. To the right of them a young couple in swimming costumes held hands and surveyed the cold water, daring themselves to dive in.

I took the timetable of the Haukeli express, the Oslo-bound bus, out of my wallet and unfolded it. I was lucky. Only forty minutes to wait. Definitely time for another beer. I stood up and stumped across the floor on concrete legs, lurching from side to side like Dr Frankenstein's monster. In a mirror on the wall behind the counter I caught sight of my reflected face, red and glowing. My whole body ached.

Seated back at the table, after another long drink of the ice-cold beer, I sensed, like reluctant homing pigeons, the slow return of the concerns of everyday life.

On Friday the turf roof for the cabin would be delivered. I had to be there.

On Saturday Nina was due back from France. I must remember to shop.

On Sunday we'd visit my father-in-law and watch the football on TV. First division Stabæk – our team – against second division Ålesund. It was a relegation play-off. Henning Berg was manager of Stabæk now. He'd done well enough in charge of Legia Warsaw in Poland, but could he save Stabæk from relegation? I wasn't too confident. And from there I began thinking about how, if I ever came to write about this mountain walk, I would definitely have to recast it as a Slingsbyan triumph that focused on the ecstasies and delights of a walk on the Hardangervidda, and not on how I had almost spoiled it for myself by hopelessly overloading my rucksack and failing to stick to the waymarked footpath.

I would also need to find out whether those cylindrical brown stones I had seen up on the plateau really were petrified tree trunks. I recalled something I had read in Peder W. Cappelen's book *Alene med vidda* (*Alone with the vidda*), a diary-type description of the spring and summer he spent fifty years ago at a remote fishing cabin at Skjerhøl, in the very heart of Hardangervidda. Cappelen writes lyrically about the field mouse that had moved in during the winter; about the pine marten, the fox, the golden plovers and linnets he sees and hears as he works at putting the cabin back into shape after the long hard winter. Suddenly, without any warning, he slips in a sentence about seeing a *flock of cuckoos*. I was no ornithologist. For all I knew it might be true that, in certain circumstances, cuckoos do gather in flocks. But I felt instinctively that it must be a mistake. And if it was, didn't that undercut the authority of the whole account? Wouldn't I, by even bringing up the subject of these petrified tree trunks, risk something similar?

The more I thought about it, the more unlikely it seemed that what I had seen was petrified timber. There had been a series of articles in the Norwegian press recently about how global warming in the north would mean the treeline moving ever higher up the *vidda*. In time, the mountain plain itself would be forested. Geologists pointed out that this would be nothing new. Fossil finds of timber from the beds of lakes on the *vidda* showed that during the early part of the Stone Age, more than seven thousand years ago, much of Hardangervidda had been covered in trees. In some parts the treeline was about two hundred metres higher than today's level. In the warmest and best areas, pine dominated. Where the soil was less good, and in the higher regions of the *vidda*, mountain birch thrived. The scientific explanation was that the summers were warmer back then. To add to the complications, summers on the eastern side of the *vidda* – the Numedal side, our side of it – are warmer than in the west. So while the treeline in the east can be as high as twelve hundred metres, in the west the range is between nine hundred and a thousand.

I began to wish I'd never seen the bloody things in the first place. In all of the newspaper articles I had read on the subject, the timber finds came from the sediment at the bottom of lakes. I hadn't seen any reference to petrified, pale brown trunks lying open and scattered on rocky heights. Instinct told me what I had seen and touched were large, fossilised tree trunks; common sense told me they couldn't be. It wasn't possible for an amateur rambler carrying an overpacked rucksack and in a constant state of anxiety about his exact location on the *vidda* to have made such a unique and important discovery.

Someone pushed open the glass door of the otherwise deserted cafeteria. It was the woman with the blind dog. She stopped at the till and bent down and whispered something in the dog's ear. The dog sat down. She saw me watching her and raised her hand in a brief gesture of greeting. The young Swedish girl appeared behind the counter and asked what she wanted.

Now my attention was distracted by the shrieks and shouts of the couple I had been watching through the window. They broke into a run and dived head-first into the lake. Moments later I heard the mournful sighing of hydraulic brakes. I turned and saw that a white bus had pulled up outside the window on the far side of the cafeteria. By the time I realised I was looking at the Haukeli express I had forgotten all about the tree trunks and scarcely even knew whether it mattered or not.

Drifting in and out of sleep on the long journey back to Oslo, I found myself rehearsing how I would describe the walk to Nina when she returned from France. I would touch only lightly on the sudden cold bite of panic, the sense of being lost and alone in the midst of a bewildering and malevolent vastness. There would be little of the mysterious dread of Peder Balke's paintings from the Arctic north

and none of the sense of threat so vividly conveyed by Theodor Kittelsen.

Instead I would dress the mountains in the ruggedly romantic light of a nineteenth-century painting by J. C. Dahl, with every step of the way offering some new enchantment for the eye. The dark magnificence of Nupseggi. The long, paradisal descent into Dyredokk. The wild mountain framing of Slettedalen, the bouncing, foaming rush of the Kvesso, the pockets of year-round snow high up on the mountains, the wind-polished brilliance of the waters of Valldalsvatnet. I was confident that, by the time we reached the bus station in Grønland in Oslo, the reinvention would be complete.

# 8

## Friday 7 September

The 'living roof' arrives – country and

western music in Norway – A. B. Wilse

the photographer – construction and

maintenance of the living roof – DAB radio

in Norway – conversation about Norwegian

national dishes – on the early trade routes

across Hardangervidda – the pre-

Christian burial ground at Kjemhus

The lorry carrying the turf roof arrived at two in the afternoon. Watching from the windows it was easy to identify the dark green scarab crawling towards the sharp turn at the end of our lane. It was moving so slowly I had time to walk out and meet him while he was still halfway round the turn. On arriving a couple of hours earlier I had discovered a hole about a metre in diameter in the middle of the lane, where the rock and rubble foundations had partially collapsed. I had called Reidar the builder and he'd promised to get it fixed as soon as possible. In the meantime, though, a lorry that size might easily collapse the whole track and leave it with its front wheels headed for Australia. It would also leave us a problem of access.

As a hazard warning to the driver I had wedged an old ski pole into the hole, but I wanted to alert him in person too. Making my way along our drive to the main track I stood by the side of the road and held up both hands in a hang-on-a-moment gesture. Through the window I could see he was making a call on his mobile. He was wearing a cowboy hat. He braked and brought down the passenger-side window... *by day I make the cars, by night I make the bars...* I could hear the sounds of Bobby Bare's old country hit 'Detroit City' drifting down from the cab.

I stepped up onto the footplate:

'*Hei. Det er et stort hul midt i veien. Tror ikke det går an å kjøre her.*' ('There's a big hole in the middle of the track. I don't think your lorry would make it.')

He nodded, the window glided back up. Even before it had reached the top I saw his hand go up to his ear and he was on the phone again. He released the handbrake and crawled on up the hill, disappearing round the bend by the Fjellstue.

About half an hour later he was back. I was reading Melville's short story 'Bartleby the Scrivener', in an old Dover Books edition I had taken with me from Oslo. Ever since the title had popped into my head on the walk I had been wondering if Bartleby's enigmatic refusal to do anything at all really was an appropriate reference point for the mood that had overcome me as I made my way through Slettedalen.

I put the book down. Stepping to the window I saw a fork-lift truck come bouncing along the track towards the house with a load of bulging sacks made of grey netting balanced on its extended prongs. Our *levende tak*. The driver was wearing a grey cowboy hat, with shoulder-length brown hair and a full beard. There is a wide city–country cultural divide in Norway, and it has always seemed to me that this particular look is part of the country-dweller's rejection of urban fashions, whether conscious or unconscious I've never been quite sure. Taste in music out in what the Norwegians call *distriktene* – which basically means everywhere apart from Oslo – reflects the look. The musical heroes are American stars of the post-Hank Williams golden age, singers like Willie Nelson and Waylon Jennings and the other 'Highwaymen'. But there is also a rich subculture in which native performers like Bjøro Håland, Ottar 'Big Hand' Johansen and Claudia Scott are among the better-known names, although their record sales are largely over the counters of rural petrol stations. I can still recall my surprise on discovering the existence of this Norwegian version of American country-and-western culture, complete with singers who dressed the part in big hats and checked shirts, but sang in Norwegian. It seemed dream-like, but the more I learned about the close ties that link Norway and the United States following the huge Norwegian emigration to America towards the end of the nineteenth century, the less strange it seemed.

For the next hour I listened, and occasionally watched, as the roofer – his name was Lars – went about his business of laying the turf roof. Technical advances had made the task of laying the *levende tak* rather easier than it would have been in days gone by. Starting at the ridge, over which he carefully draped the plump, pillow-sized sacks of turf, he worked his way down the roof, fitting the sacks neatly together until the whole of the black plastic underlay was covered. When he was done I invited him in and we sat on the sofa and drank coffee.

'You live locally?'

'Did do,' he said. 'Not for much longer.'

'On the move, eh?'

He nodded.

He leaned forward and touched a book that was lying on the coffee table next to the Melville, reading the title out loud: 'Leif Ryvarden. *Hardangervidda: Naturen, Opplevelsene, Historien.* (*Hardangervidda: Nature, Experiences, History.*) I haven't seen this one.'

He picked it up and began flipping through the pages.

'Looks alright,' he said. 'Mind you, there's so many of them.'

He stopped leafing through the pages and rested the tip of his index finger on a black and white photograph that showed a group of men leading *kløvhester*, or packhorses, across a mountainous landscape. The group had stopped and appeared to be posing informally for the camera.

'I used to do this,' he said. 'Before the roofing. My wife and I had a stables down in Veggli. We used to take tourists out on horseback along the old *slep* and the *kløvhest* trails. Stay out a few nights. Sleep out. It was a wonderful time. We had six horses.'

'Why did you stop?'

He shrugged. 'Not enough money in it. Well, enough. But not enough, if you know what I mean.'

'So then you started doing the turf-roofing?'

'Well, I always had it as a part-time job. A fall-back.'

He peered down at the photograph and read the caption out loud: '*Driftene over vidda hadde til tider stort omfang med titalls hester og kløvkarer, som her ved Langedalen nær Hårteigen i 1919.*' ('At times activity on the *vidda* could be extensive, involving dozens of men and horses, as here at Langedalen near Hårteigen in 1919.')

It was one of A. B. Wilse's pictures. I knew about Wilse from research I had done for Knut Hamsun's biography into the years Hamsun spent in America as an immigrant. Wilse was the great early photographic chronicler of Norwegian life. He left home at thirteen, emigrated to America in 1885, bought his first camera the following year and by the time he returned to Norway in 1900 was a master photographer. There's hardly an aspect of contemporary Norwegian life that he didn't document with his camera in a career that spanned over fifty years and produced over two hundred thousand photographs. In his way he was as important a part of Norwegian nation-building as writers such as Henrik Ibsen and Bjørnstjerne Bjørnson, the folk-tale collectors Asbjørnsen and Moe, and painters such as J. C. Dahl, Thomas Fearnley and Nikolai Astrup. It was no surprise to me that Wilse had been up on the Hardangervidda too with his camera.

'See this man here?' Lars said suddenly.

I stood up and leaned over his shoulder.

The figure his finger was resting on was a portly, middle-aged man on the left of the picture. He looked as if he had a black moustache but it was hard to be sure. Like the rest of the party the man was dressed in what looked like the normal, everyday clothing of the period: homburg hat and dark suit. No state-of-the-art waterproof fabrics or woollen beanies here. Part of a large bag slung over his shoulder was visible by his left thigh. He carried a stick in his right hand.

'What about him?'

I thought he was going to tell me it was his grandfather or something like that. Instead he said:

'Would a man like that tell his troubles to another man? What do you think?'

'What do you mean? What kind of troubles?'

'Any kind of troubles. Something he had on his mind, that was bothering him.'

'This man here, in the hat?'

'Yes.' He turned from the book and looked up at me expectantly.

'I don't know,' I answered. 'You can't tell just by looking at a photograph of someone what they're like. Maybe he'd tell his troubles to his brother. Or his best friend.'

'No,' he said, a slight note of exasperation in his voice. 'I don't mean him specifically. I mean, would a man *like that, like him,* tell his troubles. To these other men, for example. When they stopped for the night.'

I shrugged. I really couldn't see what he was getting at.

'Maybe,' I said. 'Maybe not.'

He closed the book and put it back down on the table.

'What I mean is, people were different in those days, don't you think? Husbands were different. Wives were different. A man knew how to be a man. A woman knew how to be a woman. Nobody had to tell them how to do it. But now nobody seems to know any more.'

He fell silent for a few moments. Then he tipped the brim of his hat upwards and looked at me again.

'What about *you?*' he said. 'Do *you* tell other men your troubles? Or do you think that's weak?'

'I tell my wife my troubles.'

'No, other *men.* Do you talk about your troubles with *other men?*'

I recalled having a similar conversation with an Englishman in a bar in central Oslo a few years ago. He was a jazz musician, an expatriate like myself, but younger by some years. Married to a Norwegian, which is almost always the reason the English will give when you ask what brought them here, he played the saxophone and had a day job teaching at the Music College. He had a very complicated private life. On that particular evening, after a few beers, he had started talking about some of the problems he was having at home. He'd met someone else, and now he was wondering whether he should leave his wife and two young children, or wait it out and see what happened. I didn't know the situation nearly well enough to feel comfortable talking about it with him and shut him up rather bluntly by saying a person shouldn't talk about their troubles, that *a trouble shared is a trouble doubled*. He gave a spluttering laugh into his beer and changed the subject. He'd just been reading *Straight Life*, the autobiography of the tenor saxophonist Art Pepper – Pepper's life sounded at least three times as troubled as his own – and started talking about this instead.

*A trouble shared is a trouble doubled*: had I really meant that? Or had I said it just to shock? I didn't know then and I didn't know now. Either way, I decided to say the opposite this time.

'No, I don't think it's weak.'

I must have taken too long to answer because in response he just grunted and looked away. Again he picked up his phone from the table, stared at the screen, cursed the temporary lack of a signal and stepped outside onto the terrace. He stopped, tapped a number onto the screen and then waited for a reply, face turned towards the sky, his lips moving and his head nodding as if he was conducting a silent conversation with himself.

After a minute he closed the phone and walked slowly back in through the terrace door.

'Where are you moving to?' I asked.

'Don't know yet,' he said dismissively. 'Have you got a pair of binoculars?

'Yes.'

'In the spring next year, soon as the snow goes, get them out and have a look at the roof. Look particularly around the ridge, the chimney and the air vent pipe. Pay special attention to the area around the *vindski*.'

He stepped out onto the gravel in front of the terrace and pointed up at the gable.

'The *vindski*, that's the planks running down either side of the gable there.'

He headed off round the side of the house and I followed.

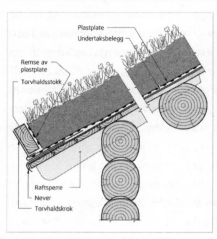

Plastplate

Undertaksbelegg

Remse av plastplate

Torvhaldsstokk

Raftsperre

Never

Torvhaldskrok

'And here,' he said, stopping again and pointing to a long, faintly green-tinged plank running the length of the roof at an angle and fastened with a series of wrought iron fittings. 'This is the *torvhaldstokk*. This keeps the turf in place. It's got a lot of work to do. It's impregnated, but you might have to replace it if the wood starts to rot. If you do, then take care and don't let the turf slip down the roof. It'll cause you a lot of extra work.'

'*Bør jeg beise den?*' I asked. 'Should I paint it with wood dye?'

'Some people do. I don't.'

'Any other maintenance apart from that?'

'No.'

'What about snow on the roof?'

'The rule of thumb is, if it's more than half a metre high, get up there and clear it. If there's a lot of snow, clear it regularly. But not right down to the turf. Leave a layer of about ten to twenty centimetres. But don't worry. This is a new cabin, it's built to withstand a lot of snow. Cabins built before 1979 were only expected to withstand up to around a hundred and fifty kilograms of snow per cubic metre. But remember, when the weather turns mild you need to be especially careful. The snow attracts water, and wet snow can weigh as much as four hundred kilos per cubic metre. Once you're up there, clear the snow from the top downwards, and clear the sides of the roof evenly, and gradually. That way you won't get disproportionate weight. These new cabins are sinking anyway, and they'll go on sinking for another two or three years. A lot of snow will speed up the process, but you need to make sure it's evenly distributed across the roof. And when snow is wet, that's when it lets go. And you don't want to be standing underneath when that happens, believe you me. Several tons of snow falling on your head, or your car, and you're looking at a new head, or a new car.'

'And the grass just grows by itself? I don't have to water it or put fertiliser on it?'

'The bags are presown,' he said. 'And there's a grass guarantee. If the grass doesn't grow we come back and lay you another roof. But don't worry, it'll grow. It always does.'

I very much liked the idea of the roof of the cabin looking like a meadow in the spring, with splashes of red and yellow and blue across the green, and had bought a packet of mixed seeds from the *felleskjøpet*, the farm shop down in the valley. I planned to sow them in the spring, but Norwegians have so many micro-rules governing things like that I asked about it anyway:

'What about flowers? Is it okay to have flowers growing on the roof?'

'Of course,' he said. 'Just make sure they're native to the area.'

He pulled the phone out of the breast pocket of his jacket

and again wandered off a few paces, again tried to make a call. Again he failed to get an answer. I heard him swear quietly as he slipped the phone back into his pocket. It must have been the ninth or tenth time.

'Not a very good signal up here,' I volunteered. 'It comes and goes. It's the same with DAB. One day the radio works on the windowsill, next day you have to take it over to the kitchen work-surface. Next day it's back to the windowsill again.'

'Yeah, bloody DAB.' It was a sore point with Norwegians, the peremptory haste with which the government had decided to close down the FM network completely and go over to digital radio. You heard people complain about the results all the time.

We went back inside and sat down. He picked up his coffee mug, mechanically blew across the rim of it and took a sip.

'So,' he said, leaning back. 'Now you've got a garden on your roof. You've got a piece of the great *vidda* draped across the top of your own cabin. It's a hat to be proud of. A layer of peat across a lining of bark, the bark to keep the rain out, the peat to hold the bark in place and keep the heat inside the house. In the old days it was the only way. It's just decoration now. In the old days they couldn't have survived without it. You'd mow it, and trim it like a field. It was a part of the farm. I've seen goats grazing up on those roofs. So you don't have *levende tak* in England?'

'Not that I've ever seen. We have thatched roofs.'

He nodded. 'I've seen them,' he said. 'They have them in parts of Denmark too. In Fyn. Why don't they have them in England?'

Norwegians will often put me on the spot like that, as though being English made me an authority on matters as varied as the educational system, the rail network in the UK and why people who live in English coastal towns don't eat more fish. In fact, after thirty years away from my home country, the sheer extent of the changes in almost every department of social and institutional life in England, coupled with my own inattentive nature, have left me knowing less about my own country than the average newspaper-reading Norwegian. And yet so deeply rooted is the idea of a nationality that I myself am still capable, after all these years, of treating Norwegians in exactly the same way, as though being Norwegian made them experts on their own history and culture, when very few of them are.

'I don't know,' I replied. 'There are so many things the English don't do that seem odd when you come to think about it. Look at the winter and Christmas food Norwegians eat – *ribbe, pinnekjøtt, fårikål* – you'd think, with all the pigs and sheep in England, that they would be bound to have stumbled across the pleasures of eating ribs of salted mutton steamed over a layer of birch twigs, even if only by accident.'

'What about *lutefisk*? What is that in English?'

'I suppose it would be "lye fish". Cod soaked in lye. But I've never seen it in England and I've never heard of anybody eating it.'

'Do you like it?'

'Yeah. I like the trimmings best. The mushy peas. The bacon bits you scatter over it. Do you like it?'

He grimaced. 'Fish I like. We always had fish for Christmas back home where I come from. But *lutefisk*? Can't stand it. I feel ill just looking at it quivering on the plate.'

'Where are you from originally? Bergen?'

I knew that a lot of Bergensere typically ate fish for their Christmas meal, and the guttural way he pronounced the word for 'dish' (*tallerken*) was pure Bergen. It's an accent thick enough to slice, like Brummie or Scouse or Geordie, and has the same singing tonality.

'Long time ago.'

'So you're a *Nordmann*?' I responded, glad of the chance to show off a bit of esoteric knowledge I had recently acquired.

'You know about that, do you?' he said with a little laugh. 'Well then, you must have been here a long time.'

I told him that Normann, spelled without the 'd', was my wife's maiden name, which accounted for my interest. A few weeks earlier I had bought a copy of Reidar Fønnebø's 1981 book about the Nordmannsslepene from Ruud's second-hand bookshop on St Hanshaugen, in Oslo. From earliest times the Nordmannsslepene were the trade routes across Hardanger-vidda for hunters and traders heading east for the great cattle and trade markets on the other side in places like Kongsberg, Drammen, Tønsberg and Christiania. They used packhorses, sometimes strapping the goods on to their backs, sometimes harnessing them to two parallel poles that rested on the ground but were curved at the ends, so they could be dragged across the terrain. They carried dried fish, hops, salt, the type of rough wool fabric known as *wadmal*, tallow for use in the Kongsberg silver mines. Over the years the passage of these trade trains ploughed three or four distinct, wide furrowed tracks over the *vidda*, as though God had leaned down and drawn his spread fingers across the land. The most southerly of the trails was the *Søndre Nordmannsslepe*. It came down off the *vidda* and into the Numedal valley at Veggli. For obscure reasons, traders arriving in the valley from the west seemed to those greeting them to have come from the north of the mountainous plateau, and were accordingly referred to as 'Nordmenn', men from the north.

This great network of trails is now little used by walkers. Like me on my walk over in the south-west of the *vidda*, walkers prefer the security of the trails waymarked by DNT with the red 'T's. But for the adventurous and the independently minded, these great historical arteries are still navigable, and the waymarking cairns of centuries still stand in many places to guide the traveller. The Hardangervidda wasn't a wilderness back then. It was used. I read somewhere that ten thousand place names have been known on the *vidda* over the centuries, although only a handful of these ever made it onto a map.

'Me and my wife used to take tourists on horseback over the last part of the trail, up at the top here,' he said, pointing vaguely upwards through the window. 'From Lufsjå and down into the village where it comes down. Have you got a map? I'll show you.'

'There's one in the back of the Fønnebø book.'

I got up and climbed the steep wooden stairs to look in the little bookcase on the landing. Through the upstairs window I could see him standing on a rise in the land, phone in his hand, holding it up in the air and turning in a slow circle as he searched for a signal. He shook the phone, then hit it against the palm of his hand as though it were an old-fashioned mechanical object that could be made to work with a thump.

As I reached the bottom of the stairs he was standing in the terrace doorway, in the act of slipping the phone back into the thigh pocket of his cargo pants. He seemed momentarily surprised to see me, as if he'd forgotten where he was and what he was doing.

'What's the point of a bloody phone if you don't answer it?' he said mysteriously.

He sat down on the sofa again, still shaking his head.

I handed him the book, open at the inside back cover where

there was a line-drawn map of the *vidda* with the *slepene* marked.

'Here,' he said, pointing. 'It comes down here at Kjemhus. It's just down at the bottom of this hill. Kjemhus means "arrival place", "destination". Something like that. There's a burial site there. People used to die on the way over. That's where they buried them. In the days before churches and cemeteries. It's signposted,' he said. 'You've probably seen it on the drive up.'

I was surprised to hear about this and said I had never visited it, nor even seen the signpost.

'You should go,' he said. 'It's beautiful. No one ever goes there, of course. People nowadays don't care about the past at all. They think the world began the day they were born. It's a pre-Christian burial site. You can park your car there, then there's a bit of a walk and along at the end of a track you come to a clearing surrounded by trees with all these stone-marked graves. It's beautiful. Very peaceful. I go there a lot. Used to.'

He took out his phone yet again, but this time it was only to show me an image of the burial ground. 'Kjemhus,' he said. 'That's where I'd like them to bury me. No name. Just a pile of stones. That'd do me.'

He closed the phone and stood up.

'*Nei, jeg må se å komme meg hjem.* I best be getting back home. Thanks for the coffee.'

'Are you going back down to Veggli?'

'Yes.'

'Any chance you could give me a lift down? I'd like to see Kjemhus. If you drop me off I can walk back up.'

'Okay,' he said. 'But I'll have to show you. The sign is over-grown, you can hardly see it from the road. Someone should do something about it. I'll wait up on the bend for you. I'll be about half an hour.'

He gave a little wave of his hand, walked over to the forklift truck and swung up into the cab. I watched him reach out his hand to start the engine, then change his mind and sit back in the seat. He sat quite still for a few moments, then slowly and deliberately took out his phone. This time, instead of trying to place a call, he simply stared at it. He said something to it, shaking his head, then returned it to his pocket. Abruptly he put the fingers of both hands to his forehead and leaned all the way forward until the backs of them came to rest against the big steering wheel. He held the pose for just a few seconds then sat bolt upright again and slid the window open.

He didn't speak for a long time. Then he said: 'This has got to be a rehearsal for life, *ikke sant*? ('Right?') This can't possibly be the actual thing itself, can it?'

The questions were rhetorical, and although he was looking hard at me I made no attempt to answer.

'I don't have time to take you,' he said finally. 'I have to get home. She's not answering.'

He turned on the ignition and the raucous rumble of the engine filled the air. He made a three-point turn in the gravel in front of the terrace then headed off at a slow wobble up the track, carefully rounding the jagged edge of the black hole in the middle. In the low sunshine the tough little vehicle looked suddenly fragile and almost toy-like. It was bright yellow.

# 9

## Mid-September 2018

Problems with the *komfyrvakt* ('cooker alarm') – morning

coffee in the village – how cabin settlements rescue village

economies – the neighbouring plot of land sold – on

Norwegian newspapers – formation and political fate of

the Christian Democratic Party – blasphemy laws – abortion

law reform – the price of alcohol – visit to the Kjemhus

burial ground – reading about Chinese hermits – a street party

in the mountains – waiting for a lunar eclipse on

Hardangervidda – food and fuel at walkers' cabins – an idea

from London – the Resistance and the Jews in Occupied Norway

F riday morning. Nina was away for the weekend running an exhibition stall at the Alternative Fair in Lillestrøm. The plan was for her to pick up the dog on Sunday afternoon from her brother in Oslo, then take the train out to Kongsberg. I would drive down from Veggli in the car to pick her up at the station. It gave me most of the weekend to myself. It was chilly and I started a fire before breakfast. Even before doing that I had stepped outside and made a circuit of the cabin to admire the new roof. It seemed to me, or it may have been my imagination, that already I could see a faint, pale undershine of green coming through up there. It was probably just a trick of the light. Nonetheless, the blanket of turf gave the cabin a finished look. Where before it had looked naked and unprotected, exposed in spite of the stoutness of its timbers, now it looked ready for winter.

For breakfast I decided on my usual porridge with cinnamon and brown sugar. As usual, the *komfyrvakt* started to peep, this time before I'd even turned the oven on to heat the porridge. It's attached by a magnet to the back of the fan hood. According to the lengthy instruction book the electrician left behind it's a 'smart' device supposed to 'learn' your cooking habits and not start peeping unnecessarily, but I swear it frequently began giving off its little chirps when the oven was turned off after use and sometimes, as now, even before I'd turned it on. Once it even woke us up in the middle of the night. According to the booklet, if it's a false alarm you're supposed to be able to intercept the series of preliminary cheeps prior to the full bells and whistles alarm by a single, long thumb-press on the large button in the centre of its underside. It never works like that. It just ignores the thumb-press and then leaps ecstatically into full alarm register, at the same time as it cuts off the current to the oven. Naturally I had thoroughly investigated the possibility of disabling it, but no such possibility exists. Removing it completely from the oven doesn't work either, since the oven can't then be turned on. It certainly isn't smart, and there's nothing to be done about it because these things have been mandatory on all new cookers since 2015. A sort of relentless Norwegian egalitarianism means that everyone is treated as though they're short-sighted, hard of hearing, or suffering borderline dementia and incapable of negotiating the hazards of everyday life such as boiling an egg or making porridge without help. Norwegian culture is a wood culture, of course, and fire is always a hazard, which is the main reason there are so few really old buildings in the country – most of them burned down before they could reach venerable old age. But even so, Norway is a bit of a nanny-state, and it's dispiriting when the nanny inflicts beta-technology like this on a whole population.

After breakfast I decided to let the fire go out and drive down to the café in Veggli for my morning coffee. As recently as the 1960s, Veggli was still a remote village on a country road with a petrol station on one side and a *kro* or bed-and-breakfast on the other. I had finally managed to track down the *Rollag Bygdebok* at the National Library and spent an hour scanning the pages pertaining to Veggli and the central section of the Numedal valley. The cabin-building boom of the past twenty years was showing no signs of abating and the heart of the village was now the recently extended shopping mall opposite the old *kro*.

At the northern end of Numedal is the small town of Geilo, where my wife's family had rented a cabin every winter in the 1960s. One day in the spring, we drove the hundred kilometres up the Fv 40 to see how the place had changed since Nina's childhood days there. Geilo has developed into one of the country's major centres for winter sports, with slalom slopes and cross-country skiing tracks extending in all directions. Dr Holst's Sanatorium, the magnificent white castle-like walls of which used to dominate the town, was now hidden behind a series of commercial terraces. Every other shop sold winter sports clothing and equipment. This boom is the most obvious manifestation of Norway's post-oil affluence, these endless racks of brightly coloured anoraks made of the latest lightweight, windproof fabrics. We left after an hour, vowing not to return. With the overdevelopment of Geilo, pressure on space means that Norwegians are now quite happy to buy an apartment in one of the new blocks that have been built in or near the town rather than build or buy a cabin further out. The overcrowding of Geilo and its environs has opened up opportunities for landowners further down the valley. While places like Veggli and Blefjell couldn't offer the downhill facilities of Geilo, their height above sea level meant they could guarantee snow, and that is enough for most winter-sports-mad Norwegians.

As a result, Veggli had changed and expanded dramatically, attracting buyers interested in cabins not just from Oslo but from other regional population centres like Tønsberg and Kongsberg. The cost is the loss of privacy and remoteness traditionally associated with the cabin in the mountains. As of 2019, about 80 per cent of the cabins built in the Østfold, Oslo and Vestfold regions in the last two years have less than seventy-five metres separating them from their nearest neighbours. In the spacious and remote north of the country only 15–20 per cent of new cabins are built in these concentrated groupings.

The local Coop in Veggli was one of the largest supermarkets I have ever shopped in. Over the last ten years its turnover must have increased several hundred per cent. During particularly busy periods like Christmas, Easter and the *vinterferie* (corresponding to the English half-term holidays) it can even be hard to find a parking space. On this particular Friday morning, however, it was still pleasantly deserted as I drove past the giant, blue-trousered troll who welcomes shoppers from his sentry-post beside the road, turned in and parked.*

The Coop took up most of the ground floor of the new, extended shopping mall. It now also boasted an 'interior' shop selling small items of furniture, ornaments, candles and suchlike, as well as a coffee bar. I bought an *Aftenposten* from the supermarket and spent a few moments puzzling over the alien terminology of the coffee menu before deciding on an 'Americano'. Norwegians drink a lot of coffee. They have embraced the new 'barista' culture wholeheartedly, without wholly abandoning their fondness for the more traditional and – to me – scarcely drinkable *kokekaffe*, in which coarsely ground coffee is brought to the boil in a pan, removed and left

---

* In what is probably another sign of the ongoing gentrification of the area, I noticed on a recent visit that this troll has now been banished to a site behind the supermarket.

to brew for a few minutes before drinking; and the slightly more civilised *filterkaffe*, coffee powder in a conical paper filter through which water drips from a percolator into a glass jug. Every time a shop closes down in Norway, be it a shoe shop, an estate agent's or a hairdresser's, the odds are that it will reopen as a coffee shop. Norwegians do drink tea, but it's a minority taste. And you will often find that the tea you are offered in a coffee bar or restaurant is not tea at all but instead a choice of finely packaged herbal or fruit drinks. Ask if they have any proper tea and they might offer a lemon-yellow packet of Earl Grey, and be surprised when you explain that what you want is a cup of tea you can put milk in.

I took my coffee and newspaper and settled in a bench seat by the window looking out onto the almost deserted car park. The café was on the ground floor, which in Norwegian is very logically referred to as the *første etasje* (first floor). This is a crucial difference and a fruitful source of misunderstandings for English visitors. An even richer source is the difference between 'half-ten' in English and 'halv-ti' (half-ten) in Norwegian. You may think, when your Norwegian friend suggests that you meet at *halv-ti*, that she'll be there at ten-thirty. She won't. She'll have been there at nine-thirty, waited a quarter of an hour and then given up and gone. The reference is always to the next hour.

At the table in front of me a middle-aged delivery-van driver, pot-bellied in a grubby orange boiler suit, was talking to two young checkout girls from the supermarket on a break. They were talking about 'Lothepus', a reality TV star in the news lately because he had just revealed to the press that he had recently recovered from throat cancer.

Before starting on the newspaper I turned on my phone to check my emails. A real one arrived as I was busily deleting the threats from PayPal scammers and 'the Microsoft team'. It was from the builders, formally notifying us that the plot of land adjacent to ours had been sold. If we had any objections these should be addressed to the appropriate authorities within the appropriate time span.

So we would be getting neighbours.

The new cabin would be sited in front of us, but slightly to the left, and so far below us that, in terms of view, we would lose only a rather uninteresting pine-clad hillside in the south-east. From the start we had been reminding ourselves regularly that this day would come, and that the privacy we had enjoyed during the first three months of occupation could not last, so the disappointment was not too great, nor the news a real surprise. Like our own cabin, the new place would have an open and unimpeded view across the valley to the Blefjell peaks in the distance, unimpeded because both cabins were at the eastern limit of the permitted development. As I closed the mail programme I felt a sense of relief. We had told ourselves repeatedly that the longer the plot remained unsold and undeveloped, the more difficult it would be to adjust to the cabin's 'new' reality. The quick sale meant that within a few weeks the experience of our mountain cabin would be a settled and realistic version of the dream. There would be marginally less privacy, but Nina and I had already talked about the need to extend the terrace around the cabin and have some kind of fence put up.

I put the phone away in my inside jacket pocket and spread the newspaper out next to my coffee. *Aftenposten* is a national institution in Norway. It was the last of the mainstream broadsheets to go tabloid, and for some time afterwards had retained its historical conservatism. Inevitably, however, the paper has moved with the times, a fact of which I was reminded on page 12, when my eye fell on a story headlined '*Forsker fant korthåret og glattbarbert Jesus i ørkenen*' ('Scholar found short-haired and clean-shaven Jesus in desert'). The story recounted the discovery of a sixth-century mural in the ruins of Shivta, in Israel's Negev Desert, which the researcher advertised as 'the oldest known mural depicting Jesus in the Holy Land'. Whether Jesus had a beard or whether he wore his hair long or not were matters of no consequence to me. The catalyst of my dismay was a *Fakta* ('Fact') box that broke up the central text of the article. The box held four bullet-point sentences. The first read '*Jesus fra Nasaret eller Jesus Kristus var en jødisk forkynner og religiøs leder*' ('Jesus of Nazareth or Jesus Christ was a Jewish preacher and religious leader'). The second added the information that '*han er den sentrale skikkelsen i kristendommen*' ('He is the central figure in Christianity'). Even before reaching the third I had turned the page, frantically searching for the football section and news of whether Stabæk were any closer to escaping automatic relegation. But I was too late. Already I found myself floundering in a familiar despair. Was it really possible, I asked myself, that there was an adult Norwegian reading this story who needed to be told in this Wikipedia fashion that Jesus of Nazareth was a *Jewish preacher and religious leader*? The thought was almost unbearably dispiriting. Or was there some hopelessly misguided egalitarian instinct at play here? Another possibility: was the dogged dullness of the biographical note in its way a typically 'safe' and conventional piece of politically correct provocation of the kind that characterises so much of the culture of Norwegian public debate? Within certain strictly defined limits, an ability to provoke strongly, and a capacity to be strongly provoked, are regarded as intrinsically laudable social qualities to possess. Some years ago the mass-market

daily *Dagbladet* ran a series of interviews that always concluded with the celebrities answering the same short series
of questions. Among these was *Når ble du siste provoserte?*
('When was the last time you were provoked?'). I waited in
vain for someone to answer that it was so long ago they
couldn't even remember.

As I closed the *Aftenposten* and pushed it to one side, I
reflected that I should have bought *Klassekampen* ('The Class
War'), the newspaper of the far left in Norway and nominally
the polar opposite of *Aftenposten* in its editorial stance. I
rarely agreed with the Marxist spin the journalists put on their
stories, but they had the supreme virtue of treating their readers
as adults. I drank up the rest of my Americano – just ordinary
black coffee in a slightly bigger cup – and slid out from the
table, leaving the *Aftenposten* behind. From a farewell glance
at the back page I learned that an eclipse of the moon was due
that evening. It was probably the only piece of unspun news
in the whole paper and brought me an unaccountable feeling
of relief. I made a firm resolution not to miss it.

*

Some train of association from the story about the mural
depicting Jesus led me, as I left the café and headed for the car,
to think about another religiously themed story that had been
preoccupying the Norwegian newspapers recently. Norway
had been governed by a coalition of right-wing and centre-right
parties under Erna Solberg, leader of *Høyre* (the Conservatives)
since the election in 2017, but without an absolute majority
in the *Storting* (House of Commons). This left the *Kristelig
Folkeparti* (the Christian Democrats), one of the smaller parties,
in so-called *vippeposisjon*, meaning that it could overturn the

government should it choose to vote with the Opposition *Arbeiderpartiet* (Labour Party). In 2018, for the first time since the formation of the Christian Democrats in 1933, its leader, Knut Arild Hareide, had proposed a change of direction, from its traditional alignment as a *borgelig* ('bourgeois') party to a new and unprecedented political alliance with the Labour Party. Hareide's proposal was founded on an unwillingness to persist in an alliance that included *Fremskrittspartiet* (the Progress Party). The Progress Party had attracted many of Norway's working-class voters away from what had become, increasingly since the 1980s, a Labour Party led by middle-class personalities. The Labour leader, Jonas Gahr Støre, was himself the wealthy son of a shipbroker.

Hareide's difficulty with the traditional alliance was that he found the values of the Progress Party, notably its sceptical attitude towards mass immigration, incompatible with his Christian beliefs. He had come to believe he could take the Christian Democrats with him, and he had gone public with his suggested change of direction. It was political dynamite, and had to be discussed before the party could make this historic change of direction. After weeks of intensive campaigning for and against, at the annual party conference Hareide's proposed new direction was rejected by the narrowest of margins. The Christian Democrats were then formally invited to begin negotiations with a view to joining the sitting government.

It emerged that the party's deputy leader, Kjell Ingolf Ropstad, who was not in favour of Hareide's realignment proposal, had already had confidential discussions with Erna Solberg from which he had felt able to take back to the faithful the prospect of minor changes to the abortion law should they agree to be part of Solberg's government. As one would expect, a belief in the need for reform of Norway's liberal abortion laws has long been one of the party's central tenets, and Solberg's offer had been enough to decide the vote, by the narrowest of margins. Hareide had staked his political future on taking the party with him into the unprecedented alliance, and promised to resign once discussions about which ministerial post or posts the Christian Democrats could take up had been concluded.

Turning left out of the car park onto the Fv 40 I debated briefly with myself whether or not to drive the thirty kilometres further up the valley to the town of Rødberg. The nearest '*pol*' or *vinmonopol* ('state-run off-licence') is there, the only place in the area where you can buy wine and spirits (supermarkets like the Coop are not allowed by law to sell anything stronger than beer). Recalling the impending eclipse of the moon, it occurred to me it might be a good idea to take a half-bottle of Gammel Opland *akevitt* onto the *vidda* with me, in case a Li Po mood overtook me after the eclipse was over and, like that hard-drinking Taoist poet of the eighth century, I felt like drinking by moonlight.

Aquavit is Norway's national spirit. It's distilled from a potato base and acquires its characteristic flavour from the caraway seeds introduced into the process. There are a number of competing brands on the market, but for many years I had been loyal to Gammel Opland, a rich, dark drink, ideal as a chaser with a glass of ice-cold Frydenlund's beer. Recently my brother-in-law had introduced me to *Fjellvitt*, a brand produced locally in Numedal, which I had enjoyed enough to want to try it again. I was curious to see the *pol* at Røldal, since it was reputedly the smallest in Norway, but at the last moment I remembered I was trying to cut down on my drinking and so took another left at the roundabout and began the fifteen-minute drive back up the mountain to the cabin.

On the drive back up, still thinking about the Christian Democrats and their diminishing influence on Norwegian society over the eighty years of the party's existence, I found myself pondering the party's origins; why had Norwegian Christians felt the need to express their values in this secular form back in the 1930s? On the surface of things, weren't the values of socialism so similar to those of Christianity as to make such a party redundant from the outset? It seemed illogical, until you realised that it was precisely the increasingly secular nature of public and political life in Norway in the 1930s that was the problem, with both Communist and Labour Parties adopting attitudes of unrelenting hostility towards Christianity. One of the most urgent catalysts for the formation of the Christian Democrats in 1933 was the trial, in the same year, of Arnulf Øverland, on a charge of blasphemy. Øverland was one of Norway's most famous poets and a passionate proselytiser of his communist beliefs. On 21 January of that year he delivered a series of three lectures to the Oslo Students Union that were subsequently published as *Tre foredrag til offentlig forargelse* ('Three lectures intended to outrage public sensibilities'). The lectures were a sustained attack on all branches of Christianity, Norwegian Protestantism as well as the much rarer Norwegian Catholicism. The rite of Holy Communion, so important to Roman Catholics, was dismissed by Øverland as 'cannibalistic hokum', a typically scurrilous jibe. The blasphemy laws had not been invoked in Norway since a successful prosecution in 1912, and when Øverland was summoned to appear in court and face charges over the three lectures, the case attracted considerable attention. Øverland was found Not Guilty, although only by the narrowest of margins; six of the ten jurors voted for a conviction, the required number was seven. Øverland was free to go, but his acquittal was seen as a sign of the times and hastened the formation of the Christian Democrats as a political party dedicated to defending and promoting the values of Christianity in an increasingly secular age. The blasphemy law became a 'sleeping paragraph', until it was finally repealed in 2015.

The party's opposition to abortion is probably now the only arena in which it is seriously out of step with the secular majority. As I progressed up the side of the valley, I reflected on what an extraordinarily emotive issue this remains. No sooner had the Christian Democrats made their decision to join Solberg's government in exchange for a promise of two reforms to the existing abortion laws than large and well-supported demonstrations against the proposals were held in towns and cities across the country. The reforms involved removing a paragraph that allowed one of a pair of twins to be aborted, and amendments to a paragraph permitting abortion after twelve weeks in cases where the foetus is diagnosed as suffering from a serious illness or disability. The Christian Democrats argued that these provisions served the needs of what they termed a *sorteringssamfunn,* a society that is actively engaged in a process of birth-selection. Of the nearly 13,000 abortions carried out in 2017, 287 women had invoked this option. In sixty cases the reason given was Down's syndrome. Other cases involved a club foot or a cleft lip. Between 2016 and 2018, thirteen abortions were carried out on one of two otherwise healthy twins.

Alongside the abortion law reforms the Christian Democrats requested as the price of their support for the Solberg government, the press also reported that once the party was officially in government it would be pressing for a reduction in the amount of wine and spirits returning travellers were allowed to bring into the country. For public health reasons – in earlier times couched in the language of religious disapproval, later as a socialist measure to improve productivity at work, and finally because successive governments have become dependent on the money it brings in – alcohol is taxed at an exorbitant rate in Norway, whether bought at the *vinmonopol* for consumption at home, or in bars and restaurants. One result of this is that buying alcohol at airports is a very big business indeed, and the size of the traveller's quota a matter of life and death importance. No matter how late the plane touches down, Norwegians will make a ritual detour through the duty-free shop to load up a trolley with the full quota of wine and spirits to take home. So it was hardly a surprise when the Christian Democrats' proposal to reduce this was greeted with a howl of outrage that almost, if not quite, equalled the response to the proposed changes in the abortion law.

Secularisation has left the Norwegian countryside dotted with beautiful little white wooden churches that are regularly used by almost no one. There is one at the first bend of the road up the mountain after it leaves Veggli, and as I rounded the bend I was reminded of Lars's enthusiastic recommendation of the pre-Christian gravesite at Kjemhus and on the spur of the moment decided to pay it a visit.

I located the sign on the next bend in the road, obscured, as the roof-layer had warned me, behind the leaves of a wayside birch. I indicated left and turned off the road. Drawing up at the single parking space marked out in the small clearing at the edge of the forest, I stepped out of the car. The roof-layer had told me that there was a particularly well-preserved section of the Nordmannsslepe here, and in the trees a few yards away I saw a wooden post with 'Store Nordmannsslepe' carved onto its mossy finger. Following the grassy track up an incline through birches I presently came to a weather-beaten hoarding displaying a simplified map of the *vidda*, with the various *slepe* trails marked by dotted lines. Down each side of the map were paragraphs in Norwegian, German and English outlining the known history and use of the ancient tracks, but the protective plastic film covering the board had whitened with age and it wasn't possible to read anything but the paragraph headings.

I carried on walking up the track and after about two hundred metres another sign directed the visitor to leave the *slepe* and head right. In another five minutes I came to a second, smaller hoarding with information about the grave field. Like the first one, harsh weathering over the years had made most of it illegible beneath the protective film.

The grave field had the same name as the farm lower down the hill, where the trains of traders and cowboys gathered after the rigours of the journey over the *vidda*, to rest their horses and cattle before moving on further down the valley. The graves themselves were visible a few paces further on,

in a clearing. There looked to be about thirty mounds, none more than about half a metre high. Most were roughly square, constructed of medium-sized round-edged stones encrusted with dark green moss. The site was little visited and there was no obvious route between the gathered stones so I wandered between the graves in a haphazard way. After a few minutes, I sat down on a stone. A watery sun floated behind a veil of grey, featureless cloud. There was a slight chill in the air and I turned up the fur collar of the leather jacket I was wearing. Some magpies chattered briefly and noisily to each other in a nearby tree and flew off. Then came a silence so deep and palpable I closed my eyes and let it fall down over my shoulders, like a cloak.

\*

Back at the cabin I spent the rest of the afternoon reading. I was halfway through *Road to Heaven,* Bill Porter's account of the trip he made to the Chungnan mountains to explore what remained of the tradition of Chinese hermits after the ravages of Chairman Mao's Red Guards. After heating up a packet of something called either Turkey Jerk or Jerked Turkey from the Veggli Coop's unnecessarily well-stocked selection of globalised convenience foods, I set off in the evening to walk up onto the *vidda* in plenty of time to see the rising of the eclipsed moon.

The track winds up around a hairpin bend to pass through the ten cabins that make up the upper part of our settlement before narrowing to a footpath that leads through a small stand of pines. Being fifty metres or so higher up the mountain, these were the plots that had sold first. There was one left by the time we had decided to buy and build on Vegglifjell.

But in winter that hairpin bend would definitely cause problems for a car without *piggdekk* (studded tyres). That was one of the reasons we chose to build on the lower arm of the settlement, which had the further advantage of a lack of visible neighbours either behind or to the side of us. The people living on the top had better views across the valley, but for most of them the view included near neighbours, jacuzzis, trampolines and all.

As I rounded the bend I saw that the cabin-owners up there were having some kind of street party. Fifteen or twenty adults and children were seated around a homemade *langbord*. It was about five metres long and had probably been knocked together just that afternoon. Faint wisps of blue smoke emerged from the two *bålpans* ('fire-pans') that stood a couple of metres away from each end of the table. These are tripods on long black metal legs with a deep pan suspended on chains from a hook. They can be used for barbecuing, and also function as log fires for sitting around. It looked like most of the party-goers had finished eating, though a couple of the children were still playing with their half-eaten frankfurters, squirting tomato sauce at each other from cone-like potato-cake wrappings. There were a few cans of Frydenlund beer on the table and a couple of open bottles of wine. Feeling as if I was intruding on something I walked past, nodding a greeting to a bespectacled boy of about thirteen whose eye I happened to catch as I passed by. He was wearing a black 'I ♥ New York' T-shirt. I recognised him. I'd met him a couple of times, out walking with the family's dog, a friendly little dachshund called Stella.

*'Skal du gå forbi uten å hilse?'* I heard someone say.

The visit to the Kjemhus cemetery and then reading Porter's book had left me preoccupied with the idea of death and I really didn't feel all that sociable. Since turning seventy earlier in the year, I had noticed this increasing and suspiciously *programmatic* preoccupation with death. What was particularly frustrating was to discover that, after years of engaging with minds like Søren Kierkegaard and Arthur Schopenhauer, the older I became, the more did these monumental wrestlings with the meaning and purpose of it all dissolve into verbal dust. 'You need the fish trap to catch the fish. Once you've caught the fish you can forget about the trap,' Chuang Tzu writes in one of his chapters. 'You need words to catch the meaning. Once you've caught the meaning you can forget about the words. Show me a man who's forgotten about words; I'd like a word with him.'

I had always loved that sentiment. But in life it doesn't work like that. Come what may, the mind goes on sprouting words with the same meaningless exuberance. A phrase from Porter's book was preoccupying me as I made my way past the diners: 'I was impatient to die', one of the few female hermits he encountered in the Chungnan mountains had said to him. The phrase struck me as attractive. I was trying to work out whether it expressed a negative or positive attitude to death. I felt a curious affinity with this woman; I think it was she who interrupted Porter at one point to ask him, with a puzzled frown, *Who is this Chairman Mao you keep talking about?* It seems the whole Chinese revolution had passed her by completely.

For all these reasons I was slightly too late in realising that someone from the table had been addressing me, in a friendly-but-challenging way, asking if I intended to just walk by without stopping to say hello.

I looked up. At that precise moment I felt hardly capable of engaging with a crowd of strangers. I was certainly hoping to do my best when I opened my mouth to reply. But my old fear of being the outsider who says the wrong thing completely could not prevent me from replying *Hvorfor ikke?* ('Why not?')

The speaker was Jan Erik, the father of the boy in the T-shirt. He was sitting at the middle of the *langbord* on the far side. Seeming to sense my discomfort he at once stood up, stepped out from the bench and walked round the table to greet me privately.

'Didn't you get an invitation?' he asked, perhaps thinking I was being deliberately unsociable on that account.

Relieved to have been put ever so slightly in the right as someone who obviously *should* have had an invitation to the *langbord* but never received one, I replied no, I hadn't.

'Aren't you in the group?'

'What group?'

'The Facebook group.'

He explained what it was. I knew my wife regularly visited a page called *Vi som bor på Vegglifjell* ('We who live on Vegglifjell'), which contained matters of interest to cabin-dwellers on the Veggli mountain (the weather; the impending beer festival at Veggli Fjellstue; why haven't the roads been gritted? Will the person flying the drone please stop? etc.), but this turned out to be something even more local. It was a Facebook page confined to the interests of those of us living in that particular pocket of the mountainside development.

'We're in the process of forming a residents' committee,' he said. 'We think there should be a representative from down below the bend. Someone like you, for example.'

A middle-aged woman wearing a black fleece jacket approached. She held an iPad in her hand and asked for my email address. She tapped it down on the keyboard and said she'd just sent me an email. That way we would be part of the new residents' group. Before the thing got out of hand I had to tell them I wasn't on Facebook, where news of the group's activities would be posted, but that I would pass the invitation on to Nina. My bouts of unsociability are at times a source of regret to me, but I knew I lacked the strong sense of community that seems native to all Norwegians and that I was not the right man for the job. That sense of community is everywhere. On arriving in Norway back in 1983. I remember how surprised I was to discover that it was considered normal almost to the point of obligatory for writers to be members of one of the *Forfatterforeninger,* the Writers' Unions. While living and working in England, I had not even been aware of the existence of such organisations.

Over time I came to a better understanding of the need for solidarity. Solidarity is the basis of Norway's social stability and of the high degree of social and sexual equality that characterises Norwegian society at every level. Perhaps the absence of social and political arrogance, which is another aspect of the same quality, can be traced back to the four centuries the country spent as a Danish colony, and the century after 1814 as a junior partner under the Swedish crown. It may be that Norway's experiences of an almost colonial subservience during this period created a mindset always wary of the possibility of abuse by authority and a determination never to let it happen.

Even so, I had not expected the solidarity imperative to manifest itself up here in the Norwegian mountains. But it was only another way in which the reality of owning a cabin deviated from my dream of it, now that the dream was coming true.

On an earlier walk I had seen, through the terrace windows of Jan Erik's cabin, a Meade telescope mounted on a tripod and tilted upwards. At the time he was feeding branches into a twig cutter at the back of his cabin but turned it off as I walked by and stumped down the slope to say hello. I mentioned the telescope, and asked if astronomy was his hobby, since it was one of mine. He'd said no, not really. The telescope had been a surprise birthday present from his wife. Apparently he'd once said that astronomy was something he thought he might like to get into, now that they owned a cabin in the mountains, miles from the light pollution of Tønsberg where their regular home was, so she'd bought it for him. On a whim, and because I felt the need of company to lift me out of the trough of death-thoughts in which I had been sunk for so much of the afternoon, I asked if he wanted to walk up onto the *vidda* with me to watch the eclipse of the moon.

'I'd like that,' he said. 'When is it?'

I told him just after a quarter to ten.

'I'll see you up there.'

And he went back to his seat at the *langbord*.

★

Ten minutes of steep walking later I passed the barrier that is brought down to close off the track in winter, and in another ten minutes I was on the top. I rested for a few minutes and stood looking into the west. The sun was roasting the mountaintops as it slid towards them, basting them in flames of fiery orange and yellow. It was a riot of colour, a carnival of bronze light and deep blue shadow, a sight to make you grateful merely for the privilege of being able to witness such a scene and to forget every cramped little complaint you ever voiced about life. *Who can have made all this?* you ask yourself in bewilderment. *Who had the time and the imagination to put on a show like this?*

I had suggested to Jan Erik that we meet at the fingerpost where the path to Lufsjå takes off, and I set out along the track towards it. It's a pleasant forty-minute ramble. While painting the cabin, Nina and I had been in the habit of ending the day by walking up there with the dog. The section of path we usually walked, between Veggli and Lufsjå, followed the exact route of the Store Nordmannsslepe. In Fønnebø's book I had read that the best time to see the tracks is when the sun is low in the sky, and bending down now I could make out in places as many as fifteen or twenty ruts worn into the grassy ground by the long poles dragged along by the horses.

On reaching the signpost I lay down on a bed of crisp, hard heather and folded my hands behind my head. A light wind ran swift and rushing up the side of the mountain. Somewhere nearby I heard, as one always hears up there, the mournful monosyllabic cry of the plover. The sound of loneliness, as if it's calling to someone. In another minute I heard the low, almost frog-like croak of the ptarmigan. I leaned up on one elbow and looked round for him. He's hard to see, his brown and black mottled feathers against the grey, lichen-coated rocks and the heather, and the red tendrils of the dwarf birch that cover the ground above the treeline. He croaked again and this time I saw him. He was standing on the edge of a flat rock a little above me, his small head and large body silhouetted against the pale blue of the sky in the east. He croaked again and then abruptly flew off. Again the only sounds were the rushing of the wind through the mountain undergrowth and the sad, repetitive cry of the plover.

Still with my head turned, I now saw, on the side of the rock where the ptarmigan had been sitting, half-turned away from me, my wife's face. I wondered where she was, who she was with, what they were talking about. I recalled, suddenly, one of the first times we had walked up there. It was about a year ago, before we had bought the land and the cabin, before we had even thought of doing such a thing. We had been visiting my brother-in-law and his family at their cabin. I was still on crutches after a hip-replacement operation in the spring. After three months I felt like taking the chance of walking in the mountains, using the lightweight metal crutches as a pair of *gåstaver*, or Nordic walking poles. It had been a day rather like this one, blustery and sunny, and the first time since the operation I had been in the mountains. The most depressing aspect of the arthritis of the previous two years had been the thought that this harbinger of old age might mean that this chapter of my life was now over for ever, and I recalled the ecstasy I felt as I humped and stumped along the track, so relieved to know that it wasn't.

Not wanting to push my new hip too hard, we stopped frequently and leaned against rocky outcrops to rest up for a few minutes. Each time we stopped I had been puzzled by a low, musical, rather ghostly whistling sound. For some time I couldn't figure out the source of it, until I worked out that it must be the sound of the wind whistling through the nooks and crannies of the small cairns that travellers in the past had built along the track, in the centuries before the DNT and the big red 'T' markings.

'Listen,' I said to Nina. 'That's the sound of the *vidda*. The *vidda* is talking to us in the wind.'

Nina listened to the eerie fluting sound for a few seconds.

'It's your crutches,' she said. 'It's the wind blowing through the height-adjuster holes in your crutches.'

I listened again. She was right. I felt mildly deflated, and irrationally annoyed. I marvelled at a central and recurring paradox in our marriage, that she, who believed instantly and fiercely in the wildest claims of any clairvoyant and spirit-channeller of some long-dead Native American chieftain, should, in almost all other matters, be so consistently more level-headed and logical than I, who derided all such claims in the name of ordinary common sense.

As the sun finally slipped behind the peaks in the west, I felt the temperature drop immediately and wished that I had had the foresight to wrap up a little warmer. Looking around, I saw the pale silver slivers of seven or eight glow-worms nearby in the long rough grass and made a mental note to find out when I got back to the cabin exactly *how* it is they glow like that, and *why*, following it up with an equally firm resolution not to do so and content myself instead with the undisturbed experience of wonder.

Several times I peered north along the track and wondered what had happened to Jan Erik. Perhaps he'd forgotten. Perhaps the social claims of the *langbord* and the new Facebook group had proved too strong. And did it even matter? Because now that the sun had set, when I turned and looked into the east I saw only a bank of blue-grey cloud on the horizon.

I looked at my watch. It was just past nine. Having drawn the eclipse to Jan Erik's attention I felt burdened by an illogical personal responsibility to make sure it actually took place.

But suppose it didn't? The wind was still blowing strongly from the west. Suppose it wasn't strong enough to drive the clouds back over the horizon? I recalled the anxious disappointment of the Japanese poet Matsuo Bashō, described in melancholic detail in 'The Visit to the Kashima Shrine', when his pilgrimage to this mountain shrine to experience the rising of a full moon was frustrated by the presence of cloud. Through the greying light I could just about make out a yellow anorak, and Jan Erik's stout figure hurrying along the path, still about half a mile distant. I crossed my fingers that we would not suffer a disappointment similar to Bashō's.

When he joined me we walked on for a few more minutes, clambering off the path and up a nearby rise to a rocky outcrop that gave us a still better vantage point. We sat down next to each other with our backs against the rocks. I mentioned my worries about the clouds.

'They look like they're breaking up now,' he said, pointing.

He was right. The cloud had started unravelling at its edges. In another five minutes it had all but dissolved. Light now held the air in a cold, hard brilliance. We waited, our eyes fixed on the south-east horizon.

'Have you been to Lufsjå yet?' he asked.

Lufsjå was the nearest DNT cabin to us, but most of us who had bought cabins in Veggli were new to the region, and we had been so busy painting and furnishing them that it would probably be another year before our exploration of the nearby regions of the *vidda* could begin in earnest. Anyway, as I quickly realised, Veggli was first and foremost of interest to my Norwegian neighbours as a winter resort, a place to ski in.

'Not yet,' I said. 'Have you?'

'We spent the night there last week. Just a there and back trip.'

'Is it *selvbetjente*?' ('self-catering')

'Yes.'

I shook my head. 'You know, I still can't get over it, the way some of these DNT places are stocked with food that you pay for on a trust system. I don't think there are many countries in the world that would have that much faith in the honesty of its people. You just take the food you want, fill out a giro before you leave and pop it in a box. Six months later, when you've forgotten all about it, you get the bill.'

I'd been reading about the history of these self-catering cabins in a recent issue of *Fjell og Vidde* ('Mountains and Wilderness'), the members' magazine published quarterly by DNT. It seems the initiative came from a man named Gunnar Sønsteby, better known as a leader of Milorg, the Norwegian resistance movement during the Occupation years of the Second World War. After the war ended in 1945, Sønsteby went back to his old job as a route inspector for DNT. The end of the war saw a rise in membership of the organisation and a growing interest in spending time walking in the mountains. More cabins were built to extend the network; but it soon became clear they weren't being used much. The problem was the availability of food, or rather the lack of it. DNT experimented briefly with providing some cabins with military rations. These satisfied the hunger, but not much more than that. Towards the end of the 1950s, Sønsteby had the idea of providing visitors with something a little more appetising. Some cabins began to be stocked with supplies of tinned fish, like *fiskeboller* (fish-balls), tinned meat, packets of soup and powdered fruit drinks, spreads, coffee, tea, biscuits, even exotic varieties of tinned fruit like peaches and pineapples.

The initiative was an instant success and is one of the reasons why long-distance walking in the mountains has become so popular among Norwegians today that you could properly describe it as a national pastime. As of 2018, 173 of the Trekking Association's 540 cabins offered self-catering. A handful of the larger ones at popular hiking centres, like Finse and Haukeliseter, offer considerably more than that. You can get three hot meals a day there, beer, wine and whisky from the bar, and they have their own small souvenir shops. But the great majority of cabins are still *ubetjent* ('uncatered'). These offer bunk-bed sleeping accommodation with foam-rubber mattresses and duvet, cooking facilities and fuel in the form of wood or gas. Walkers need to bring their own food and their own *lakenpose* ('sheet bag') to sleep inside. This is a sheet-thin, one-piece bag with an attached pillow slip and a nightmarish thing to wriggle in and out of, especially if you need to get up in the night to pee.

'But for me,' I went on, 'the really curious thing is that when Sønsteby was asked where he had got the idea from, he said England, when he was in London during the war. He'd noticed how the boys selling newspapers on the street corners and outside the Underground stations would leave their flat caps behind when they went off to get something to eat.* People would pick up a paper and drop the money into the cap. If they didn't have the right money they would help themselves to change from the cap. Sønsteby figured that if an honour-system like that could work in the middle of one of the biggest cities in the world then it ought to work in the Norwegian mountains too.'

Jan Erik smiled and nodded his head in pleased appreciation of this unexpected paradox. Then he added, in a kindly way, that I had got the wrong man. It wasn't Gunnar Sønsteby I was thinking of but Claus Helberg.

'But they were both involved in Milorg, so you're right there.'

'I keep getting them mixed up,' I said. 'It's probably because I've been following the debate in the papers about Marte Michelet's new book.'

Michelet was a journalist who had just published a book in which she claimed that the anti-Semitism of Norwegians

---

* I used the obsolete English word 'sixpence', meaning a coin from the pre-decimal age. For some unknown etymological reason it remains the standard Norwegian term for 'a flat cap'.

in general, and of the Norwegian resistance movement in particular, had let down the Jewish population of the country during the war. The issue had a personal interest for me. For over a year, back in the 1980s, while working on my biography of Knut Hamsun, I had occupied a desk next to Oskar Mendelsohn in the bowels of the Oslo University Library in Solli plass.* Mendelsohn was working on a massive, two-volume *Jødenes historie i Norge* (*The History of the Jews in Norway*), his attempt to rescue from historical oblivion each individual member of the Norwegian branch of a people brought almost to the verge of extinction as a result of the war. I had grown to like him and to admire the almost superhuman dimensions of the task he had set himself. I still remember one occasion when we were talking at my desk. Abruptly he broke off and asked, with a chill in his voice: 'What is that "J" on the cover of your book?' Puzzled, I replied that it stood for 'Journal', and that it was my way of distinguishing between different notebooks among the set of several identical ones I was using for my research. Moments later I realised the source of his alarm, a still-vivid memory of those identification cards stamped with 'J' that all Jews had been forced to carry by the Nazis. In absolute mortification I hastened to show him my notebooks marked 'L' for 'Letters' and 'C' for 'Contacts'.

At the heart of Michelet's argument was a claim made by Gunnar Sønsteby in an interview in 1970 that Milorg leaders had known of the Nazis' plans for the Norwegian Jews a full three months before the campaign of deportations and executions had got under way in the autumn of 1942. According to Sønsteby, information from his sources within the Nazi-controlled state police had left members of Milorg in no doubt

---

* This is now the National Library.

about the intended fate of the Norwegian Jews. 'Our job was to fight, not to help people' was how he explained the fact that the rescue of the Jews did not then become a Milorg priority.

Michelet argued that the failure to warn the Jews of what awaited them could only be ascribed to an anti-Semitic bias on the part of the Norwegian population as a whole at that time. She made this alleged complicity explicit in the title of her book: *Hva visste hjemmefronten? Holocausten i Norge: Varslene, unnvikelsene, hemmeligholdhet* ('What did the Home Front know? The Holocaust in Norway: warnings, evasions, secrecy').

The media debate that ensued was bitter and acrimonious, and for obvious reasons. Milorg veterans like Sønsteby are among Norway's greatest heroes. Their stars shine as brightly as those of Nansen or Amundsen, and their right to this status had never been even slightly questioned before. Ethically, the war has been a more troubling subject for the Norwegians than for the British. Britons had not, after all, suffered the trauma and humiliation of Occupation. And once it was over, Norway, a country with a population so small it feels like a family, was faced with the problem of how to deal with the significant numbers who had joined Vidkun Quisling's far-right, collaborationist party *Nasjonal Samling* ('National Unity') during the Occupation. Many were committed Nazis, many were influenced by a fear of Bolshevism, most were probably motivated by the improved access party membership gave to hard-to-come-by rationed goods like meat, jam, butter and sugar, as well as by the human fear of ending up on the losing side. They all had to be dealt with.

In the world of the arts, film has been the medium that has concerned itself most consistently with these subjects. From the end of the war until the early 1960s, Norwegian filmmakers were concerned to depict a *dugnad* spirit among the population as a whole in the face of the misery, shortages and unpredictability of daily life during the five years of the Occupation. Arne Skouen's *Ni Liv* (*Nine Lives*, 1957) described what happened after a sabotage mission by the Norwegian Resistance was betrayed to the Nazis. Based on a true story, it follows the escape of the badly wounded Jan Baalsrud as he makes his way through Troms county for the safety of the Swedish border. Skouen's concern was not so much to depict Baalsrud's individual heroism as to show that he would never have made it without the help of others. In this respect, it was a typical reflection of Norwegian social values.

Skouen's *Kalde spor* (*Cold Tracks*, 1962) inaugurated a second phase in this cultural self-analysis, one in which attention was focused on the failings and existential distress of individual Norwegian resistance fighters. Toralv Maurstad played a self-tormenting former resistance member who tries in vain to escape his personal demons by seeking out the solitude of the mountains once the war is over.

A third phase emerged by the end of the 1960s, characterised by films that considered the fate of ordinary Norwegians who were not members of the resistance, in particular the experiences of women and children during the war. The ethical problems surrounding such phenomena as black marketeers and those owners of construction companies, known as *brakke-baroner* ('barrack barons'), who profited by building for the occupying forces, were also explored. Women directors such as Laila Mikkelsen and Bente Erichsen were prominent voices in this phase. Mikkelsen's *Liten Ida* (*Little Ida*, 1981) looked at events through the eyes of a seven-year-old child bullied because her mother has had an affair with a German SS officer. Erichsen's *Over grensen* (*Across the Border*, 1987) re-examined the case of two Norwegian border guides who were alleged to have robbed and murdered two Jewish refugees whom they were supposed to be leading to the safety of the Swedish border in 1942, and who were acquitted when the case came to trial after the war.*

Erichsen's film raised all sorts of uncomfortable questions about culpable silence, anti-Semitism, and greed among Norwegians during the Occupation. The ferocity of the debate it aroused was a harbinger of what was to come with Michelet's book, and the film's appearance may have been one reason the war disappeared as a theme for the next twenty years.

It was not picked up again until 2008, in Joachim Rønning and Espen Sandberg's *Max Manus*. Based on the memoirs of its eponymous hero, the film describes Manus's involvement with the illegal press in Norway during the war, and his activities as a saboteur while a member of *Kompani Linge*, one of the most admired of all resistance groups in Occupied Europe. By local standards *Max Manus* had a huge budget, and it was marketed as an event of national significance so successfully that the premiere was attended by King Harald V and several government ministers, as well as surviving relatives and associates of Manus's.

*Max Manus* was the first in what was a new genre for Norwegian film, a Hollywood-inspired celebration of the heroes of the resistance. Harald Zwart, a Dutch-Norwegian director with a number of real Hollywood films to his credit, followed up with *Den 12. mann* (*The 12th Man*, 2017), essentially a glamorised remake of *Nine Lives*. Like *Max Manus*, *The 12th Man* took liberties with the known historical facts of the

---

* Erichsen's film was based on Sigurd Senje's documentary novel *Ekko fra Skriktjenn* (*Echoes from Skriktjenn*), published in 1982.

stories they were based on. Both films did extremely well at the box office.

The commercial success of this approach meant that Michelet's attack on the Home Front gave a severe jolt to this romanticising of its activities during the war years. I asked Jan Erik if he'd read her book, and what he made of the accusations of anti-Semitism it contained.

'No, I haven't read it,' he said. 'But I've been following the debate, the contributions from the Holocaust Centre, the Resistance Museum, the war historians and so on. It's a difficult thing to talk about.'

He looked at his watch.

'Shouldn't the moon be up by now?'

I glanced at mine. 'Any moment now,' I replied. 'I think maybe your watch is a little fast.'

'Hmm.'

Jan Erik frowned. He shook his head several times and then fell silent for a few moments. He seemed to be struggling with his thoughts.

'Michelet is young,' he said suddenly, pulling up his hood and zipping his anorak up to his neck. 'She has no idea what it was like to be at war. She has empathy, but it's luxury empathy, the empathy of the spectator. What happened, happened. You can't change it. The past isn't a film. You can't rewrite the script and shoot it all over again until you get the result you want. Every war, all wars since Vietnam – Afghanistan, Iraq, the Balkans – they've all been television wars. You watch them. You take sides. But none of it is *about you*. Your daily life goes on just the same. Young people have no idea of how *uncivilised* a real war is. It's brutal beyond their conception of what brutality can be. Listen: in October 1942 Josef Terboven, Hitler's Reichskommissar in Norway, issued an order announcing the death penalty for thirty-eight different forms of resistance and civil disobedience, including anyone caught spreading news from London, anyone found in possession of a weapon, and anyone caught helping refugees to escape.'

He pulled the hood back off his head again and turned towards me, wagging his index finger in my face.

'You could be arrested and locked up in Grini* just for wearing a *binders* ('paper clip') on the lapel of your jacket.'

'Why a paper clip?'

'Because it was a symbol of support for Milorg,' he said. 'Like a red woollen hat – Norwegians were banned from wearing red woollen hats in public during the war. And the paper clip was invented by a Norwegian, a man named Johan Vaaler, so that gave it an added dimension of symbolic power.'

I had heard this widely believed but erroneous claim several times before. I was still feeling slightly silly for having mixed up the names of two of Norway's greatest resistance heroes and saw my chance here to redeem myself by correcting Jan Erik's mistake.

'Actually, Jan Erik, it wasn't invented by a Norwegian. Vaaler *did* patent a design for a paper clip in 1901, but the Gem paper clip – that's the one everyone uses today, with the two metal loops – was already widely available. Vaaler's clip stopped halfway round. It didn't have the second loop that would enable it to exploit the torsion principle, so it didn't actually work. Vaaler's design was never even put into commercial production, but most Norwegians still think he invented the paper clip.'

---

* Grini prison camp in Bærum, a western suburb of Oslo, was used as a concentration camp by the Nazis during the Second World War. After the war it housed Norwegians convicted of treason and collaboration.

Jan Erik looked at me and nodded his head slowly several times. 'Well, you learn something every day. Thank you for telling me that. But even so,' he went on, raising his voice, 'the fact that Norwegians *believed* it was invented by a Norwegian gave the act of wearing one on the lapel of your jacket an added patriotic force during the Occupation.'

I knew that even this wasn't true, since one of the most curious aspects of this particular cultural myth was that it arose *after* the war, decades after Vaaler's death in 1910, and instead of being debunked grew more and more powerful, even making its way onto a commemorative postage stamp in 1999 and into the pages of the *Norsk biografisk leksikon* ('Norwegian Biographical Encyclopedia') entry on Vaaler in 2005. But this wasn't really what we were talking about so I let it go.

'You could get shot for listening to the radio,' Jan Erik continued, 'never mind helping complete strangers cross the border into Sweden. My grandfather was a Milorg leader in Grimstad. He was an XU agent, an undercover intelligence agent working under the command of the British Special Operations Executive. He was arrested in January 1943, tortured, sentenced to death and executed in the Trandumskogen forest in May 1944. The Milorg leader for the whole of the south was shot along with him. While they were still at Grini prison they were told that Milorg could rescue them as they were being driven out to the place of execution at Trandum. They said no. They knew the Germans would kill dozens of innocent civilians in retaliation, so they said no. I never knew him, of course. But my father often talked about him. So…'

He let the sentence drift as he raised a bladed hand to his forehead and peered across at the horizon. It was lit by the first counterglow of the setting sun, a soft pink light now that the blue had been filtered out.

Again he looked at his watch. It was one of those large, self-winding mechanical watches on a thick brown leather strap. He held it up close to his ear to make sure it was ticking and then flapped his wrist vigorously.

'Maybe it's already risen,' I said. I was surprised I hadn't thought of this before.

'I'll have a look.'

He unbuckled the straps on his blue Swedish rucksack, took out a pair of binoculars in a black case, opened the case, pulled off the dust caps from the eyepieces and raised the glasses to his eyes.

'You're right,' he said, standing up and holding out the glasses to me. 'It's well up.'

I stood up, took the glasses and looked for myself. Faintly, behind the powdery pink sheen, I saw the pale, round shadow hovering two or three centimetres above the horizon. I leaned my elbow on Jan Erik's shoulder.

Now that we had located it we were easily able to see it with the naked eye. For a few moments the whole clock of understanding stopped and we just stood there watching. I thought of Caspar David Friedrich's *Two Men Contemplating the Moon*. Where did I read that this painting was the inspiration for Samuel Beckett's play *Waiting for Godot*? Or had I dreamed that? So many things nowadays, it seemed to me, occupied a hinterland in which dream and reality resembled each other so closely it had become hard to tell the two states apart.

After almost two minutes the moon pulled slowly free of the Earth's shadow and began to climb into the sky. As though deliberately breaking the spell of the moment, Jan Erik belched. He roughly beat the dust from the seat of his trousers with his hand and said it was time he was getting back, as it was his turn to take Stella for a walk.

We clambered down onto the track through the heather and started walking back towards Veggli. Jan Erik was in front of me. After about five minutes he stopped and turned to me.

'Bloody eclipse,' he said, shaking his head. 'Did we actually see it, or not?'

And without waiting for an answer he turned and carried on walking.

# 10

## Saturday, 6 October 2018

Wood delivered for the first winter –

stacking the wood – I buy a tarpaulin – some

*byoriginaler* ('street eccentrics') – Willy the

Jesus Singer – Norwegian comedians –

lack of comic writers in Norway – a closely

observed delivery man – conversation with

an anarchist – walking the dogs – Frisbee

golf comes to Norway – Willy and

the newspaper seller

Before leaving Oslo we had arranged for Jørgen the landowner to deliver a *favn* of wood to the cabin on the Saturday. That's the equivalent of about fifty-five full, forty-litre sacks of wood. I had earlier sent Jørgen an email asking if he could cut down the tall, dead pine that stood just over the boundary of our land on the western side. Since this plot was still unsold it would be his responsibility if the tree came crashing down in an autumn storm and went through the roof of the car, the cabin, or even both.

No reply.

But an order for firewood meant money, and at about two o'clock on the Saturday afternoon we heard him chugging along the track towards the cabin, dragging a trailer along behind his bright red Massey-Ferguson tractor.

In our absence work had already started on the new cabin to be built on the plot below ours. It was surprising and impressive to see how quickly things happened. The site had been completely grubbed, and for much of Saturday morning a digger had been pushing and shaping the earth and rubble platform into place ready for the concrete footing. Odd, the same young man who had cleared our site, was driving. I watched him navigating back and forth across the narrow space in the large yellow caterpillar, braking expertly, the large treads hovering over the edge of the mound. One more metre and the whole cab would have gone somersaulting over and down into the valley below. I had missed this stage in the building of our own cabin, and watching the process unfold at close quarters on the neighbouring plot I was filled with a peculiar pride at being a member of the human race, so daring in its dreams of what is possible.

The access track to our cabin had acquired a branch down and to the left to service the new cabin, and Jørgen turned down into the lower arm of this Y and then reversed back up and around the bend towards us. Since I planned to stack the wood under the long overhang of the shed I asked him to drop the load as close to the shed as possible. He couldn't get in much closer than about ten metres. Then, with its tailgate open and the trailer tilted down at the back, he pulled forward a few metres and the enormous jute sack slowly slid off and onto the gravel, logs tumbling out of its gaping, pale green mouth. It was an extremely satisfying sight.

Over a cup of coffee we talked briefly on the terrace afterwards. After about ten minutes Jørgen thanked us for the coffee and said he had to be on his way, he had a meeting set up with a drone-photographer who was going to take aerial views of the remaining plots that were still for sale.

As I watched him chug away on the Massey-Ferguson I reflected on how his life must have changed since he had been granted permission to develop his mountainside into a cabin village. Until then the land had been good for little but sheep-grazing. All his time and effort now went into this new career of selling off the land. It must have brought about a dramatic change in his financial status. That was probably true of the whole village. This was a boom time for the carpenters, plumbers, electricians, shopkeepers, café-owners and petrol stations of the middle stretch of the valley.

I stood for a few moments contemplating the task of getting the logs out of the enormous sack and over to the wall of the shed. But with Nina sorting out the smaller pieces of wood that would make good kindling, it was all done within the hour. The stack stood about chest high against the wall and I reckoned it would be enough to see us through the winter. If we did run out we could always replenish supplies from Plantasjen, the big garden centre we passed at the top of the hill just before the road descends into Kongsberg.

We'd already lit the fire a couple of times on chilly evenings, and I remained thrilled both by the economy and efficiency of our Jøtul stove, and by the aesthetic pleasure it gave. The exposed black cylindrical chimney radiated heat all the way up to the ceiling, so that guests sleeping up in the *hems* found the whole floor naturally warm when retiring for the evening.

From the end of October to well into April, heavy snow is inevitable at almost a thousand metres above sea level. The overhanging eaves of the shed provided natural protection from above for the stacked wood. Most of the wind seemed to come from the north and the east, and the long wall of the cabin provided good cover from that direction. But I was concerned to find a way to cover the stack and protect it from the snow that blew down through the channel formed by the shed wall and the long wall of the cabin just two metres away, and from snow that would inevitably slide down into this channel from the roof of the cabin.

We paid Jørgen an annual sum to keep the access track clear of snow, but the size of the snowplough meant that he had to stop well short of the shed and the terracing at the front of the cabin. There was cleared space for the car in front of the shed, but the path between the car and the main entrance to the cabin had to be made by hand each time we came. We had snow shovels and scoops, but that wouldn't necessarily solve the problem. When fresh, snow is easy to push about from place to place. Old snow that has lain awhile, impacted, wet, often frozen at the bottom, is another matter.

I needed to find a way to cover the wood that did not at the same time trap moisture inside it. Some cabin-owners simply placed a sheet of zinc over the top of the stack and anchored it with stones. Some attached a small jutting roof to the side wall of the shed and stacked the wood under it. Neither solution offered much protection from snow that would slide down off the roof into the space between the front door and the shed and presently I settled on a tarpaulin as the best solution. I knew the Clas Ohlson back home in Oslo stocked these, primarily intended for use as boat covers, with metal-ringed eyelets along the edges. My plan was to wedge one end of this behind the woodpile, let the body of it fall like a curtain over the wood, and anchor it at the bottom with three or four large stones on the gravel in front of it.

It seemed a simple and environmentally sound solution and I briefly outlined the plan to Nina. After thirty-five years of marriage she still has remarkably little faith in my often homemade and unorthodox solutions to practical problems. She believes this 'impracticality' is something I inherited from my late mother. Her scepticism can be traced back to a visit my mother paid to us some thirty years ago, when she came to spend a few days at the cabin in Nøtterøy. At that time, in the late 1980s, Norwegians still decorated and furnished their cabins in a conventional way quite distinct from the style of their permanent homes. In the living room you would often see wooden platters, usually painted red or blue and decorated with *rosemaling*, displayed on wall-mounted plate-racks; small, stiff-backed and not very comfortable wooden armchairs; and woven tapestries on the walls. In the kitchen, old brass cooking utensils might hang from the walls, with a flounced pelmet across the kitchen window.

Quite often, in the kitchens of those old cabins, you would see a tray or dish hanging on the wall between attractively braided cloth straps decorated in a distinctive regional pattern. One of these *brettholder* was hanging on the wall next to the kitchen sink of the old cabin at Nøtterøy. My mother must have been greatly charmed by it, for when we visited her at her little house in Edenfield a few months later we saw that she had attempted to recreate the effect in her own kitchen, using a pair of frayed maroon braces bought from the local Oxfam shop in place of the braided straps to support a pale pink metal tray.

Nina was as charmed as I by the inventive and bohemian nature of this tribute, but in time it became a fatal reference point whenever the question of my practicality, and not least my aesthetic sensibilities, arose. But as the man of the house, having willingly handed over most of the interior aesthetics of the cabin to my wife, I was not about to relinquish my control of the way the woodpile was going to be covered. I firmly believed that her objection to my plan was aesthetic rather than practical and as such could safely be ignored.

Early on Monday morning, back in Oslo, I headed up Bogstadveien to Clas Ohlson and bought the tarpaulin (olive green) and a ball of red and black twine. Afterwards I sat on the concrete bench outside Baker Hansen at the corner of Kirkeveien and Slemdalsveien with an Americano, the large blue plastic Clas Ohlson bag at my feet, ready to resume the study of Norway and its inhabitants, my hobby and pleasure as well as my job. Almost immediately it occurred to me that I now saw both, the country and the inhabitants, not so much with the eyes of a foreigner as with the eyes of an elderly man who has lived most of his adult life in Norway and become prey to a double nostalgia. For almost as long as I can remember, visiting England has been like visiting Mars. In the days before Ryanair, the cheapest flights between Norway and the UK were called Apex fares. They cost around £200 return and had to be booked months in advance. This was a prohibitive sum of money for the penniless student I then was and the penniless writer I later became, and it was rare for me to manage more than one trip a year back home. Perhaps the long periods that elapsed between each of these visits left me more vulnerable to the cultural changes taking place there. I recall my shock at the speed at which cars now sped along leafy country lanes; and my surprise on realising that redevelopment had rendered the centres of most of the English towns I was familiar with more or less indistinguishable from each other.

Experiences like these left me feeling alienated and un-English. Born and raised in England of Scottish parents, with the coming of the age of identity politics I had even toyed for about three minutes with the idea of *identifying* as Scottish. Nostalgic for a vanished England, I suddenly realised I had become equally nostalgic for a vanished Norway. Coming to this country at the comparatively late age of thirty-five, I had felt reborn. Now, thirty-five years later, I was no longer dewy-eyed about everything Norwegian. There were times when I feared I might have exhausted my enthusiasm and replaced it with an unattractive cynicism. What, I might ask myself, what if a thousand years of almost religious reliance on the rule of law in this country revealed not so much trust and faith in its community as *the exact opposite*? A cynical acceptance of the fact that people cannot be trusted to behave well and require the constant supervision of law to keep them from cheating, robbing and killing each other, and an unremitting insistence on conformity as a way of enforcing the law?

At such times, few things could cheer me up as much as the sight of Willy Danielsen setting up on the other side of Slemdalsveien. I knew from a profile interview I read years ago in *Aftenposten* that Willy had at one time been addicted to heroin. Somewhere along the way he had found Jesus and had never looked back. A tall man, slightly bow-legged, he had been singing and preaching around the streets of Majorstuen for as long as I could remember.

Willy is what Norwegians call a *byoriginal*. He's one of a vanishing number of Norwegians who live out their eccentricity on the streets of Oslo, in a city centre still small enough to make them impossible to ignore. They inhabit a sort of *un*-celebrity. People know their names and their particular eccentricities, and lament their passing. Until quite recently Justisen, the pub on Møllergata, had a gallery of photographs of these characters on the walls of the ground floor bar. One was Einar Olsen, known as 'El Jukan', a street singer who also gave pavement-fakir shows in which he swallowed razor blades and light bulbs. Another was Advokat Hermansen ('Hermansen the lawyer'), a gymnast and former lawyer, a fascinating and oddly frightening man who astonished passengers on the T-bane ('tunnel track', or Metro) by performing feats of strength on the handrails and grab handles and doing somersaults and cartwheels up and down the carriage floors. 'We're getting more and more stupid,' he was once quoted as saying. 'We turn into standard issue people. Norwegian standard

issue. The children start school under the sign of the Department of Education and Religious Affairs. Look at children before they start school. Their spirits haven't been broken yet. You just can't behave naturally in society. Everything is rules. That's why I'm crazy – but not insane.'

Alas, in 1993 he was beaten to death at the age of eighty-three by a man who couldn't tell the difference.

Every morning, between eight-thirty and nine o'clock, Willy arrives at Majorstuen, his wooden guitar, Bible and tracts fastened to the small blue trolley illustrated with a picture of Jesus that he trundles along behind him. He stops, raises the peak of his faded blue forage cap, scratches his forehead and looks skyward for a few moments. Then he unhooks his guitar, slings it around his neck and for the next forty minutes sings hymns in praise of Jesus. His voice is quiet and you have to stand close to him to hear it above the constant roar of traffic – the crosstown number 20 bus passes every six minutes, and three separate tram lines converge here. His guitar playing is similarly quiet, and so hesitant you sometimes wonder if he's actually touching the strings at all.

In between songs he leaves the guitar dangling in front of his chest, closes his eyes and addresses Jesus directly, waving his arms above his head in slow, fluid gestures and rocking from foot to foot in a series of tiny, delicate, almost balletic steps. He holds a tract or Bible in one hand. Now and then he stops in mid-dance and, without lowering his arms, uses his free hand to point insistently to the words of some particular verse. He accepts money to pay for the independent social work he does among the drug addicts and the homeless. In return he'll give you a copy of his CD *Jesus Lever* (*Jesus Lives*). There's no track listing on it, just a quotation from the Bible, Matthew 11:28. His favourite pitch has always been the raised concrete apron outside the main entrance to Majorstuen T-bane station. In recent years, however, he has faced competition from the travelling Roma musicians who have become such a feature of Norwegian street life. If some accordion player has beaten him to it then he'll wheel his guitar over to the far side of the road and set up on the corner of Bogstadveien and Kirkegaten, between Thune the jewellers ('Please Ring for Attention') and McDonald's.

The entrance to the T-bane station is popular with other people besides street musicians. Most weekday mornings a salesman for *Klassekampen* will set up his four-poled tent on

the station concourse. He lifts it out of an oblong black box on wheels and, like someone coaxing a new-born giraffe to its feet, he prods and pokes it upright with a few practised nudges. Once it's up he lifts a pile of newspapers out of the box, closes the lid, and the box becomes his counter. He starts offering free copies to passers-by. Quite a few people are willing to take up his offer, fewer are willing to stop and enter into a conversation that always ends in an invitation to take out a subscription to the paper.

The young Roma bloods gather there too, after they've driven the older family members around and dropped them off at the entrances to the suburban supermarkets and shopping malls where they are to sit begging for the day. Four or five of them stand for a half hour, smoking and chatting, taking and making calls on mobile phones, watching the girls go by, before starting their own work. For many of them this involves trudging the streets collecting empty cans and plastic bottles from rubbish bins. An average deposit of two kroner (about 20p) per item soon mounts up, so by Roma standards the money is good. Towards the end of the day you'll see them heading into the supermarkets with bulging black sacks of empties slung over their backs to feed into the deposit machine, which afterwards issues them with a note redeemable at the checkout.

The younger Roma women concentrate on the city centre. They dress in long, colourful skirts and stride swiftly and purposefully about among the crowds, using all the bright, bird-like charm at their disposal to get people to buy a copy of *Folk er folk* ('People are People'). This is a magazine, in Norwegian, about the Roma. Produced by idealistic Norwegians who wanted to give the Roma an alternative to begging, it puts them in direct competition with the Oslo drug addicts and homeless who sell a magazine of their own, a Norwegian version of the *Big Issue* called = oslo (*Equals Oslo*). A mutual tolerance seems to exist between the two groups, although I did once see an = *oslo* seller crossing Kirkeristen to remonstrate angrily with a *Folk er Folk* seller whom he had spotted squatting with her knickers down and peeing in the bushes behind Oslo cathedral.

I sit drinking my coffee and watch the ever-changing stream of people. When the traffic lights on Slemdalsveien are against them they bunch two metres away from me, and then swarm across as soon as the green man shows, some peeling off to the right towards the side entrance to the station for the eastbound trains, others marching purposefully towards the main entrance and turning into a short passage that has a kiosk on each side selling an almost identical range of small items – newspapers, magazines, train tickets, coffee from a machine, hot sausage wrapped in a choice of potato cake or bread roll.

In a gap in the crowd I catch a glimpse of one of the young Roma men with a broom in his hand, busily sweeping up the cigarette butts that litter the pavement outside the little tobacconists on the corner. He must have come to some arrangement with the proprietor. I often buy my scratch cards there and I know that the shop is owned by a man named Bjørn Sand, who is now in his eighties. In his prime he was one of Norway's best-known and most popular comedians. Using the format of the radio phone-in, he created a figure called 'Stutum', an articulate and opinionated reactionary hostile to every new development in Norwegian public life and discourse, from feminism to Pakistani immigration to the environmental movement.

For some twenty years this wickedly well-caught caricature delighted Norwegians, most of whom recognised the satirical thrust behind the act. By the 1990s, however, Sand was alarmed to discover that his Stutum had become a hero in some quarters to people who felt that at last they had been given a voice, and he retired the character forthwith. Clips of the act can still be seen on YouTube, but the Oslo public libraries hold no copies of his one and only CD, a 1995 collection entitled *Stutums verste* ('The Worst of Stutum').

Thanks largely to the impact and influence of Henrik Ibsen and Edvard Munch at the end of the nineteenth century, Norway has acquired an enduring cultural reputation as official purveyor of melancholy to the rest of Europe. But the country has also had its share of great comedians, from the George Formby-like goofiness of Leif Juster to the avuncular bluster of Rolv Wesenlund. Comedians like Harald Heide-Steen, Grethe Kausland, Øivind Blunck, Hege Schøyen and the Dizzie Tunes group all made their names on the stages of such theatre-cum-nightclubs as the *Chat Noir* on Klingenberggata, in central Oslo, a venue that for decades nurtured a peculiarly Norwegian form of the theatrical entertainment known as the 'review'. The rise of the cheeky, anti-establishment young stand-up comedian marked a break with this tradition, although recent developments seem to suggest a peculiar grafting of traditional Norwegian seriousness on to the comedy. Some of the best-known of the current crop of Norwegian stand-ups now offer their audience confessional acts that come close to the 'misery-memoirs' familiar from the world of book publishing: Rune Andersen, Bjarte Tjøstheim and Else Kåss Furuseth have all recently put on shows of an overtly therapeutic nature built around apparently un-comedic themes such as childhood with an abusive father, angst and suicide.

It may be that the pervasive influence of Ibsen and Munch explains the absence from Norwegian literary history of a single humorous novelist of note. Mark Twain was one of Knut Hamsun's crucial influences and there's a strong touch of Twain in Hamsun's late trilogy featuring the wanderer August; but beyond that there's never been any writer with a body of work comparable to a P. G. Wodehouse or even a Tom Sharpe. And with the historical exception of the Enlightenment writer Ludvig Holberg, whom the Danes like to claim as their own, and the now largely forgotten Helge Krog, there has never been a Norwegian playwright writing in the same vein as an Oscar Wilde, a Noel Coward, a Tom Stoppard or an Alan Ayckbourn.

Glancing down Bogstadveien I saw a violently orange, fan-shaped cloud occupying the sky at the far end of the road. It seemed to rise up from behind Ekeberg, the hill to the south of Oslo where Edvard Munch had the vision that led him to paint *Scream*. Looking up I saw in the awning lights that snow was falling, the flakes so well-spaced, their descent so slow and sedate, you could have almost counted them as you walked around between them. Looking straight ahead into the street, however, I saw nothing. It was strange, disturbed weather. Time to head home.

But as I bent down and picked up the Clas Ohlson bag with the tarpaulin and the twine, the snappy tones of Miles Davis's *Milestones* came tripping out of the café's street-speakers and I put the bag down again to listen. Just then the Baker Hansen delivery van pulled into the delivery bay outside the wool shop next door to the café. I watched the driver jump out and walk round to the kerbside of the van, open a metal flap on the side and pull a lever that released the lock on the back doors. He opened the doors wide, pulled out a little metal ramp, walked past me and placed it up against the step in the shop doorway. Then he walked back to the van, unhooked a remote control on a coiled cable and pressed a button on it. He watched intently as the tailgate slowly slid down to ground level, stepped onto it, hoisted himself up and stepped inside the van. At once he set about releasing the Acrow props that prevented the towers of food cages from rolling around the floor of the van, wheeling one tower out of the way so that he could get at another, shunting them about with an inspired and practised efficiency. Next he unhooked a box-cart from the side wall of the van. Slipping its long metal tongue in under one tower, he tilted back on the handles, wheeled the cages to the tailgate and pressed the button on the remote control. The moment the tailgate brushed the ground he trundled the load of pastries, cakes and bread past me, up the ramp and into the shop.

It was a pleasure to watch a man so good at his job and I was tempted to stick around for his second run, and even wait for the conclusion of the whole delivery. I had seen him go through his routine many times before and was always curious about how it would end. I knew that the turning circle of his van would in principle allow him to turn and join traffic heading the other way, up into Bogstadveien. But if the queue of cars at the lights in Slemdalsveien was more than three or four vehicles then his luck was out and he would have to slip into the traffic stream going his way and take the first right into Harald Hårfagres gate. This was a much quieter road with an especially wide turning circle in front of the big wooden doors to the tram museum. A couple of minutes later I would see him heading past on the other side of the road.

But *Milestones* came to end just about then and I knew I had run out of excuses for not starting work. I picked up the Clas Ohlson bag and headed towards Harald Hårfagres gate. Passing the newsagents I glanced at the headlines on the pavement display rack. *Dagbladet* and *VG* both had front pages about the trouble the coalition government was having with the demands of the Christian People's Party for a change in the abortion laws as the price of their support.

I passed under the arched gate that leads into my block. Simen was on the central grass enclosure, playing with Aina, his Yorkshire terrier. He was holding a red, long-handled plastic tennis-ball thrower in his hand. Raising the cup and twirling it a couple of times around his head, he sent the bright yellow ball spinning up into the air. We watched as Aina scampered off round the privet hedge in search of it.

I enjoyed Simen's company. He was about half my age, and in spite of the fact that he had grown up in what seemed to have been some sort of Scandinavian post-family commune – or possibly because of that – he showed a vestigial respect for the elderly. Simen was the only person from whom I would accept man-hugs instead of a handshake. He was free and fluid and unpredictable in his opinions, and confounded most of my ancient prejudices about what an accountant should be like. He was an anarchist, he told me, and from his learned references to Kropotkin and Proudhon I knew he was serious about it. I asked if he had heard of Stuart Christie, the Scottish anarchist who served jail time in Spain for plotting to kill General Franco, and to my great surprise he told me that not only had he heard of Christie but that a friend of his, a fellow anarchist, was writing a book and *that Stuart Christie was giving him editorial advice by email*.

As Aina returned and dropped the tennis ball proudly at his feet, I suggested I go upstairs to my flat and get Alex and that we take our dogs for a walk along Hammerstads gate to Tørteberg. This is a large open green space that occupies the space between Slemdalsveien and the science department buildings of Oslo University. It's where the juniors from Frigg, a lower-tier Oslo football team, train. We could let the dogs run free there in the autumn and winter, when the *båndtvang* (leash-law) was not in force.

We crossed Gydas vei and the passage between the musical academy and the premises of STAMI, and by the time we got to Tørteberg the slight, misty snowfall had turned into drizzle. A gaggle of twelve toddlers in bright orange vests were being shepherded diagonally across the grass towards the nursery school at the far end by three young men. Well away from them, a middle-aged man was standing beside a pole fixed in the ground. It had what looked like a bag or basket mounted on top of it. At the man's feet lay a pile of brightly coloured plastic discs, and he was mechanically bending down, picking the discs up and throwing them as far as he could across the field, where another, similar pole had been planted. Once he was through the pile he trudged over to the other side, gathered the discs up, and started throwing them back in the direction of the first pole.

I'd seen him doing this before and stopped to talk to him about it. He told me he was practising Frisbee golf. It was a sport I had never heard of before. The 'golf' part of it involved getting the Frisbees into the container on the top of the pole. In fluent but heavily accented Norwegian he told me he was originally from Spain, and that he had been responsible for bringing the sport to Norway. Quite naturally, he had also been captain of Norway's first national Frisbee golf team and was now the manager.

For about fifteen minutes Simen and I chatted and watched as Aina and Alex chased around after each other, and after these brightly coloured Frisbees. We spoke of cabins. He and his Swedish wife, Helene, had recently taken possession of a cabin in the Romsdal valley. Helene had just passed her driving test at the third time of asking, he told me. It was good news. Travelling would be a whole lot easier now for them and their three young children, August, Juni and Oda. Simen himself didn't hold a driving licence, and had no interest in getting one. His phone pinged and he took it out and read the text message. I'd noticed before that he didn't use a smartphone but one of those old-fashioned flip-open phones. He texted a reply, called Aina to heel and said it was time for him to get back to work. His mother had a flat nearby in Hammerstads gate and he had the use of a room there as his office.

On the walk back I asked him about his record – was it out yet? He'd made a CD of songs for children, which he'd written himself and recorded in a studio on St Hanshaugen, accompanying himself on guitar with a few musician friends helping him out. He'd once been in a punk band. He told me they'd even played a gig up in Veggli, at Veggli *vertshus*, the little wayside *kro* opposite the petrol station, just before you turn off to drive up to our place. People tell me that if you flipped Norway over a hundred and eighty degrees on the map it would reach all the way down to Rome, but when Simen told me that his band had played at Veggli I thought, for about the thousandth time, what a wonderfully small country this really is.

No, he said, the record still wasn't finished. He never seemed to have the time...

Back home, after the obligatory five minutes of ferocious play with the dog, kicking a special bite-proof, cloth-coated balloon I had bought from the local pet shop around the flat, I stopped, totally exhausted. Alex muttered a few mysterious schnauzerian oaths, then stepped inside the round grey dog's bed at the end of the sofa, lay down and immediately fell asleep.

I stood panting, hands on hips, looking out the window and

waiting to get my breath back. Above the white stone turrets of the tram museum on the other side of the road I could just see the station forecourt in Majorstuen. Willy the Jesus Singer, briefly neither singing nor raising his arms to the sky in praise of God, the guitar hanging loose around his neck, wearing as always the same frayed, pale blue denim cap, was talking to the *Klassekampen* vendor. The mood looked warm and friendly. Both men laughed frequently. Both wore faded red anoraks. From that distance it was hard to be sure, but it seemed to me, as they parted company, that they handed each other a gift. Willy gave Klassekampen a Bible tract, and Klassekampen gave Willy a free copy of the newspaper. I knew that Willy would now return to the kitchen of his little flat nearby to prepare *matpakker* ('packets of sandwiches') with the help of his wife, Randi. He'd pack them up on his blue Jesus trolley and then wheel it down to the lower end of Karl Johans gate and the area around Oslo central station to hand them out to the rough sleepers and junkies who sit or lie on the pavement behind handwritten notices asking for help. Turning from the window I wandered into the kitchen to put the kettle on and thought how that simple scene, had you witnessed it, might have explained a great many things about Norwegian society that had been puzzling you.

# 11

## 12 October 2018

We arrange for a terrace to be built – architecture of a

mountain cabin – Kåre the carpenter – on the Norwegian

*lusekofte* ('louse jacket') – the NOKAS robbery – puzzling

Americanisms in British English – Norwegian fans of English

football – the plan to hang the cupboard on the wall – on the

English *lakselords* ('salmon lords') – history of Anglophilia

in Norway – clearing a salmon river – the Fjordmog Club

– nostalgia – in the footsteps of the *lakselords* – a musical

entertainment – on Lady Arbuthnott – Knut Hamsun, an

Anglophobic Norwegian – hanging the cupboard on the wall

The news that the plot next to ours had now been sold reminded us that it was time to get moving with our plan to extend the terrace around the cabin and have the cabin property fenced before the winter arrived. Privacy was one reason, but sheep had always been our main concern. The local farmers' rights to graze sheep on the mountainside during the summer months remained unaffected by the decision to develop the land for cabins. It meant that almost from the moment you passed through the barrier halfway up the mountain you had to keep a sharp lookout to avoid sheep resting or sleeping in the middle of the road. Arriving at your cabin in the summer and autumn, you would often find sheep relaxing on your wooden terrace. Their droppings and urine penetrated the wood and once the smell was established it was impossible to get rid of it. Weeks could pass between visits to the cabin so finding a way of dealing with this was one of the first problems cabin-owners had to deal with.

The terrace of the Fjellstul 2 ran along the front of the house and extended outwards for about a metre and a half, just beyond the three pillars that link the house to the traditional architecture of the region. The most popular alternative design is the so-called Numedal cabin. There's nothing particularly cabin-like about it. It's about the same size as the Fjellstul model but it looks more like what it is, a second home that happens to be in the mountains, without any attempt to suggest a link with the regional past. The Numedal design doesn't use the heavy timber of the Fjellstul cabin.

It's all wood-panelling and a rough-edged planking called *vildmarkspanel*.

There are a lot of improvisational possibilities within the two basic designs – a storage extension can be incorporated into the main body of the cabin itself; changes can be made to the height of the windows; there is an option for extra windows that most people take up in order to maximise the wonderful views – but you soon notice that the styles tend to occur in similar groups, creating Numedal and Fjellstul neighbourhoods. It's as though as buyers we have unconsciously been attracted to the visual symmetry this creates.

Both designs featured the same short, aproned terrace at the front and both faced the same problem with sheep. For most of the summer we had dealt with it by fastening twine in parallel strips between the pillars and anchoring it to hooks at the sides of the cabin each time we left. It was effective enough, but it didn't look good, and it was a fiddly job taking this improvised fence down when we came back. The small wooden platform-steps outside the main entrance and in front of the shed were easier to protect from the sheep by simply placing seven or eight medium-sized rocks spaced across them. But that wasn't a long-term solution either.

Our plan was to extend the existing terrace to something like three times its original size, and surround it with a stepped fence, high at the front, where it would obscure the view of the neighbours' parked cars, and lower along the valley side so that the view would remain unobstructed. Enjoying this view one morning with a cup of coffee I noticed something that had escaped my attention previously, that from the rear corner of the cabin there was a superb view of an otherwise hidden pyramid-like peak holding up the sky at a point just east of the pine knoll. It was not especially high, and to this day I don't know if it even has a name, but the mere sight of it was pleasurable, and the prospect of being able to look at it while eating breakfast on a sunny summer morning irresistible. As soon as I pointed this out to Nina, she agreed that the terrace should extend all the way down to the end of the cabin on the valley side.

We decided to get started straight away. Nina posted a message on the community Facebook page that evening asking if anyone could recommend a good carpenter in the area. Kåre's wife posted a reply the same day saying she couldn't recommend her husband highly enough. She added a link to his website. We followed it, read the few testimonials it contained and decided that this was our man. I gave him a call and he said he would drive up in the morning to take a look at the job.

About three in the afternoon the next day Kåre's maroon Subaru pickup turned up the lane and headed towards the cabin. I stepped outside to greet him. He was a tall, white-haired man who looked to be in his late fifties.

The afternoon was bright and cold, and before showing Kåre the job we had in mind I went back inside and shrugged on a *lusekofte* ('louse jacket') for warmth. This is a traditional knitted woollen cardigan, usually in black, with a pattern of small white markings across it that supposedly resemble the lice that give it its name. Originally a garment worn by people in rural districts, the *lusekofte* retains a central status in Norwegian public life. It is often worn by politicians

anxious to stress their commitment to social democracy, the country's rural heritage, and their own absolute normality.

Wearing a *lusekofte* is a common ploy too among men who wouldn't normally be seen dead in one until they find themselves in court charged with a crime of violence. David Toska was one example. Toska was adjudged to be the mastermind behind the theft of fifty-seven million kroner from the cash-handling centre of the security company NOKAS, in Stavanger, in 2004. It was the largest robbery in Norwegian history. Fifteen years on, more than fifty million kroner of the stolen money are still unaccounted for. The theft of Edvard Munch's *Scream* and *Madonna* from the Munch museum in Tøyen a few months later was almost certainly an attempt, planned by Toska, to divert police resources from the investigation into the NOKAS robbery. The *lusekofte* ploy didn't work and Toska was found guilty and sentenced to eighteen years in jail, which perhaps indicates he wasn't such a mastermind after all.

Partly as a result of this and similar attempts to use the *lusekofte* to make psychological capital out of the ever-present nationalism in Norwegian public life, a sort of irony has attached itself to the wearing of it, in the cities at least. For foreigners like me, however, the sheer exoticism and romance of the *lusekofte* remains untarnished. It does up at the front with round metal buttons – or sometimes elaborate silver clasps – that fasten all the way up to the neck. The basic shape reminded me of the jackets the Beatles wore in the days of their breakthrough in the early 1960s. These so-called 'Beatle jackets' also had round necks and round metal buttons with some kind of device stamped onto them. They were usually made of black, pinstriped corduroy. The Beatles abandoned the jackets after they became hippies, but I remember reading once that the fashion had lasted long enough to rescue the British corduroy industry from the oblivion into which it had sunk in the 1950s.

To possibly slightly surreal effect, I topped off the *lusekofte* with a black woollen Blackpool FC beanie, which I still wore occasionally as a connection to my northern roots and the club I had followed, through all its declining fortunes, since 1959. I then walked Kåre round the cabin, pointing out the various points at which the fencing would change heights. I also suggested a matched pair of wooden gates that would be attached to the wall on either side of the front door. They could be left open while we were there, and during our absence they could be swung across to prevent sheep getting round to the back of the cabin.

Within about ten minutes Kåre had, I think, worked out how he would do these two jobs, how long it would take him, and what price to ask. I was getting ready to bring up these matters when he suddenly gestured towards my hat:

'I've been to Blackpool,' he said. 'I saw Liverpool play there. Blackpool beat us.'

Given the gap in status between the two clubs – Liverpool challenging for the title in the Premier League, Blackpool floundering away as usual in the lower reaches of Football League One – I assumed he meant Blackburn Rovers. It's a mistake commonly made by Norwegian football fans who follow the English game in the winter, when their own season is over for the year. There was a golden age of Norwegian football in the 1990s when the national team qualified for two World Cup finals in succession under Egil 'Drillo' Olsen and had upwards of twenty players holding down regular places with English Premier League clubs. Clubs like Blackburn Rovers, who signed Norwegian players such as Henning

Berg, Stig Inge Bjørnebye, Lars Bohinen and Egil Østenstad during this period, naturally attracted a lot of support from Norwegians.

He pulled a soft, cellophane-wrapped packet of Tiedemanns Rød Nr. 3 out of the chest pocket of his blue boiler suit, teased up a cloud of dark brown weed, flicked a paper up from a packet of Big Ben and slowly began to roll himself a cigarette.

'It was a few years back. About ten years ago,' he said.

Then I realised that perhaps he hadn't been mistaken after all. In the 2010–11 season, Blackpool had indeed spent a single season in the heady heights of the Premier League. The manager was Ian Holloway, an eccentric, straight-talking man with a strong West Country burr and a shaven head. On the first day of the season we had beaten Wigan four–nil away from home, and for about three hours, until Chelsea thrashed someone in the late kick-off, we were top of the Premier League on goal difference. Inevitably, with tiny gates and severely limited financial resources, it was mostly downhill after that and the season ended in relegation. I told Kåre how I'd gone down to Bohemen, a football pub in the centre of the city, to watch the final game, an impossible must-win fixture away from home against Man United.

'Who won?' he asked.

'Who d'you think won?'

We laughed.

'But it went to the wire,' I said. 'We were leading two-one until halfway through the second half. Then they equalised and then Michael bloody Owen scored the winner. I left the pub before the final whistle. Couldn't bear it.'

'He was a great player, Michael Owen,' Kåre said, declining to commiserate with me. 'But he was always a Liverpool player, even when he was playing for Man United. Is that what "went down to the wire" means?' he continued. 'That you have to wait until the end before you know what happens?'

'Yes.'

'What is "the wire"?'

I couldn't help him there. It was an Americanism that had only come into British English after I left the country. Like something being a 'double whammy'. Or an event not being over 'until the fat lady sings'. From the contexts I knew how to use these phrases, but I had no idea of their origins.

'There's a tower there,' he said, returning to memories of his visit to Blackpool. He raised his hand a few inches into the air, palm downwards, to indicate height. Blue smoke drifted around his fingers. 'Like the Eiffel tower. We're all Liverpool fans here,' he added. 'There's a group of eight of us. We watch all the games on TV. A couple of times a year, for big games, we go over.'

'What about the Champions League? Did you get over for that?'

Liverpool had been beaten three–one in the final by Real Madrid earlier in the summer.

Kåre made a sour face: 'We don't talk about that game,' he said. 'Ramos should've been sent off for what he did to Mo Salah. And our goalkeeper was a joke.'

We carried on like this for some time. Norwegian football fans tend mainly to support big city Premier League clubs such as Manchester United, Everton, Arsenal, although I did once meet a doctor who supported the Scottish minnows Stenhousemuir, solely because he believed – erroneously, as it turns out – that the name was straight Norwegian for 'stonehouse wall' (*stenhus mur*).* So my contribution to such discussions would

---

* The place-name Stenhousemuir is in fact Old English in origin: *stan* (stone) + *hus* (house) + moor.

often take the form of a sort of corrective lecture about how my Blackpool had for many years been a top-flight English team. It was the team of Stanley Matthews, the 'wizard of the dribble' and the man who 'taught us how football should be played', according to the great Brazilian star Pele. I would relate how Matthews' Blackpool had won the greatest of all FA Cup Finals at Wembley, against Bolton Wanderers back in 1953, coming back from three–one down with fifteen minutes of the game remaining to triumph four–three. And, as a kind of clincher, I might conclude by saying that an England team at one time featured no fewer than four Blackpool players in its starting line-up. I didn't add that the game in question was against Hungary, at Wembley in 1953, and that England lost six–three, the first time they had ever been beaten at home.

With a last deep drag on his cigarette Kåre extinguished it, squeezing the tip between his fingers and dropping the butt into his breast pocket. We shook hands and he said he'd be in touch soon. Then he climbed into his Subaru, waved and reversed away down the track.

Nina was on the sofa, knitting. The dog was stretched out and dozing beside her.

'Well, he seems like a nice man, Kåre,' I said. 'But I noticed he didn't take a single note or measurement. I suppose he's been doing that type of thing so long he can work it all out in his mind's eye.'

'I sent him an email with the measurements,' Nina said without looking up from her knitting.

'Last night?'

'Yes.'

'Including the different heights for the fence?'

'Yes. Everything.'

'How did you know them?'

Now she looked up. 'Because I measured them.'

'Last night?'

'Yes.'

'What was I doing?'

'I don't know. Listening to music. Reading.'

'And you're sure he got the email?'

'People always get emails.'

'Oh. Well, that's alright then. Did he say when he was going to start?'

'On Monday.'

'And how long will it take?'

'About ten days. He works with his brother.'

'Brilliant.'

I turned and headed back onto the terrace and stood looking up for a few moments. The sky was a darker, colder blue. Looking hard, you could just see the first silver stars. As it had done so many times before, my wife's casual efficiency astounded me. Suddenly I felt an urgent and compelling need to do something necessary and important.

But *what*, exactly?

Then I had it. Ever since we had bought that beautiful old Numedal patterned rose-painted cupboard it had been standing

on the table in the corner of the living room. It had small brackets mounted one on each side at the back, but it was heavy and would need two strong screws to mount it. Nina, with her deep faith in the expertise of anyone who works in a hardware

shop, had come home one evening last week, after a long and detailed conversation with the man in the Jernia store at Røa, and handed me a small clear plastic pouch containing exactly two screws. They were long and black, and instead of the conventional flat or Phillips head they had a peculiar, counter-sunk shape, which I had never seen before and which I knew nothing in my toolbox would fit. Privately I thought that she may well have overcomplicated things in describing the job to the assistant. Out in the shed there was a jug of assorted screws, nails, and mysterious pieces of metal that I had accumulated over the years. There was bound to be something I could use among them.

Entering the shed, I switched on the light and located the screw jug on the top of the Ivar shelving system I had assembled along one wall. It was cream and had the words *Poubelle de table* written around its belly in an elegant, ornate script. Four round timber offcuts had been left behind when the builders departed. They were about thirty-five centimetres high and made great stools and occasional coffee tables. We kept them in the shed and I rolled one of these forward, sat down on it, spread out an old copy of *Aftenposten* on the concrete floor in front of me and emptied the contents of the jug onto it. The sheer variety of all that came tumbling out detained me for a few moments as I picked through some of the stranger and more mysterious objects and wondered once again what on earth they were for, and why I would never dream of throwing them away.

I then settled to the monotonous task of sifting through the contents in search of matching, ready-rusted screws suitable for hanging our rose-painted cupboard on the cabin wall. As I did so I began thinking about Kåre and his love of Liverpool football club, and how symptomatic that was of the Anglophilia that is characteristic of so many Norwegians. Its roots are firmly in the nineteenth century, and in the British discovery of what the Yorkshire mountaineering pioneer W. C. Slingsby called 'the Northern playground'. Slingsby and his fellow British mountaineering enthusiasts gave Norwegians a new way of looking at their own country. The need for local guides meant that, from the start, the British visitors met and mingled with the rural farmers, reindeer hunters, herdsmen and *budeie* (milkmaids and herdswomen) and developed an intimate and respectful familiarity with the way of life in the remote Norwegian countryside. Wealth and education dictated the terms of the professional relationship, but Norway had abolished its native aristocracy as long ago as 1821, and most of the written testimonies to the nature of the relationship stress the natural and straightforward way Norwegians treated their wealthy visitors.

Of perhaps even greater significance in the creation of this mutual tribal admiration, asymmetrical as it may have been in terms of money and possibilities, was the enduring influence of another group of nineteenth-century summer visitors from the British Isles whom Norwegians call the *lakselords* (salmon lords). In fact, few of the *lakselords* were aristocrats. Like William Slingsby and the mountaineers, they were from wealthy middle-class industrial families. They included Welsh and Irish, as well as English, but a great many of them were Scottish. Nineteenth-century Norwegians rarely made the distinction. All Britons of the imperial era were 'Englishmen' to them.

Unlike the climbers, these *lakselords* would spend months in Norway. They built homes in the English style that seemed both palatial and impractical to the locals, as well as fishing and hunting lodges along the banks of Norwegian rivers like the Driva and Suldalslågen in Ryfylke, in the west of the country. A dynasty of *lakselords* built and fished as far north as the Vefsna river in Nordland, just twenty-eight kilometres south of the Arctic Circle.

The influence of these British visitors was considered benign. Families like the Archers, the Campbells and the Hunters brought money and jobs and the outside world to some of the poorest and most remote parts of Norway. They provided employment for dozens of people, from the carpenters who built their houses and lodges to the chambermaids, serving maids, cooks, gardeners, boatmen, pilots and gaffers who served them once they were in residence. When the summer was over many of the Norwegian staff would be invited to England with their employers, where they could extend their knowl-edge of the world as well as their ability to *spikka English*.

Walter Archer was a forerunner of the conservation move-ment. An assistant secretary at the Board of Agriculture and Fisheries who went on to become chief inspector of salmon fisheries in Scotland, Archer rented the whole of the Suldals-lågen for a period of forty years. Over a hundred and fifty owners had to be individually persuaded of the benefits of entering into the contract, and Archer made his case at meet-ings in schoolhouses up and down the valley, stressing the financial impact the British presence would have on the region. The rights thus obtained in 1884 also included all the salmon spawning grounds and the tributaries leading to them.

Once the deal was settled he arranged to have the river cleared of the debris of centuries. This was mostly in the form of old *garn* (gillnets anchored at the bottom of the river and floating on the surface like tennis nets) that had clogged the waters and made them impassable for the fish. Under Archer's stewardship, for the first time in at least a hundred years the salmon enjoyed the freedom of Sandsfjord and the whole ninety kilometres of river. He also started a hatchery, built salmon traps and carried out the marking of about seven hundred and fifty salmon as part of a scientific study of their travels.

The only hazard the salmon faced was from the rods of the fly-fishers. Slingsby paid for the privilege of using Norway's beautiful mountains by introducing climbing as a sport to the Norwegians. In like fashion, Archer and his fellow *lakselords* repaid the loan to them of some of the country's rivers by introducing the natives to fly-fishing; as a sport and as a method of catching fish it was unknown before their arrival. No doubt it seemed to a man like Archer that he was spending his summers in paradise, but his connections with the larger world and its problems pursued him even here. With tensions between the British and the Germans mounting, in 1912 it seems that he and his son were recruited as British agents and given the code names 'Sage' and 'Sagette', with a brief to report on German naval movements around the coast of Norway.

Even while living in Norway, these *lakselords* observed the strict formal customs that governed life back home. Archer, for example, insisted that guests dressed for dinner. As I slowly and methodically sorted the contents on the spread newspaper before me into two piles, which I mentally labelled 'screws' and 'miscellaneous', I reflected that, even today, Norwegian Anglophilia shares this characteristic with the American version of it, that it is based on a type of Britishness that disappeared after the end of the Second World War and the dismantling of the British Empire.

Many Norwegians still indulge this harmless nostalgia. They include my wife, and on days when I find myself wondering why on earth she married me, the mere fact of my Englishness sometimes seems the only possible explanation. Something similar is probably true of me too; that in my boundless love for all things Norwegian, her very nationality was a crucial part of the intense initial attraction I felt for her, overtaken as it soon was by any number of much more profound feelings.

Not long after coming to Norway, marrying and realising there was a strong likelihood I would remain here for the rest of my days, I went through a period in which I listened to little else but the English music of composers such as Ralph Vaughan Williams, Patrick Hadley, Herbert Howells, Gerald Finzi and Frank Bridge, gazing with a kind of rapt sadness at the covers of LPs that depicted, almost without exception, views of the verdant English countryside, with the occasional picturesque ruin in the distance.

But there was always a double edge to this luxuriant wallowing in nostalgia. Putting on a treasured recording such as Peter Dawson's singing of Vaughan Williams's setting of D. G. Rossetti's 'Silent Noon', from 1922, I might find my pleasure rudely sabotaged by an involuntary vision of the singer, standing with his hand resting on the lid of a grand piano in an empty room in an empty mansion. He's wearing a lovat green three-piece tweed suit and brogues. There is a bristly, sandy-coloured moustache on his upper lip. A starched collar with a bow tie encircles his neck. It's so tight it makes his eyes bulge. When I look closely I can see beads of perspiration glistening on his forehead. Suddenly I realise the strain of the performance is almost killing him and I cannot listen any more. I turn the music off.

This sense of ambiguity towards a nostalgia for a time before I was born has never quite left me. I feel it most keenly when my wife and I join the annual autumn outings of *Fjordmog*, a club for Norwegian owners of Morgan motor cars. These outings are always referred to as the *trebilfestival* ('wooden car festival'), a humorously ironic reference both to the famous *trebåtfestival* ('wooden boat festival') held annually in Risør on the south coast and to the fact that the frame of a Morgan is made of ash.

My wife bought the car with her share of the sale of the summer cabin at Nøtterøy. Not long afterwards her brother bought the mountain cabin in Numedal, but for the past ten years the open car has been our 'cabin-on-wheels'. And being in a club and going on outings turned out to be great fun. The *trebilfestival* each year usually has a historical or geographical theme, such as 'Follow the Vikings' or 'The Silver Mines of Kongsberg'. Last year it was '*I lakselordenes fotspor*' ('In the footsteps of the salmon lords').

The goal of the trip was Oppdal, up in Trøndelag county. It's nearly four hundred kilometres from Oslo and a long day's drive even in the comfort of a saloon car with a heater. About half of us took the option to break the journey and stay overnight in the village of Skåbu, at the head of the Espedalen valley. Nina and I had spent a couple of hours there about four years ago, when we first started looking for somewhere in the mountains to have a cabin. We spent an afternoon driving round and looking at various sites with the builder, but in the end decided that the distance from Oslo was too great.

The highlight of the overnight stay was a concert in the village hall given by three young students studying folk music at Vinstra secondary school. All three wore *bunad* (Norwegian national costume) for the occasion. A young woman got things under way, playing two *stev* (a kind of Norwegian folk-dance tune) on the *hardingfele*. She was followed by a lad who played a medley of folk tunes on the mouth harp. Unable to speak while playing, he told us once he was finished that he could dance too.

And he certainly could. The climax of the mini-concert brought all three students together. A young maestro entered the stage carrying a *hardingfele* and a wooden chair and sat on the small stage. The woman who had opened the concert entered with a second wooden chair. She put it down on the floor in front of the stage and climbed up onto the seat. She was carrying a pole about two metres long. She took a soft grey felt hat from her pocket, hung it over the end of the pole and then held it out horizontally in front of her. The youth who played the mouth harp now entered the hall and began pacing around the open space in front of the girl on the chair as the fiddle player played. The music quickened, the boy's pace quickened. He danced and spun round, his eyes flicking ever more frequently up to the hat on the end of the pole. The fiddle player was playing 'Fanitullen' ('The Devil's Tune'), a wild and brilliant virtuoso number said to have been learned from the playing of the devil himself. Inspired by the music the dancer sped up, running and spinning, dropping low to the ground then up again, eyeing the hat with nervous, flashing glances. Abruptly he left the ground in a wheeling, acrobatic backward leap. His upper leg shot out and he kicked the hat high and spinning into the air. It was a feat of astonishing agility and our small audience burst into rapturous applause. The three young performers joined hands and bowed deeply before running out through the door. As the applause died away and we all stood up to leave, smiling and commenting on the performance in appreciative delight, I found myself wishing, not for the first time, that I was Norwegian, that I'd been born here and spent all my life here, and this was my culture, my world.

The main part of the outing was the two days spent at Oppdal, and all forty-one cars assembled there the next day,

gathering at a beautiful old timber hotel with a *levende tak* a few kilometres outside the town. The main building stood on top of a grassy rise set back from the road, with a dozen or so free-standing *stabbur* refurbished and adapted for use as en suite hotel bedrooms behind and beside it. The dining room and bar were in a large converted barn at the bottom of the slope. Entry to the bar was up a *låvebro*, a grass-surfaced barn bridge made of earth. In the old days hay and feed was stored up here on the upper floor, with the livestock kept down below, where the restaurant now was.

As things turned out we followed in the footsteps of only one *lakselord*. This was an Englishman named Edward Ethelbert Lort-Phillips, who came to the region for the first time in 1886 to fish for salmon in the Driva, in Nordmøre. In short order he built five or six houses and fishing and hunting lodges, establishing a connection with the area he continued to visit regularly until 1937.

One of these hunting lodges was at Vangshaugen. We drove there, parked our cars and made our way on foot to a villa built in a neo-colonial style, where we were invited upstairs to listen to a short presentation of the whole 'English connection' in the region. Everything in the house had been kept as close as possible to its original state, which meant no electricity. It was a bitterly cold morning and we were glad of the log fire roaring away in one corner of the room where we sat, most of us in sheepskin-lined leather flying jackets, most of us with the large collars turned up, cradling very welcome paper cups of coffee between our icy palms. Our guide was clearly a very knowledgeable lady, but I found I was becoming increasingly confused by the whole conception of the English *lakselord*. Lort-Phillips wasn't an aristocrat, but until I saw the name written down I had thought – as I imagine most of the rest of our group did – that she was referring throughout the presentation to a certain 'Lord Phillips': 'Lord Phillips' wife, Louisa, designed the house herself in a neo-colonial Swiss style...', 'Lord Phillips was also a noted ornithologist...' and so on. The situation was made more confusing by the fact that, in Norwegian, the word *lort* means 'shit'. It's not an infantile word, but even so I could not help but be impressed that not a single member of the party made any reference to this, once the penny dropped that it was a name and not a title.

After about forty minutes we returned to the cars and were on our way again, further down the valley to Sunndalen and a house called Elverhøj. Under the direction of our guide, Tommy Fossum, a heavily bearded man wearing a kilt and full Highland outfit, we parked our Morgans nose-outwards in a line alongside a leafy, streamside car park, and then traipsed off behind him and into a field, where we stopped and grouped and waited for the stragglers to arrive. Tommy then gave us a succinct account of the history of the house. We were off-season and Elverhøj itself was closed for repairs, although the roof was just visible over the hedge we had stopped beside.

Elverhøj's most famous owner was Barbara Arbuthnott, and from everything we were to see and hear that morning it was clear that it was *her* life, and *her* fate, that lay at the heart of the region's tourist activities, and were of the greatest interest to Norwegians. Born in Ireland in 1822 to a Scottish officer, she was married three times, widowed twice and divorced once. She and her third husband, a Scottish aristocrat named William Arbuthnott, had come to Sunndalen for the first time in 1866 to fish the salmon rivers and hunt bear and deer. They came again in 1867 and 1868, accompanied by James, the epileptic son of her first marriage. Barbara had fallen in love with the region and in 1868 she arranged to have a permanent home built.

Elverhøj was ready the following year. But the marriage was failing, and when James died in 1868 at the age of twenty-one, following a fit at Fokstua in Oppland, she blamed her husband, William, the boy's stepfather. William returned to Scotland, able to live in the style to which he had become

accustomed thanks to an annual sum from Barbara. It seems that in his absence Lady Arbuthnott began an intimate relationship with Oluf Endresen, the man who had been their guide on their first trips to the region, and whom she now employed as her estate manager. She indulged her interest in horses, bred poultry and wrote books about the art that were highly regarded among British experts. She mastered Norwegian well enough to translate the novelist Jonas Lie, now largely forgotten outside his native country but in his day one of *de fire store* ('the four greats') of contemporary Norwegian literature, the three others being Henrik Ibsen, Bjørnstjerne Bjørnson and Alexander Kielland.

Rumours of her affair with Endresen reached Scotland and caused a scandal there that led to her being ostracised from her husband's circles. She may have hoped the rumours and disgrace would be sufficient to persuade William Arbuthnott to grant her a divorce. Instead he made his way out to Norway again, armed and determined to avenge his honour, but apparently too drunk to pursue the plan in meaningful detail.

Once he had returned home Lady Arbuthnott came out of hiding and resumed her life, now as a permanent resident of Norway. When Endresen died in 1879 she appointed a young local schoolteacher named Lars Hoås to succeed him as her business manager. Hoås's sweetheart, a local beauty named Karen Lønset, was taken on as her maid. A close relationship developed between these three and they would spend the winters on the French Riviera at Lady Arbuthnott's expense. These appear to have been the only occasions on which Lars made use of a baronial title Lady Arbuthnott had bought for him, presumably to dissuade the curious from looking too closely at their unorthodox ménage.

In 1885 a series of financial reversals and the collapse of the banking concern on her mother's side of the family obliged Lady Arbuthnott to begin selling off her assets. After a last auction in 1892 she moved into Lars Hoås's modest little home. Karen Lønset moved in with them. In 1897 the unusual trinity took up residence in Einabu, a house partially financed by Sunndalen locals, grateful for all she had done for them over the years. She died there of a stroke on 28 August 1904 and was buried beside her son in Løken cemetery.

All of this we club members heard from Tommy Fossum as we stood in the long grass beside that hedge, blinking in the faint and chilly autumn sunshine outside Elverhøj. Afterwards we strolled on into the overgrown but still recognisably exotic arboretum Lady Arbuthnott had designed behind the house and listened as Tommy told us the story behind this particular Victorian enterprise.

At this point my attention began to wander slightly. Bordering the field outside Elverhøj a long and rather featureless ridge cast its dark shadow almost as far as the house, and I wondered idly why Lady Arbuthnott had chosen for her home a site so poorly favoured by the sun. I looked around at my group, all of us politely paying attention to these tales from the life of a remote and long-dead woman. We were almost exclusively couples. Most of us were around sixty. Many were retired from working life, many were still hard at work. Quite a number were self-employed. The blonde woman there in the leather jacket is a former ambassador. The tall man in the woollen earmuffs is her husband. The man in the red trousers and mustard yellow jacket is Petter Ellefson. I think he runs a security firm. A naturally hilarious man, even when hungover. That big man over there, so huge that I once made a point of watching to see just how he managed to spoon himself down into the tiny space between the bucket-seat and the wooden steering wheel of his Morgan, is a waver-on of cars on the Kiel ferry. In this regard the club is very Norwegian, very socially democratic. Snobbishness of any kind is frowned on, whether in regard to your job, or how powerful the motor of your Morgan is. That man there is one of the few who comes on every outing and is always alone. He's a car salesman and an amateur poet. Someone surprised me once by telling me he was married. The big blonde woman there is Karen. She manages a rock club. Morgan Freeman is her idea of the perfect man. We must be finished, everyone's heading back towards the car park.

Tommy leads us past the cars and over a little bridge across the stream to the local museum. It seems to be heavily dependent for its exhibits on the British presence in these parts in the nineteenth century. I take the chance to sidle up beside him and ask about the kilt. A guide wearing a full Highland outfit was probably the last thing I had expected to see on our visit to Elverhøj, but the mention of Lady Arbuthnott's Scottish roots solved the mystery.

'What tartan is that kilt you're wearing, Tommy?'

He glanced down at the kilt as though he hadn't quite realised he was wearing one.

'*Jeg vet ikke*,' he said. I don't know. 'I saw it in a shop window in Edinburgh and I liked the look of it so I bought it.'

I pointed to the scarf I was wearing and told him my name and that this was a clan scarf. He made the usual joke, asking if I was related to Sir Alex. I gave my usual response, that Sir Alex was my uncle.

We had reached the small

museum. Tommy stood on the steps and after briefly telling us what to look out for in the three or four small rooms, he let us loose. High tea would be served in half an hour in the main building on the other side of the museum compound.

Tommy was what Norwegians call an *ildsjel*. The word means 'a passionate spirit', with the passion usually concentrated on some quite specific goal or issue. In the cultural life of small or remote villages and communities it is these *ildsjel* who keep things going and make things happen. Tommy turned out to be not only the museum guide, he had also written a book about the British *lakselords* in the region, and was the moving spirit behind the creation of a musical based on the life of Lady Arbuthnott. Since its premiere in 1996, more than seventy-five thousand Norwegians have seen performances in Sunndal's *kulturhus* of *Lady Arbuthnott – frua på Elverhøj* ('Lady Arbuthnott – the Lady of Elverhøj').

After our wander through some of the occasionally quite bizarre Victoriana left behind by her ladyship, including an

uncomfortable-looking chair made from the horns of several water buffalo, we all made our way over to the *kulturhus*, where the three long tables that took up almost the entire room were just enough to seat us, for what was formally announced as 'high tea'.

We collected our plates and cups and saucers from a table laid by the window and returned to our seats. Tommy rose from his chair at the centre of the table in the middle, tapped a glass tumbler with the blade of his knife as a signal for the chattering to die down, and announced a brief account of the history of 'high tea'. First of all: did any of us know why it was called 'high tea'?

He looked around. Seventy-five faces looked back at him. Gradually, several of them swivelled towards me: Robert, you're English, surely you can tell him why it's called 'high tea'? Eyebrows lifted. Encouraging nods. Tell us. Let's hear it from the horse's mouth... How I wished then I could have got to my feet, pushed the chair in, and resting my hands on the back of it given an authoritative and entertaining half-hour talk on just *exactly* what high tea is, and exactly *why* it's called high tea.

Naturally, I hadn't the faintest idea what it was or why it was called that, and I was mightily relieved when Tommy went on to answer his own question.

The 'high' element, he said, referred to the fact that at 'high tea' the tea is drunk sitting up at a table, and so in some way drunk 'on high'. 'Afternoon tea' by contrast, is taken sitting down. I found the explanation a little disappointing, and in the privacy of my own mind couldn't help wondering if it had come straight off the internet.

I had failed to pass the test of a true Englishman. I had let the side down. But no one seemed to mind, and soon we were getting stuck into our tea and scones and jam and cream, pausing now and then to applaud songs by performers from the year's production of *Frua på Elverhøj*. They were expertly accompanied by a man on the electric piano. It was a magical and unusually dreamlike afternoon.

Back at the Bjerkeløkkja hotel we had two hours to relax and change before the evening meal. It was still a pleasant day, windy and with bright sunshine. My wife joined a number of other drivers who had decided to give their cars a wash after the exertions of the day. We had driven more than two hundred kilometres, often along rutted, one-lane tracks, up and down steeply descending and tortuously twisting gulches, passing through scenery of such wild beauty it would be fruitless to attempt to describe it.

I made my way up the *låvebro* to the bar to buy a local craft beer. It came in a half-litre bottle and cost the local equivalent of fifteen pounds, a price that seemed high even to Norwegians. With elaborate care I carried it down the *låvebro* and walked back up the grassy slope. I sat down at one of the wooden tables set out at the top that gave a fabulously uncluttered view of Snøhetta, the highest mountain in Dovrefjell range.

After a few moments, during which I was bothered by a drowsy wasp that seemed to like the taste of the craft beer rather more than I did, someone sat down beside me. I looked up and registered with pleasure that it was Hjalmar Lid. At the biannual gatherings of the whole Fjordmog club I had grown used to the fact that conversation in general would be light and bantering, and that when it wasn't it would be about the cars. The Fjordmog is a man's thing. I was probably unique in that club in being the only man who had joined to please his wife. Nina and I would share the driving when we were out, but for most club members it was a case of the wife comes along, and the husband drives. As anything more than a means of transport, cars have never been of much interest to me. The only exception to this indifference I can recall was my dazed admiration for the Citroen DS19, once described by Roland Barthes as looking as if it had 'fallen from the sky'. To admit as much in a club setting, however, would have been what Norwegians call *å banne i kirken*, akin to swearing in church. Hjalmar Lid was the only other man I had spoken to in the club for whom the literature, painting and history of his own country meant as much as his motor car. Certainly he was as avid about his Morgan – a beautiful grey and maroon 4/4S – as any other club member; but he happily wore his other hat for me.

As we sat sipping our champagne-priced beers and keeping a cautious eye on the wasp, occasionally wafting it away, we expressed our pleasure at the day's outing 'in the footsteps of the *lakselords*'. It brought us presently on to the general subject of Anglophilia. I was interested in its possible roots beyond the presence of so many English aristocrats for sporting purposes in nineteenth-century Norway and the general admiration people seem to feel for the citizens of a nation powerful enough to have policed the world. Hjalmar pointed out to me that when Norway was suing for independence from Sweden in 1905 and it appeared that the Swedes might attempt to prevent secession from the union by military force, Britain had anchored a warship off Kristiania (Oslo) harbour as a warning to them not to do so. British support for Norwegian independence was certainly a factor, he said.

I knew that Hjalmar, like so many Norwegians, had a great love for Knut Hamsun's novels, at the same time as he took great exception to Hamsun's political stance in the 1930s and 1940s, when he expressed his admiration for Adolf Hitler and support for the German occupation of Norway. I asked him if he knew that Hamsun, then well over forty years of age, had actually enlisted in Colonel Stang's volunteers in Drøbak to fight the Swedes should it have come to military conflict in 1905.

'Yes. And he praised the British for their support because it made fighting unnecessary,' Hjalmar said, adding, with a smile, 'It was about the only good thing he ever had to say about the British.'

Ever since I first heard of the prejudice, Hamsun's Anglophobia had interested me. I described its manifestations at length in a biography I wrote of him some thirty years ago. The earliest example I had come across was in a travel book called *I Æventyrland* (*In Wonderland*), published in 1903, which contains his account of an episode on a tram in Munich in which an English passenger arrogantly demands his money back when the tram runs over a child and his journey is delayed. Among its most extensive statements was *Et Ord til Os* ('A Word to Us'), an essay published in 1910, in which Hamsun expressed his fears concerning the detrimental effects English tourism was having on the farming communities of rural Norway. He lamented the way that wagons and horses that should have been hard at work on the farms were being instead rented out to transport affluent visitors from one beauty spot to the next. He objected to the way the farmers put themselves at the service of these tourists as drivers and guides, doffing their caps as they opened and closed the farm gates for them. In due course he added examples from history to bolster his dislike. These included the British starvation blockade of Norway during the Napoleonic wars and the bombardment of Copenhagen in 1807; and the British invention of concentration camps during the Boer War. Early recognition of his talent as a writer from the Germans, combined with a lack of interest from British readers, served to deepen the prejudice, and on the outbreak of the Great War he was passionate and open in his hopes of a German victory and a crushing defeat for the British.

The Scot William Archer, who played such a crucial role in introducing the work of Henrik Ibsen to British audiences as his translator, took issue with some of Hamsun's newspaper articles on the subject of the war. Hamsun conceded in response that his was a lone voice: 'I know that ninety-nine per cent of my countrymen support the English,' he wrote. 'But I do not.'

I drank some more of my beer and, instinctively moved to defend a novelist whose books had meant so much to me, remarked to Hjalmar: 'People forget the historical context in which Hamsun developed his dislike of the English. They condemn him for supporting the Nazis when the Second World War came along, but in a way the political system in Germany didn't matter to him. It was Germany itself he was in love with and that meant that in the event of war, any enemy of Germany's was an enemy of Hamsun's.'

'Well, that's the charitable response,' Hjalmar replied. 'I think you would have to call him a Nazi. You just have to separate the books from the man. We Norwegians have been doing it for decades.' He lifted the bottle and took another drink of his craft beer. 'Doesn't his hatred of the English bother you?'

'No,' I replied. 'I can't take it seriously. It's difficult to, when the Norwegians in general are so positive about the English.'

'And do you think it'll last? This Anglophilia?'

'It's fading already,' I answered. 'England used to be special. Now it's just another European country. America is where the power is now. America is the policeman of the world. America is where the cultural focus lies. Norwegians under forty you meet, they don't speak English, they speak American.'

'What's the difference?'

'Well, the accent. King Harald speaks beautiful Oxbridge English. But his kids speak like members of the cast of *Friends*.'

Hjalmar gave me a puzzled look. I said I was talking about that quizzical lilt young Americans add to their speech, which makes everything they say sound like a question.

'The older generation that admires the English for their self-deprecating irony, stiff upper lips and Oxbridge accents, that'll soon die out and it won't be replaced. How could it be, when the original no longer exists? Mind you, you still have outposts of it. Like Fjordmog.'

We raised our glasses and drank a toast to the club.

'I read in *Sliding Pillar* that over seventy per cent of the Morgans made at the factory in Great Malvern go for export,' said Hjalmar.

He lost me for a moment until I recalled that *Sliding Pillar* was the name of the club magazine.

'So I don't think nostalgia for old England will ever go out of fashion,' he went on. 'As a matter of fact, I'm going over later this year.'

He finished off his beer, yawned, and stretched his arms above his head.

'I'm going to the vintage air show at Biggin Hill. Meeting up with six Englishmen. We're staying in a caravan. You want another?'

He stood, held up his empty beer bottle and wiggled it at me. I didn't like the price, or the taste, but I liked the company so I said yes.

I watched Hjalmar as he strolled down the hill and then up the barn bridge and vanished in the shadows of the barn door. As I waited for him to return I glanced over to my left, to where my wife was standing in the sunshine by an outdoor tap on the side wall of the hotel. She was filling a red plastic bucket, holding it by its white handle and staring with great intensity down into the frothing water. It was an extremely pleasant and almost dreamlike sight.

★

I had entered so deeply into these reminiscences that when the faint barking of the dog recalled me to the present I was, for a moment, thoroughly disorientated to find myself sitting on a log in a shed at Veggli, a newspaper spread on the floor at my feet, my gaze focused with hallucinating clarity on two quite ordinary wood-screws. Half-obscured in the central fold of one of the newspaper's pages, they lay some fifteen centimetres apart. For several seconds I sat there, literally scratching my

head as I wondered what on earth my interest in these two screws might be. And then it came to me: they were ideally weathered and the perfect length for attaching the rose-painted Numedal cupboard to the wall of the cabin.

Pocketing the screws, I shuffled the remainder of the nuts, bolts and other assorted items into the central fold of the paper, lifted it up by its two wings and poured the tinkling metal stream back into the jug. I then stood up, returned the jug to its place on the top shelf, rolled the cylindrical wooden stool back to its home beneath the two pairs of skis hanging from the side wall, picked up the combination screwdriver and drill, closed the door behind me, headed back into the cabin and within ten minutes had the cupboard mounted on the wall.

Perhaps disproportionately content with my afternoon's work, and for some reason feeling slightly more Scottish than either Norwegian or English at that moment, I picked up my phone, navigated to a recording of Jimmy Shand playing 'The Birks O' Invermay' on his accordion, and for the next few minutes danced in celebration around the living-room table, quite forgetting what lay in store for me for the rest of the weekend: a fight to the death with two IKEA sofa beds we had bought some weeks previously and which lay in wait for me, piled and unopened, in a corner of the upstairs bedroom.

# 12

## Friday evening,
## 21 December 2018

The difficulties of sofa beds – the terrace in place – decide

to clear snow from the terrace – on making a dream come

'true' – on Bernhard Herre's *Recollections of a Hunter* – a love

triangle – influence of mountains on Norwegian philosophers

– Arne Næss and Peter Wessel Zapffe – Næss's mountain

cabins – how smoking saved Bertrand Russell's life – Næss,

Else Herzberg and Zapffe climb Stetind – failure of my efforts

to clear the snow – on Zapffe's 'Anti-Natalist' philosophy –

Zapffe's extreme environmentalism – we sit down to eat

Geirr Tveitt's *Vél Komne med æra* is less than four minutes long, and once the music came to an end the spell was broken, the sky was just sky again, the stars in the valley below just electric light. I stood up, turned off the radio, crossed the room and climbed the *hønsetrapp* to the first floor. It's narrow and steep. Going down is best done backwards, like a seaman on a boat. We had talked about fixing a rope to the wall as a handrail, anchoring it through three wrought-iron loops. Jørgen's in-laws, who owned the first cabin we looked at, that day I had to take the dog out of the christening in the chapel, have already sold and moved on. I heard someone say, as I was passing that *langbord* gathering of cabin-owners a few months ago, that it was because they couldn't manage the stairs.

At the small landing at the top, where the thick black pipe from the stove passes between the floor and the ceiling, I turned into the smaller of the two rooms in the *hems* and looked at the sofa beds again. It had been six or seven weeks since I had finished assembling them. I had had no particular purpose in climbing the stairs, but looking at those two sofa beds I recalled the difficulties I had experienced in getting one of them into place. It was fractionally too wide to fit against the wall where it had to stand, and, with some trepidation, I had had to saw about fifty millimetres from the outer edges of each of the four legs. The room is small, and as nearly as possible the sofa bed had to be assembled in the position in which it would eventually stand. One tends not to look too far ahead in the instruction brochures that accompany IKEA products, and the thing was at least two-thirds built when it dawned on me that the four support bolts that secured the back legs of the bed to the frame had to be screwed into the frame from the outside. With the bolt in position and ready to be screwed in with the metal key, there was simply no room between the wall and the bed for the hand to turn the key. And yet by an amazing piece of luck it turned out there was just enough free space to wriggle the whole construction until there was enough of an angle to the wall to slide a hand in and turn the bolt.

As promised, Kåre and his brother had built us the apron-terrace. It took them nine days from start to finish, and they'd done a beautiful job. We had managed a single symbolic break-fast out there on a bitterly cold November morning, wrapped in scarves and thick pullovers and enjoying the view of that Blefjell pyramid over a bowl of porridge swimming with butter, brown sugar and cinnamon. There were a few jobs left, but they were small ones: an inside wall of the shed needed painting, which we'd put off doing because it meant taking down the shelves I'd put up when we first started work on the cabin; and the cornices above the kitchen area still needed painting. We weren't content with the discus-like light fittings provided in the living room and bedroom and had bought two black, wrought-iron replacements that seemed to us better suited to the rustic atmosphere conjured by the thick timbers of the interior walls. But our visits to the cabin were no longer dedicated to working on it. Assembling the two sofa beds up here had been the last big job, and now we would be ready to receive visitors. There is a strong tradition of hospitality attached to the Norwegian *hytta* culture. Nina had already booked a weekend visit just for herself and a group of friends, and I had family from England coming over in February.

I noticed in the corner of the windowsill a tiny collection of objects left over from the fight with the sofa beds. I picked them up and studied them. Two wooden dowels, a black plastic grommet, and the little silver key spanner. There's always something left over after an IKEA job, a reminder that you haven't done a perfect job, but the thing will hold. Recalling the words of the Han dynasty official Ssu-ma Ch'ien, who tells us in his *Records of the Historian* that builders in ancient China always left a tile off the roof of any house they built, 'to mirror the great imperfection', I couldn't help wondering if the oversupply was deliberate, an obscure part of the IKEA philosophy. In any case, there was no question of throwing them out.

I placed the little collection back down in the corner of the windowsill and looked out of the window across a snowy slope with the edge of a pine forest about fifty metres away. By the light of the risen moon I saw a trail of footprints, probably a fox, crossing it in a syncopated curve and sloping upwards before straightening out and heading into the forest. For a moment I thought of the indescribable harshness of its life, and shuddered. Then I walked across the small landing and into the larger of the two *hems*. There were two more sofa beds here, comfortably positioned opposite each other along the long walls. At the gable end of the room, a small wooden table and chair stood on a striped rag rug. The table was the first thing we had bought for the cabin. It didn't quite fit any more. The wood was too light for the walls.

I bent to look out of the window and down at the terrace. At its widest, here at the front, there was room for the circular table and six chairs we had bought. Come the spring we would eat out there every day. Kåre had left a gap of about twenty centimetres all the way around, between the bottom of the panelling and the terrace floor, so that snow could easily be pushed off the boards through the gap. Nina was still in the bathroom showering and shampooing the dog. Snow continued to fall heavily, and I decided to fill in the time before we ate by clearing the metre-high wall that had piled up on the long side of terrace. I would really only be making room for more, but it was a pleasure to be out in the snow.

I went down the stairs, sat on the bench by the front door, pulled on my black rubber snow boots and stepped outside to the shed. With the snow scoop broken now, there was only the shovel left. I unhooked it from its wall mountings and trudged round the back of the cabin with it. Unbolting the gate Kåre had fitted to the end of the terrace, I stepped up onto the snow and began systematically shovelling it out through the gap below the fence. The snow was a little wetter and heavier than the snow on the roof had been.

More tired than I realised from my exertions on the roof earlier in the afternoon, I very soon took a break. Resting on the handle of the shovel, I glanced up and saw the small, pyramidal peak in the east. Its sides were fairly straight, and its peak almost perfectly pointed. It looked like a child's drawing of a mountain. As I turned my head to the right to look in through the window there was a sudden spill of light in the room as the bathroom door opened and Alex came tearing out, followed at a gentler pace by my wife. She stepped over to the kitchen wall, raised her hand to the switch and the series of downlights around the edge of the ceiling lit up. The switches are wireless, there's no 'click' as they go on and off, you just touch them. It's unnerving. I watched as the dog raced round and round the furniture in a dizzying series of loops, the way he always does when he's been shampooed – he's trying to get dry, I suppose. Nina was standing in front of the open fridge, peering into its bright interior.

Clearing my throat, I spoke to myself. 'You've done it,' I said, turning to look down over the valley, 'You've nearly done it. It's nearly done. Nothing can undo it now, it's nearly done. You've nearly done it. Seventy years old and you've nearly done it.'

But *what* had I nearly done? Made a dream come true? Does it give structure and meaning to a life, to make a dream come true? Is it proof that you always secretly knew what you were doing? Of course it doesn't. Of course it isn't. Beyond the vaguest outlines, I never had the slightest idea what I was doing or where I was going. I had learned Norwegian merely to read novels written by a Norwegian author in the language in which they were written. As young people will do, I had identified with the hero of one of those novels.

A novel that moves you profoundly creates a world of its own. When you first read it, you have no interest in whatever banal truth might lie behind its invention. A desire to know what inspired its author to write the book is something that comes later. Hamsun wrote *Pan* in 1894, and I read the novel in the 1970s, but it was only some years afterwards that I discovered the true story that had provided him with his starting point. I came across it in a book called *En Jægers Erindringer*\* ('Recollections of a Hunter'), by a nineteenth-century Norwegian named Bernhard Herre.

This slender book was published posthumously in 1850, shortly after Herre's death. I bought a copy of it some years ago from an antiquarian bookseller, along with a brief presentation of Herre written by Henrik Jæger, who was later to become Henrik Ibsen's first biographer. On the morning of Sunday 15 July 1849, writes Jæger, Herre with two other men

---

\* The spelling is modernised in newer editions to *En Jegers Erindringer*.

had gone hunting in the Kristiania *marka*, part of the great belt of forest that surrounds the city on three sides. In their wanderings they came to a hill at the far end of Maridalen. The track was steep, and they needed to use both hands to claw their way up. They carried their rifles slung over their shoulders. Herre was walking alone, some distance from the others, when an overhanging branch dislodged the rifle. As it fell, the hammer struck a stone and the rifle discharged, sending a bullet in under Herre's chin and up into his brain. His companions ran to his side and found him still alive. He was capable of speech, Jæger tells us, but death had already clouded his brain and he was in great pain. An hour and a half later he was dead. Ever since reading Jæger's account I have wondered whether the precision with which he described the shot, its progress up through Herre's chin and into his brain, was his way of implying what many people have come to believe over the years: that Herre committed suicide.

Bernhard Herre, like Knut Hamsun's Glahn, was a young man who had found himself on the losing side of a love triangle. In Herre's case it involved Camilla Wergeland, sister of the poet Henrik Wergeland, and Herre's own house-tutor, the poet Johan Sebastian Welhaven.* As Glahn does in the novel, Herre made unsuccessful efforts to deal with his defeat by trying to bring the couple together; and as in Glahn's case, there is an element of tragic uncertainty surrounding his death. After Herre's death, two of his friends, the folklorist P. C. Asbjørnsen and his former tutor and rival Welhaven, went through his papers and published the few short accounts

---

* Later, as Camilla Collett, Camilla Wergeland would write *Amtmandens Døtre* (*The District Governor's Daughters*), one of the classics of early modern Norwegian literature.

that make up *En Jægers Erindringer*. Proceeds from the sale of the book went to Herre's mother.

*En Jægers Erindringer* has become a classic of Norwegian nature writing. Herre's closely observed and lyrical but unsentimental descriptions of the animal – and human – life he encountered while hunting in the forests around Oslo marked a break with the prevailing and prettifying traditions of national romanticism. Reading it, one is rarely conscious of listening to a voice that speaks to us from over a hundred and fifty years ago. This effect of timelessness and immediacy is such a striking characteristic of the best of Knut Hamsun's early writing, and of *Pan* in particular, that Hamsun *must* have derived something from Herre's style as well as his tragic fate.

*Pan* changed my life. It brought me to Norway, and to everything good that Norway has given me, and for that reason alone the novel will always have a special place in my heart. But I confess to feeling a kind of relief at the glimpse behind the mirror that came with my discovery of Herre's writing and the story of his life. Unlike the hero of Hamsun's book, he was no handsome and enigmatic soldier but a drudge who worked all his days as a copyist in the Treasury Department. A borderline alcoholic, he frequently got into fights and on numerous occasions was summoned to appear in court when one of his hunting dogs – it could have been Falkøie, Coquette, Feiom or Linge – had bitten someone.

I resumed the work of shovelling snow off the terrace, recalling as I did so a cabin with rather brighter associations than Glahn's and the sad hovels that crop up here and there in Herre's reminiscences. In 1937 the Norwegian philosopher and mountaineer Arne Næss built himself a cabin under the Hallingskarvet ridge in the Jotunheimen range. 'Tvergastein', as he called it, was over fifteen hundred metres above sea level. In 1942 he built another, smaller cabin even higher up the Skarvet, on a tiny ridge from where a thousand different climbing routes lay open to him. Næss's cabins too were born of a long-held dream: from his earliest childhood he had dreamed of one day establishing a permanent, personal relationship with the great ridge. He experienced Hallingskarvet as 'overwhelmingly powerful, mighty, solid, peaceful at its core, self-respecting – qualities I wished I had possessed myself but, in the main, never did'.

Thinking about Næss led me to reflect on the emergence during the last century of a strikingly close association between

mountains and philosophers in Norwegian intellectual life. Næss and Peter Wessel Zapffe, two of the most admired thinkers in Norway in the twentieth century, were men whose lifelong involvement with mountaineering became an integral part of their idea of themselves *as philosophers*. Næss, who died in 2009 at the age of ninety-six, held the chair in philosophy at the University of Oslo from 1939 to 1969. He has an international reputation as the foremost proponent of a philosophy of life he called 'Deep Ecology', in whose development he was influenced by Rachel Carson's seminal work of environmental concern, *Silent Spring* (1962). I remembered what pleasure it had given me, in reading his *Klatrefilosofiske og biografiske betraktninger* ('Philosophical and biographical observations on climbing'), to come across, in his description of a four-month climbing expedition undertaken alone in the Pyrenees in the spring of 1930, a reference to the books he carried in his rucksack, mostly, he specifies, on 'European and Chinese philosophy'. In its cultural openness there was something typically Norwegian about a 'proper' philosopher unafraid to pursue an interest in traditions far removed from those of his own Western disciplines; and discovering, rather as Schopenhauer did, that the conclusions reached, the one by the pathless track of paradox, enigma and poetry, the other by a painstakingly rational and logical use of language, turned out be similar to the point of indistinguishable. For Næss's 'deep ecology' is essentially a translation into Western terms of what he learned while climbing in the Hindu Kush and the Himalayas, including the first ascent of Tirich Mir, the highest mountain in the Hindu Kush, in 1950.

His early curiosity about Chinese philosophy may have been deepened by encounters with Buddhists and Taoists at the time of the trip to the Hindu Kush, and further stimulated during a trip to the Himalayas in 1971 with two younger climbers, Nils Faarlund and the philosopher Sigmund Kvaløy Setreng, who shared Næss's interest in traditions and disciplines that lay outside Western rationalism and logic. Their destination was the Sherpa's holy mountain, Gauri Shankar, in the Rolwaling valley in Tibet. But the purpose was not to 'conquer' Gauri Shankar, to Nepalese Buddhists 'the sacred dwelling place of Tseringma', in the spirit in which Slingsby had taught Norwegians to conquer mountains; it was to commune with the mountain in a mystical sense. As a guarantee of his sincerity, Næss gave a personal undertaking to the King of Nepal that he and his party would not climb all the way to the top but stop some three thousand feet short of the summit.

Næss seems to have been sobered by the exponential growth in mountaineering as a pastime that had taken place since 1953 and the maiden ascent of Mount Everest. He became increasingly imbued with the sense of respectful and devotional awe with which the Tibetans and Sherpas viewed the mountains around them, and to feel that the mountains needed protection from the large-scale expeditions that threatened the ancient religious culture – Buddhist, Hindu and Taoist – of the region. On his return to Norway he promoted a campaign to have Gauri Shankar declared a protected area: 'The attempt to protect Gauri Shankar is a small step in the direction of acknowledging that the mystical way in which the Sherpas view this mountain is as valid as the recreational, sporting and commercial approach of Westerners.'

In later years Næss would even express regret at having built on Hallingskarvet at all, coming to view it as an arrogant human imposition on a natural wilderness. He wrote of the ridge in an anthropomorphic way. Hallingskarvet had a soul. What it had to 'say to us' was 'infinitely more than we can say to Skarvet, ephemera that we are'. In *Det gode lange livs far* (*The father of the good long life*), a title that self-consciously echoed the translation of the Tibetan Tseringma as 'The mother of the good long life', he wrote that 'the 'enlightened' age, with its contempt for symbols, rituals and mythology, is over. It is no longer useful to regard such things as 'unscientific'. Næss came to feel that the Hallingskarvet ridge was numinous, and to think of it in the same way as the Tibetans in the Rolwaling Valley thought of Tseringma. It had been, to him, the father of the good long life. The 'deep' in deep ecology was simply a way of emphasising the importance of the attitude of oneness and respect he had arrived at after his journey; he wanted to stress the contrast with a 'shallow' form of environmentalism that limited itself, essentially, to feeling guilty about littering. As it was for Schopenhauer and Søren Kierkegaard, philosophy for Næss was more than an abstract and sometimes merely competitive game with words; it was a visionary endeavour that should have real consequences for the way the philosopher lives his life.

It's rare for a philosopher to become a national icon, I reflected, but during the later years of his life, and in the decades since his death, Næss has achieved a status and renown in Norway that are comparable with the regard in which Bertrand Russell was held by the British public in his old age. Thinking of Russell, I remembered the obscure story of the *Bukken Bruse*, an amphibious plane in which the philosopher was travelling from Oslo to Trondheim in 1948. As the pilot tried to land on the waters of the Trondheim fjord, the plane was caught by a sudden gust of wind. Nineteen people lost their lives when the fuselage filled with water.

The peculiar irony of Russell's survival was that he had insisted on being seated at the back of the plane, so that he could smoke on the flight – 'If I cannot smoke I will die I am sure', he had explained apologetically. All nineteen who died were seated at the front, in the non-smoking section of the plane.

Russell, then seventy-four years of age, escaped through a broken window. Still wearing his overcoat, he swam in the direction of a boat and was picked up. He had been due to deliver a lecture to students at the Trondheim Students Union the following day, and duly lectured them at the appointed hour on the twin dangers of nuclear war and Joseph Stalin, a philosophical response to adversity that would have delighted Arne Næss.

I had come across the bones of this story while reading about Russell and Ludwig Wittgenstein and had presumed for some time that the purpose of Russell's flight to Norway had been to visit Wittgenstein at Skjolden, in the county of Sogn og Fjordane and within sight of the Hurrungane mountain range, where Wittgenstein had had a cabin since 1914, and where he wrote most of the *Tractatus Logico-Philosophicus*. Once he felt the cabin had served its purpose, Wittgenstein gave it away. In similar fashion, Næss gave away his mountaineering cabin, Skarvereiret. Or at least he tried to do so, on several occasions. Somehow it always kept falling back into his hands.

All in all, it was hard to know whether to treat Næss as a philosopher who happened to climb, or a climber who liked to philosophise. From Slingsby and the Norwegian school of mountaineering he fostered in the later decades of the nineteenth century, both Næss and Zapffe had inherited the tradition of the mountain as a focus for conquest. The ice axe and the spiked shoes Slingsby introduced to his Norwegian friends were technical aids in the struggle to subdue the mountains. In his earlier years Næss had been responsible for the next step forward in the use of technology in mountaineering following Slingsby. While studying in Vienna in the mid-1930s and climbing with Austrian friends he had become acquainted with the use of bolts. He sent a carton of these home to Norway, where his friends pounced upon this new climbing aid, which, at a stroke, opened up a whole new world for them.

Zapffe, in his account of the first ascent of Stetind in 1936, described the revolutionary effects of these bolts. This Nordland mountain has a remarkable status among Norwegians. In an NRK poll in 2002, listeners voted it the country's National Mountain. It's known as 'the anvil of the gods' from its curious, flat top, as though it has been decapitated. Stetind was one of the few mountains to have defeated the great Slingsby, who described it (afterwards) as 'the ugliest mountain I have ever seen'. Long thought to be impossible, it was not finally climbed until 1910, by a team of three Norwegians, Ferdinand Schjelderup, Carl Wilhelm Rubenson and Alf Bonnevie Bryn.

Næss and Zapffe split up. Zapffe and two companions set out using the 1910 route. Næss, accompanied by his wife, Else Herzberg, the pair of them with Næss's Viennese bolts dangling from their necks, made the first attempt at a new route up the mountain since the maiden ascent of 1910, scaling the so-called Sydpillaren (South Pillar). In his essay *Stettind* (sic), Zapffe relates how, resting a moment from his own exertions, he saw Arne and Else in a single 'quick upward glance over the towering, *panserglatte* [absolutely smooth] wall up which they were "crocheting" themselves by means of their strange hardware'. The ascent of the sheer face would have been impossible without it. He loses sight of them but can always hear the tiny, far-off ringing of the bolts being hammered into cracks in the surface of the mountain as he

and his two companions continued along a route on which hands and feet find their holds 'the good old-fashioned way'. At one point they are able to locate the pair through a telescope – 'two coloured specks at the very edge of that desert of stone, dangling there, each from their own hook, like two *blodvidner* [martyrs], between the looming hammer and the dizzying depths. I think we might have paled a little, our souls have blanched a little as we rested there on our "access road" to the top, each with a large rock firmly beneath our backsides. What was going on up there was absolutely *something else,* perhaps akin to glimpsing a jet fighter plane high above while out for a spin in grandad's helicopter.'

Arne and Else's marriage lasted ten years, until 1947. A few years ago, I shared an office on Fredensborgveien with the philosopher Ragnar Herzberg Næss, the elder son of the marriage. Ragnar always had a picture on his desk of a woman standing at a ninety-degree angle on a rock-face, turning to the camera, smiling, possibly – the image isn't very clear. I asked him once whether the photograph was from the ascent of Stetind, since I knew his parents had climbed it together on other, later occasions. He confessed that he didn't know, but that it was possibly Kolsås, a wooded ridge just outside Oslo where, to this day, many Norwegian climbers hone their mountaineering skills. There was an almost poetic justice in Næss's conquest of Stetind: it seemed to me to encapsulate the scope of his intellectual achievement – the way in which he made mountaineering and philosophy indistinguishable from one another, and mutually dependent. The Englishman Slingsby had given Norwegian mountaineering a kick-start back in the nineteenth century; the two Norwegians Næss and Zapffe, had, in a sense, taken the mountains back. And just as Ibsen's career had such a strong influence in fostering Norway's position as a leading advocate of full equality between the sexes, so has Næss's advocacy of a 'deep' ecology profoundly influenced Norway's other great claim to moral authority in the modern world, as devoted protector of our natural environment.

It was still snowing heavily. My efforts had made no visible inroads at all and the snow was still piled waist-high along the length of the terrace. I didn't mind in the slightest, but there was little point in going on and I walked round the cabin to the shed and hung the shovel back up on its peg, beat the snow off my boots on the wooden step outside the front door, and stepped inside. With his unfailing courtesy the dog rushed to greet me as though it was months since we had last seen each other. Risking the embarrassment I knew it might cause my wife (for most of the neighbouring cabins were occupied for Christmas), I coaxed him into a brief session of loud, wolf-like howling. It gave me such pleasure to see his pleasure, bouncing about on his paws, curly tail waggling furiously, his little grey head and neck stretching upwards as he joined me in howling whatever it was we were howling.

I walked into the kitchen area. My wife was standing at the wooden work-surface peeling some kind of knotty orange vegetable. I kissed her on the neck.

'What's that?'

'Sweet potato.'

'What are we having?'

'Lasagne with sweet potato.' She said she'd seen the recipe for it in *Aftenposten*'s Weekend magazine that morning and thought it sounded interesting.

'How long will it be?'

'About twenty minutes.'

'Want a glass of wine?'

'Yes. There's some rosé in the fridge.'

I opened the fridge, took down the carton of wine, poured her a glass and put it down next to the chopping board. I poured myself a glass of beer and an aquavit chaser and took them over to the sofa at the other side of the room. Stepping towards the DAB radio on the windowsill with the intention of listening to NRK's Jazz station, my finger about to tap the 'On' button, I stopped in bewilderment as the opening bars of Jimmy Yancey's 'Midnight Stomp' came rolling into the room. It took me some moments to realise it was my own phone I was hearing. In an idle moment a couple of days before leaving Oslo I had changed the ringtone. No one had called in the meantime and it had completely slipped my mind.

I picked up the phone from the coffee table and looked at the display. It was my friend Eskil. I guessed he would be calling to see if I was interested in going to Herr Nilsen's tomorrow. Herr Nilsen's was a jazz club in C. J. Hambros plass with regular concerts on Saturday afternoons between four and six. Until quite recently we had never missed a session, but over the past year the demands of working on the cabin and having a dog had made it difficult for me to find the time, and it was months now since we had last met up there. But our intention to keep up the habit remained firm, and we called and texted regularly to see if we could get the arrangement up and running again. A very good tenor player named Petter Wettre was appearing with his quartet, but I had to tell Eskil, with sincere regret, that I couldn't make it as I was at the cabin. We small-talked for a couple of minutes and were about to sign off when I had a thought. Eskil worked in the philosophy department at the University of Oslo, and I knew he had taken his degrees there. He must have been studying at about the time when Arne Næss was finishing his tenure as philosophy professor at Blindern. I asked if he had had Næss as a teacher.

'Yes, I did,' he said.

'What was he like? I mean, in person?'

'He was very eccentric. There are lots of stories about him. Did you ever hear about the time he got locked out of his office on the campus at Blindern?'

'No. What happened?'

'His office in the philosophy department was in Niels Treschows building, the tall building at the back of the campus, next to the tram lines. One day he left his keys in there and locked himself out. But it was summer, and his window was open, so he climbed out of the window of the office next door to his and in through his own window, picked up his keys and let himself out. It was on the eighth floor. *Dagbladet* heard about it and sent a photographer and a journalist up to Blindern. They offered him money to do it again but he wouldn't and they left.

'A few minutes later two more journalists turned up, this time from *VG*. How exactly did you do it, Professor? they asked him. For some reason he changed his mind. I did it like this, he said, and he climbed out the window and did the whole thing all over again. So *VG* got their pictures for nothing. Another time him and Jens Bjørneboe – you know, the writer – arranged this practical joke where Bjørneboe got on the metro at the station before Majorstuen and Næss got on at Majorstuen. As soon as he boarded Næss began complaining loudly about the heat and asked whether anyone happened to have a glass of water on them. Of course, says Bjørneboe, and pulls a glass of water from his inside pocket. I'll swap you this for a spanner. So Næss pulls a spanner out of *his* inside pocket and hands it to Bjørneboe, who gives him the glass of water. Then they both go back to their seats – still pretending to be complete strangers – and get off at different stations. Why are you interested in Arne Næss? Are you writing about him?'

I told him I was thinking about writing something about Norwegian mountaineers who were also philosophers, or Norwegian philosophers who were also mountaineers.

'You should say something about Peter Wessel Zapffe. I always slightly preferred him to Næss. Just as a character. He was more melancholic, but very funny.'

'Was he one of your teachers?'

'No, he wasn't attached to the department. But he wrote some textbooks. I don't think he ever had a proper job. He studied law and practised up in Tromsø, where he came from, for a couple of years. But he gave it up, it wasn't for him. He's the only law student in Norwegian history who wrote his exam paper on the principles of judicial precedence in rhyming verse.'

'Did he pass?'

'Yes. He got *laud*. It's the highest mark you can get.'

I mentioned something I thought I remembered about Zapffe from a book I read years ago, about Salomon August Andrée, the Swedish balloonist who set off for the North Pole in 1897 with two companions and disappeared. They were not heard of again until 1930, when two fishermen came across what was left of them on the remote Arctic island of Kvitøya; hadn't Zapffe been the official photographer with the party that sailed to Kvitøya to pick up the remains of the three dead balloonists?

'Yes, he was a photographer too. And a humorous writer – his book *Vett og uvett* (Wit and half-wit) is a classic of north Norwegian humour. *Om det tragiske* (On the Tragic), a version of his doctoral thesis, is a classic of a different kind in Norwegian literature. He was a cartoonist. Satirist. And philosopher, of course.'

'Where did he stand on Deep Ecology?'

'I suppose you'd have to call him a fundamentalist. He was an Anti-Natalist. He believed it would have been better for us never to have been born. All this searching for ultimate meaning, all the agonising over ethics, to him it wasn't impressive, he viewed it more as a sort of malfunctioning of the brain. He believed that human consciousness, having solved the basic problems of comfort and survival, had developed into a grotesque and useless luxury. That there's no meaning anywhere. Like patrons at a theatre, we come, we sit awhile, and we go. Bringing children into the world, he said, that's like carrying wood into a burning house.'

'Sounds bleak,' I said.

'Well yes. But if you believe there's no meaning in life and no point in wasting time looking for one, I suppose it brought a sense of relief. I remember reading a memoir by someone who knew him when he was very old – he lived to be ninety-one. She was young, very idealistic, she liked to have deep talks with him about the meaning of life. Once he was telling her about how life is like rowing alone in a small boat on the open sea. You have no idea where you are, and no lighthouse blinking anywhere to guide you. She lost patience with him. "You're old," she told him. "You'll die soon. But I'm young and my life is only just beginning. The picture you paint is so bleak." Zapffe was quiet for a long time. Then he said to her, "Well, while you're rowing the boat, there's no need to mope about it. You can sing, for example. And open a tin of pineapples."

Eskil gave a little laugh.

'What was your question again?' he said.

'About Deep Ecology. Where did Zapffe stand on Deep Ecology?'

'He was so deep he was subterranean. He thought that marking footpaths the way DNT do it was wrong. He even thought it was wrong to put up little *varder*. *Du, hva heter det forresten på engelsk, varder?*'

'It means *cairns* in English.'

'He even thought it was wrong to raise little cairns to mark the way. Logical enough, I suppose, if you don't believe there even *is* a way to mark.'

From the corner of my eye I saw my wife gesturing to me that the food was ready. And swearing once more that we would soon get together and resume our Saturday afternoons at Herr Nilsen, even if we had to wait until the spring, Eskil and I ended our conversation. Putting the phone back down on the table, I had an odd thought: that in a voyage without lighthouses we end up providing our own. Maybe, without my knowing it, my youthful obsession with a novel had actually been a kind of lighthouse to me.

I poured another glass of rosé for Nina, helped myself to another Heineken from the fridge and sat down at the table. Before doing anything else I raised a glass to her and thanked her for the meal, and for a number of other things as well. Then I asked her what she thought of Zapffe's idea that even something as simple as building cairns might be the wrong way to go about life. It seemed interesting to me, possibly a bit extreme, and I was curious to hear what she had to say about it.

# Bibliography

Asbjørnsen P. Chr. and Moe, Jørgen: *Samlede Eventyr Vols 1 and 2*, Oslo 2000

Christensen, Arne Lie: *Det norske landskapet*, Oslo 2002

Ferguson, Robert: *Enigma: The Life of Knut Hamsun*, London 1987

Ferguson, Robert: *Henrik Ibsen: A New Biography*, London 1996

Fossum, Tommy: *Våre ladyer og lakselorder*, Sunndalen 2018

Fønnebø, Reidar: *Langs Nordmannsslepene over Hardangervidda*, Oslo 1988

Herre, Bernhard: *En jægers erindringer*, Christiania 1850

*Historien. DNT Årbok* 2017

Haddal, Per: 'Fem år som vi så dem – Norsk okkupasjonsdrama på film'. In *To Liv – Zwei Leben – Norsk tyske filmforindelser*, ed. Jan Erik Holst, forthcoming Oslo 2019

Hoff, Knut: *Rollag bygdebok: ætt og gard og grend. Vols 1–5*, 1988–1997

Holan, Jerri: *Norwegian Wood: A Tradition of Building*, New York 1990

*Hundre år i fjellet*. DNT 1868–1968, Den Norske Turistforening, 1968

Hytta, Lidvard: *Fjellfolkets Rike, Folk og virke på Hardangervidda*, Oslo 2009

Larsen, Arne: *Pionerer: Kvinnenes klatrehistorie fra dametinder til K2*, Oslo 2018

Næss, Arne: *Det gode lange livs far*, Oslo 1999

Rees, Ellen: *Cabins in Modern Norwegian Literature*, Plymouth 2014

Ryvarden, Leif: *Hardangervidda – naturen, opplevelsene, historien*, Oslo 2011

Slagstad, Rune: *Da fjellet ble dannet*, Oslo 2018

Slingsby, William Cecil: *Norway, the Northern Playground: Sketches of Climbing and Mountain Exploration in Norway between 1872 and 1903*, Edinburgh, 1904

Sylte, Tor: *Laksen og Lågen. Suldalslågen gjennom 1000 år*, Fagernes 2008

*Veiviser til vidda*. DNT Fjell og Vidde nr. 8 – 1998

Visted, Kristofer and Stigum, Hilmar: *Vår gamle bondekultur* Vols 1 and 2, Oslo 1971

Zapffe, Peter Wessel: *Barske glæder*, Oslo 2012

# List of Photographs

# About the author

ROBERT FERGUSON has lived in Norway since 1983. His books include *Scandinavians: In Search of the Soul of the North*; *The Hammer and The Cross: A New History of the Vikings*, and biographies of Henrik Ibsen, Knut Hamsun and Henry Miller. He has translated numerous books by Norwegian writers into English, including *Norwegian Wood* by Lars Mytting, which won the Bookseller prize for Non-Fiction Book of the Year in 2016.